Home Winemaking

Step by Step

THE WINEMAKERS SHOP
3517 NORTH HIGH ST
COLUMBUS, OH 43214
614-263-1744

Home Winemaking

Step by Step

A Guide to Fermenting Wine Grapes

FOURTH EDITION

JON IVERSON

STONEMARK PUBLISHING COMPANY
Medford, Oregon

STONEMARK PUBLISHING COMPANY
312 South Ivy Street, Medford, OR 97501

Cover and book design: Patricia Broersma,
www.greenhorsegraphics.com
Interior illustrations: Sarah Cribb

ISBN 978-0-9657936-4-3

Fourth edition

Iverson, Jon.
    Home winemaking step-by-step : a guide to fermenting wine grapes / Jon Iverson. -- 4th ed.
        p. cm.
    Includes index.
    ISBN-13: 978-0-9657936-4-3
    ISBN-10: 0-9657936-4-8

    1. Wine and wine making--Amateurs' manuals.
I. Title.

TP548.2.I94 2009   641.8'72
                         QBI09-600089

Manufactured in the United States of America

10 9 8 7 6 5 4 3 2 1

Contents

Vacuum aspiration
Testing free SO2 by Ripper
Procedure for standardizing iodine
Testing total sulfite by Ripper
Digital pH meters
Bench trials

Home Winemaking

Step by Step

QUANTITIES

Grapes — As a rule of thumb, 100 pounds of grapes will yield a gross total of 6 to 7 gallons (U.S.) of juice and pulp and a net of 5 to 6 gallons of finished wine after settling and racking losses. This will vary depending on the relative water content of the grapes, how hard they are pressed, whether you settle out the pulp and ferment only the clear juice, and whether you use pectic enzyme, which will release more of the liquid but also create more pulp. Red grapes will usually yield slightly more because they are fermented on the skins and more liquid is released before pressing.

Sugar — If the juice needs to be sweetened, 1½ ounces of table sugar per U.S. gallon will raise the Brix by 1°.

Acid — One level teaspoon per U.S. gallon of tartaric acid, malic acid or acid blend will raise the total acidity of a wine or must by approximately .12%. See Appendix A for testing total acidity and page 89 for further details on these acids.

Potassium metabisulfite — ¼ tsp. per 5 U.S. gallons = 45 parts per million (ppm). Use 45 ppm at crushing, 45 ppm at the first racking, and 45 ppm at the third racking before bottling. Always dissolve it in a bit of water first and stir it in very well.

INTRODUCTION

he first few chapters of this book will lead you successfully through the crushing, pressing, fermenting
and clarifying steps of making white wines, as well
as the bottling. White wines are a good place to start
in understanding the art of fermenting wines, as
they force you to appreciate the pernicious effects of air. Minimize
air contact, limit the use of potassium metabisulfite, don't over-
oak, and you will actually find it quite easy to make a good white
wine.

There are a number of reasons why white wines are easy to make.
The small amount of unfermented or "residual" sugar present in
white wines tends to conceal flaws in the grapes and makes fruit
quality a little less critical. In contrast, red wines are normally
bottled "bone dry," i.e., with no residual sugar. As a result, high
acidity, low pH or flaws in the fruit quality are more easily detected
in a finished red wine. The quality of the fruit has to be higher to
make an outstanding red wine.

White wines are also easier in that they are fermented cooler than
reds and are not as prone to spoilage problems during fermentation.
Red grapes are normally fermented at higher temperatures in order
to extract maximum flavor from the skins. The higher fermenta-

tion temperature increases the risk of spoilage and unwanted side reactions involving volatile acids.

In my experience, it has been easier to find quality white grapes than red, and at less cost. This will, of course, depend on the supply and demand situation in your area. Since most white grapes ripen earlier than reds, the white grape crop is less often affected by early rains and frosts. If you have tried white wines in the past and had only marginal success, don't give up! Follow the basic procedures discussed in Chapter 1 through Chapter 5, and you'll be well rewarded.

If, as has been said, "the first duty of a wine is to be red," it follows that the first duty of a winemaker is to make red wines! And that is probably what most readers will have in mind. The discussion of fermentation of red wines in Chapter 6, along with fermenting variations for red wines in Chapter 11 and malolactic fermentation in Chapter 12, covers all the techniques that can readily be used to good avail by a home winemaker.

You can make excellent red wines without going beyond Chapter 6, and I highly recommend that beginning winemakers do just that — stick to the basics in Chapter 6 and ignore the more advanced techniques. (But do put the wine through malolactic fermentation.) If you are a beginning winemaker intent on making red wines, be sure to read the earlier chapters on white winemaking. Some of the procedures are treated in greater detail there.

Glossaries of equipment and supplies are included at the end of several chapters. These are intended to be reference sources as needed. Note that not every term used in this book is fully defined. Just remember that "racking" means siphoning from one container to another and that potassium metabisulfite, meta, sulfite and SO_2 are synonyms, and you will get by very well!

Chapter One

GETTING STARTED

he art of making wine has evolved a great deal in the last twenty or thirty years, and the progress shows no sign of slowing. Never in the history of mankind has it been possible to make wine of such high quality from a given batch of grapes. Great strides have been made both in growing premium grapes and in extracting the maximum from the fruit during fermentation. The advances benefit the home winemaker as well as the commercial. With the expanded array of equipment and supplies now available, the home winemaker can routinely make wines that exceed the quality of ordinary commercial wines. In fact, if you ferment the same grapes from the same vineyard, your wine could very well be better than the winery's, even on your first attempt! The home winemaker has an edge in working with small quantities and being able to clarify without having to pump and filter. Follow the sound principles in this book, and the quality of your wine will be limited only by the quality of the grapes you crush and ferment.

Good grapes

This subject is as impossible to discuss as it is important! If omitted, the reader could legitimately ask why it was not included. So here goes. The reason grape quality is so important is that good grapes are the basis for any good wine. The better the grapes, the better the wine will be. Any honest vintner will admit that when the grapes come in good, the wine literally makes itself. It ferments without problems, clarifies readily and needs no adjustments before or after fermentation. On the other hand, if the grapes are poor, the best vintner in the world will not be able to make a great wine out of them.

There is no simple answer to the very elusive question of what makes a good grape. Grapes cannot be judged by appearance because sunburned grapes with broken skins are likely to make a better wine than perfect looking clusters. Nor do acid, sugar and pH readings tell the whole story because growing conditions differ from year to year. Here are some general considerations, laden with my biases.

YIELD. Tons per acre is one of the biggest factors in determining quality. Some growers like to believe that a heavy crop does not affect quality, as long as it ripens fully. But vintners, including the author, believe that a light crop is inherently better than a heavy crop. Historically, the best wines have come in years when Mother Nature imposed a low yield per acre. It is also significant that wineries growing their own grapes and making premium wines will intentionally drop fruit during the growing season.

On the other hand, the growers correctly point out that with the

Doug and Marlene Moorhead of Moorhead Vineyards, North East, Pennsylvania, examining their Viognier vines.

Peter Brehm kneeling by his Chardonnay vines at White Salmon Vineyard, in Underwood, Washington

right variety and right clone on the right site, very heavy yields of very high quality grapes can be grown, with almost no loss in quality. But these sites are relatively rare. There is no definitive answer as to the optimal yield per acre.

VARIETY. Some varieties suffer more from over-cropping than others, Chardonnay and Pinot Noir being two such that come to mind. Cabernet Sauvignon and Merlot are less affected, as are some of the other white varieties. However, over-cropping always takes a toll. This means that if the yield looks to be 30% or 40% below normal, it should be a good year and you should start in early July trying to line up a source of grapes. It may take more effort because the wineries will compete harder for the reduced crop.

IRRIGATION. This is another subject on which the interest of the growers differs from the wineries. There is an inherent conflict of interest between the two in that the grower wants to maximize the yield and the winery wants the maximum quality. The problem is that few wineries are willing to pay a grower twice as much per pound for dropping half the grapes. So unless the grower has a contract with a winery, he will be inclined to water generously to increase the yield; but this dilutes quality. The plumper the grape, the higher the ratio of juice-to-skin and the less the flavor. The best wines are thought to come from small berries because there is more skin surface relative to the volume of liquid. Although the best grapes probably come from grapes that have been dry-farmed, the effect of watering can be greatly reduced by stopping all irrigation during the six weeks prior to harvest. This allows the berries to shrink as harvest approaches. Since dry farming is a rarity in most areas, the next best choice would be drip irrigation. A vineyard with state-of-the-art drip irrigation most likely has a knowledgeable grower, and the grapes will have suffered less from fungal and pest problems.

SPECIFIC VINEYARDS. Due to a combination of factors, some vineyards will produce superior fruit year in and year out. The depth and composition of the soil are big factors. All else being equal, vines in shallow and poor soil are thought to produce better grapes than vines in deep, fertile soil. The availability of water is similarly related — grapes from a vineyard with abundant subterranean water will probably not measure up to those from a nearby vineyard with little underground water. Talk to vintners in your area to find out which vineyards and growers have the best reputation. I have found vintners to be as approachable and friendly as they are dedicated to their art! Everything else being equal, I would favor the vineyard that sells to respected wineries.

Finding Good Grapes

The first — and always the most important — order of business is lining up a source of good grapes. The earliest in the year you

Donna Lailey checking the set on her Cabernet Franc vines at her Niagara-on-the-Lake Vineyard, Ontario.

establish contact with possible sources, the more likely that you will be rewarded with quality grapes in the fall. If you live in a grape growing region, start calling vineyards in early summer. By late June, they will know the extent of the fruit set and will be more willing to make a commitment. Some will want part of the money up front, which is a reasonable request if they are expected to reserve fruit for you. Some growers cater to home winemakers because they get top dollar for their fruit. And it's all cash to the grower, which isn't always the case when they sell to commercial wineries. Once you find a good source, stay with it year after year. A continuing relationship is your best chance of getting grapes in years of scarcity and high demand.

Some wine supply stores make arrangements to buy grapes from growers and resell to amateurs. This convenience is worth the extra cost, and there is comfort in knowing that the grapes were likely picked at their peak. In the case of white grapes, some stores will even crush, press and sell you the juice, or "must," as it is called in winemaking parlance. This should have particular appeal to someone who plans to process small batches of grapes or who is uncertain about winemaking as a hobby. It saves the expense of purchasing or renting equipment.

The natural tendency is to ferment small quantities of several varieties. Although it is interesting to have several varieties, you will soon discover that it takes little more effort to process two or three hundred pounds of a given variety than one hundred pounds. A larger quantity also gives you the ability to ferment 5 gallons in one manner and 5 gallons in another. And starting with more, you are more likely to have a little left in two or three years, when the wine is reaching its peak! It is perfectly acceptable to ferment small batches; it's just that if you become serious about home winemaking, you will most likely lean toward larger quantities of fewer varieties.

When are they ripe?

It's true that great wine starts in the vineyard, but the second most important factor is when the grapes are picked. Hopefully, you will have control over when they are picked, because the degree of ripeness will affect the outcome. And the desired ripeness will vary depending on the varietal and the style of wine you want. The flavors change as the berries ripen and the extent of malic acid decreases. Chardonnay, for instance, goes from lemon when green, then to apple and pineapple and finally to tropical fruits as it ripens. If you want a crisp, dry white table wine, you would want the grapes at the lower end of the 22-24°B range for white grapes. On the other hand, if you want a Chardonnay that is big and fat, you would want ripeness at the upper end of the range, and might want to put it through malolactic fermentation as well to give it the buttery quality. Much the same could be said of Sauvignon Blanc. Riesling, on the other hand, makes a good wine with sugar levels as low as 18-20°B, if bottled with a higher level of residual sugar. If you do not have control over picking, be aware of the different fermentation styles and pick a style the fits the grapes on hand.

In the case of red grapes, look for a pH from 3.4 to as high as 3.8, with 3.6 being ideal. If you can only measure the sugar, you would want it to be 24-27°B. The stems should be woody, and the berries should have no green skin around the stem. Peel off some skins and chew them; hopefully, they will be tangy and tannic but not astringent.

Alternatives to fresh grapes

Most serious winemakers are probably reading the next section already. The rest of you, take note! There are some excellent juices available in forms which are not only easier to work with than fresh grapes but which generally eliminate the need for a crusher, crusher-stemmer or press. The reason I include this section is that many home winemakers do not live in wine growing regions. Even those who do will discover that locating a source of grapes is only the beginning. When the grapes ripen, there is a fairly short window of opportunity during which the grapes are at their peak and should be picked. This means that you might have to drop everything and go get them on short notice, often in the middle of the week. This very sizeable investment of time and planning can be circumvented by using frozen must, aseptic juice or concentrate kits rather than fresh grapes. If high quality grapes were used, some of these alternatives would probably make a better wine than fresh grapes of low quality. So, don't rule these alternatives out.

If fresh grapes were not available to me and I was intent on making high quality wine, my first choice would be frozen musts. These are grapes that have been crushed, possibly sulfited and then frozen. The buckets start thawing during shipment and can be fermented shortly after arrival. White grapes have been crushed and pressed. You ferment pure juice, so neither crusher nor press will be needed. Just follow the basic procedure for fermenting white wines as outlined in Chapter 2.

Red varieties arrive crushed and de-stemmed, so you will not need a crusher-stemmer. Just add a yeast starter and ferment in a primary fermenter for a few days, punching down as discussed in chapter 6. A 5-gallon bucket of frozen must will yield about 3½ gallons of finished wine. Five gallons can be pressed in a nylon mesh bag, but you would want a press for larger volumes. A nylon bag requires a little more effort than a press, but you will get almost as much wine. And it is quicker to use rubber gloves and a nylon bag because there is no set up or clean up.

There is virtually no loss of quality as a result of freezing a must. Frozen musts are generally available on a first-come basis, so it tends to be a seasonal proposition. It will pay to get your name on the list early. See Appendix F.

If frozen musts were not available, "aseptic" juices would be my next choice. If the same grapes were being processed, the quality should be only slightly lower than a frozen must. Rather than being frozen, the juice is flash pasteurized, sulfited, bagged and boxed. The juice has not been reduced in volume by boiling, as have the concentrates discussed below. Neither press nor crusher-stemmer is needed, even in the case of red grapes, as the skins have been processed and added back for pigment and complexity. After pasteurization, a controlled amount of sulfite is added and the juice is bagged and boxed. The home winemaker simply transfers the juice to a primary fermenter and ferments with no ado. No grapes to crush or de-stem, no punching down and no equipment to clean up! The wine can be fermented in a primary fermenter for 3 or 4 days and then transferred to carboys, topped with an air lock and allowed to ferment to dryness. However, I prefer to ferment in carboys two-thirds full from start to finish. Follow the basic procedure in chapter 2. Bottle a red wine bone dry; sweeten a white wine slightly before bottling, as discussed in chapters 3 and 4.

"Concentrate kits" are relatively new and superior in quality to

Joe Nardone, Rochester, New York, checking the Brix in primary fermenters handed down from his father.

the canned concentrates that have been around for decades. They are referenced as "kits" because they come packaged with all the essentials, such as sulfite, potassium sorbate, bentonite, isinglass or gelatin, oak flavoring, finishing agent and the like. Like aseptic juices, concentrate kits come bagged and boxed. However, after being flash pasteurized, they are reduced in volume by boiling at low temperatures in a vacuum. They are not reduced as much as the traditional canned concentrates, so the quality remains higher. Six gallons of juice might be reduced to 4 gallons or 3 gallons. The winemaker adds water to bring the volume back up to 6 gallons and ferments according to directions. The shipping and storage costs are less, so the overall cost is less.

The traditional canned concentrates have been reduced the most in volume. The instructions typically call for adding 3 gallons of water to 1 gallon of concentrate. They have been processed longer than concentrate kits and probably subjected to more heat. Fruit quality being equal, the quality of canned concentrates should be lower.

Although grapes of very high quality are sold as frozen musts, the very finest grapes will not be found in concentrates. Neither the processor nor the home winemaker could afford it. Grape quality is still critical, and some processors will use better grapes than others. In addition to grape quality, the sophistication of the industrial process used to make the concentrate is important to the ultimate quality. The better the vacuum, the lower the temperature at which the liquid will boil, and the less of the essence of the grape that is lost. Although all processors will trap the phenols and organic compounds that are boiled off and add them back before canning, a lower temperature and more gentle processing will retain more of these subtle organic compounds. Don't hesitate to ask questions about the processing method before deciding on a concentrate. (See Chapter 15 and Appendix E for more on fermenting aseptic juices and concentrate kits.)

Equipment and supplies

You will also need to decide on equipment and supplies. Some items are essential at the outset, while certain others can wait until bottling or until next year. Some pieces can be improvised. Some are luxury items that you will never buy unless winemaking becomes a serious hobby.

The first stop should be your local winemaking supply store. If the Yellow Pages for your area has no listings under "Beer and Winemaking Supplies," try a large metropolitan area. Call and ask for a catalog. Many wine supply shops have catalogs and are happy to ship. Shopping on-line and by mail is easy with toll-free numbers, FAX machines and UPS delivery.

If you will be fermenting aseptic juice, concentrates or frozen white juice, you will not have to worry about the main pieces of winemaking equipment — the crusher and the press. If you ferment frozen red grapes, you will not need a crusher-stemmer, but you will need a press for larger quantities. If you plan to process only small quantities of fresh grapes to begin with, try renting a crusher and press, as the cash outlay to purchase is substantial. If you find yourself totally without access to equipment, small quantities of grapes can be crushed with a 4X4 post or even with your foot and pressed by hand in a nylon mesh bag! (Be careful, however, not to crack the seeds if crushing with a hard object, as they contain large amounts of highly astringent tannin.) But if you have much more than 100 pounds to process, try your best to borrow, rent or purchase a crusher and press.

Once you've made the decision to invest in equipment, try placing an ad in the "Miscellaneous Wanted" section of your newspaper classified ads or on Craigslist.com. There are always retired home winemakers willing to part with used carboys, crushers and presses for much less than replacement cost. Most equipment lasts indefinitely, and used equipment is usually as functional as new. And whether you are considering new or used equipment, the initial investment can be kept even lower and more fun can be had if several people go in together and pool their resources!

Equipment Glossary

The array of equipment available to the home winemaker has improved steadily over the years. It would take a tidy sum to buy everything at once, but you do not need everything at the outset in order to make quality wines. Here's a list of standard equipment and supplies. Note that plastic, polyethylene and polypropylene materials for pails, hoses and other materials that come in contact with the wine should be of food grade quality. This is indicated by a "USDA" or "HDPE" imprint. (Parentheses indicate that the item is not essential.)

NOTEBOOK. Get a substantial notebook to keep notes. Some winemakers hang a tag around the neck of each carboy for immediately recording what was done and transfer the data to the permanent notebook later. I settled on a 3-ring binder with mylar-reinforced notebook paper. Whatever technique you use, good notes are important.

CRUSHER. The threshold question in deciding on a crusher is whether you are primarily interested in white wines or red wines. For processing white grapes, a simple crusher with two meshed rollers is all that you need.

White grapes should be left on the stems for pressing, as the stems stabilize the mass inside the press and allow the juice to flow more freely.

A crusher-stemmer, however, is needed for processing red grapes because the stems have to be separated before fermentation, and it does this automatically.

CRUSHER

CRUSHER-STEMMER

With a small quantity of red grapes, the stems can be fished out with a homemade rake, such as a white oak stick with long stainless steel screws in it, or even by hand. But with larger quantities, a crusher-stemmer is nearly indispensable. Unfortunately, crusher-stemmers are considerably more expensive than plain crushers, even if not motorized.

Whether you are looking at a plain crusher or a crusher-stemmer, consider getting one with a stainless steel hopper. It's worth the extra cost in the long run. Washing and maintenance will be less critical, and you will not have to worry about contamination with trace amounts of metals or paint chips.

PRESS. A good press is the other basic piece of winemaking equipment. The screw-type, vertical basket press of Italian origin has been around forever and works well. The larger the press, the less efficient it will be at extracting the juice, due to the diminishing surface-to-volume ratio as the size increases. If you plan to do mostly white wines and want to extract as much juice as possible, a smaller size might be preferable. The No. 30 size — about 7.5 gallons — will press 100 pounds of white grapes before it has to be split apart to dispose of the cake of skins and stems, or "pomace." Double that poundage if you are pressing red grapes after fermentation on the skins. Bladder presses are easy to use and can be adjusted to extract the desired amount of juice. But they are more expensive.

Consider building or buying a stand to mount your press on. Not only will the press be more stable, but the added height will allow the use of larger containers to catch the juice as you press.

PRIMARY FERMENTERS. At least one primary fermenter will be needed. Red wines are initially fermented in an open container, preferably one with a lid or cover. Although white wines are best fermented in carboys, a primary fermenter will be needed anyway to hold the grapes and juice as they are crushed. And they are convenient for transporting grapes. So at least one primary fermenter, such as a Rubbermaid Brute®, should be on the shopping list. Or, you could get 55-gallon poly barrels which have been used to transport fruit juices (see photo next page). Fruit juice brokers and cold storage warehouses often have them available for $10 or so, and they will accommodate up to 400 pounds of red grapes. Be sure you know what they contained before, as the juice will pick up a taint.

Fifteen-gallon beer kegs are probably the most commonly used primary fermenter as they are probably the least expensive, gallon for gallon.

OPEN FERMENTERS. If cost is not a factor, consider a 304 stainless steel vat with a floating lid. These containers are available in various

Fifty-five gallon poly barrel

sizes starting at 20 gallons. The lid has an inflatable tube around it, similar to a bicycle inner tube, which can be pumped up to make the fermenter airtight. Although a container of this type could be used to ferment almost any wine, it is especially useful when blending larger volumes and for extended maceration of red grapes after fermentation is complete.

PAILS. Two or three plastic pails will be needed to catch the juice as it flows out of the press, to dip crushed grapes, etc. Get the largest capacity pail that will slide under the drainage spout of the press.

CARBOYS. The number needed will depend on how many grapes you expect to be processing. One hundred pounds of grapes will yield roughly 6-7 gallons of unfermented must and pulp and 5-6 gallons of finished wine after loss of pulp and lees from several rackings. However, if you will be fermenting white wines and using carboys as primary fermenters, bear in mind that a 5-gallon carboy will accommodate only 60 to 70 pounds of grapes. That's because it can be filled only ¾ full, taking foaming into consideration. And an extra carboy will be needed when it comes time to rack.

TIP

Never clean your stainless steel containers with bleach as it will pit the surface. Use a cleaner designed for stainless, such as Star San.

Carboys come in 7, 6, 5, 3 and 2.8 gallon sizes, but some sizes are difficult to locate. After you have several 5-gallon carboys, get a

foam

fermenting
wine

yeast lees

3-gallon carboy, or a 7-gallon carboy. You'll appreciate the flexibility year after year. You can never have too many carboys! Avoid plastic carboys, as oxygen will eventually permeate and ruin the wine. But that's not true with respect to Better Bottle® carboys, which oxygen molecules cannot permeate. If you are doing large quantities or using 15-gallon barrels, a 14-gallon (54 liter) demi-john might make a nice equipment addition at some point.

You will also need some smaller jugs to temporarily handle the excess volume — 1 gallon, 4 liter, 3 liter, 1.5 liter, etc. Make sure your stoppers will fit as the neck diameters of jugs vary.

CARBOY STOPPERS. You will need one solid stopper per carboy and one drilled air lock stopper per carboy. Size no. 7 fits most carboys; no. 6½ fits most jugs. Rubber stoppers are better than cork as they last indefinitely and don't lose their shape. Cork stoppers tend to assume the shape of the carboy neck and seat less dependably with age. Some stoppers made of newer synthetic materials are elongated and will work in a wider range of neck diameters than rubber; they work well for gallon jugs. Stoppers can be wrapped with a layer of heavy plastic wrap to counter the tendency to back out. The type used by delis to wrap sandwiches works, as does Stretch-Tite® from Costco. Punch a hole in the plastic wrap if using an air lock so the gas can escape.

AIR LOCKS. Several types of air locks or "bubblers" are available; all work acceptably well as long as the water level is maintained.

The two-piece air lock with a straight stem and separate float requires less headspace above the carboy. It has the disadvantage, if
over-filled, of drawing reservoir water or sulfite solution into the
wine if the temperature falls enough to cause the carboy volume
to shrink. The one-piece, "S-shaped" air lock allows for backflow
of air without contaminating the wine with reservoir liquid.

PLASTIC FUNNELS. Get the largest capacity you can find for
racking into carboys. You will also need a smaller funnel to fit into
wine bottles.

RACKING STEM, HOSE & CLIP. For racking from carboy to carboy,
you will need a clear vinyl hose and a racking stem of $5/16$", $3/8$"
and/or $1/2$" diameter. I prefer the $1/2$" size for racking from carboy to
carboy as it is faster, and the $5/16$" size for bottling. Plastic clips are
made which slip over the $5/16$" diameter to cut off the flow. Be sure
your hose fits tightly on the racking stem and bottling wand.

HYDROMETER, JAR AND WINE THIEF. This is basic equipment for
testing the level of unfermented sugar in musts and sugar solutions.
A wine thief is a convenience for lifting samples out of carboys
(see page 20).

BRUSHES. A carboy brush and a bottle brush are indispensable.
Bend the carboy brush to fit the shoulder of the carboy. I have a
second carboy brush bent at 90 degrees to clean the bottoms.

WOOD DOWELS. This is a hardware store item used when stirring up lees to promote malolactic fermentation and for topping in additives rather than racking. I have a very slender one for stirring up MLF lees and a thicker one for heavier jobs.

MEDICINAL TEASPOON. The ordinary kitchen teaspoon is amazingly inaccurate! It is often 30% more or less than a true teaspoon, which is approximately 5 ml. Greater accuracy is needed for measuring chemicals such as tartaric acid and potassium metabisulfite. Get a medicinal teaspoon at the drug store, which can be used by trial and error to find a kitchen teaspoon that happens to be accurate. Then mark the kitchen version and use it to measure your chemicals by volume — it's much easier than weighing every time.

ACID TEST KIT. Total acid is such an important measurement in winemaking that you should invest in an acid test kit early in

read from the bottom
of the meniscus

Hydrometer
and jar

WINE THIEF

*Volumetric (top) and
serological pipets*

your home winemaking career. It will be well worth the modest cost. See Appendix A for details on assembling your own kit and conducting titration tests.

CLINITEST® TABLETS. These tablets for measuring residual sugar are available at some drug stores if your wine shop does not carry them. They are particularly important in making white wines in which small quantities of residual sugar are desired. See Appendix A for details on use.

PIPETS. Serological or graduated pipets are among the most useful supply items. The 1 ml size can be used for Clinitest® and for acid titration tests. When you are interested in controlling the addition of sulfite at bottling, for instance, ¼ tsp. of potassium metabisulfite can be dissolved in 25 ml of water and 1 ml dispensed into each bottle to give 45 ppm. A 1 ml pipet can also be used as a straw to sample wine right out of the carboy! I use a burette if I am testing a lot of samples, but I use pipets for testing 2 or 3 samples. I would suggest two 1-ml class A pipets for titrations, one for sodium hydroxide and one for the wine sample. It's easier than setting up a burette.

A volumetric pipet of 5, 10 or 20 ml size is needed to measure wine samples when doing titration tests with a burette (see Appendix A). It doubles as a wine thief! A lab supply house will normally carry glassware of this type if your brew shop does not.

(SCALE). Some type of scale capable of measuring fractions of an ounce (and preferably metric as well) is a convenience, but by no means a necessity. A photographer's, reloader's or digital postage scale would work, but you can usually get by without a scale. This book usually references chemicals in fractions of a teaspoon on the

Argon tank with regulator

assumption that you will not have a scale. If you have a scale, by all means use it, particularly for potassium metabisulfite, calcium carbonate and potassium bicarbonate.

(INERT GAS TANK). If you plan to ferment a lot of white wines, a tank of inert gas with a flow regulator is the answer to the air problem. White wines — particularly those from hot climates — are so sensitive to air that every effort should be made to minimize the air contact. A tank makes it easy to displace the air. I have a small tank of argon with a regulator valve that reduces the flow to 20 cubic feet per hour. Argon is heavier than nitrogen or carbon dioxide and the molecules are larger, so it does not rise or get absorbed as readily. With a tank of inert gas you can purge your carboys of air before racking into them. You can use it to protect wine in partially filled carboys. You can use it to protect the wine while running bench trials and waiting for the outcomes. One of its best uses is protecting the cap of red grapes during extended maceration — the headspace should be sparged weekly. In addition, I sometimes give each empty bottle a puff at bottling time if I am late in getting around to bottling it. The cost at a welding supply shop was less than $100 filled, and a refill a year and a half later was only $15. While I would not classify a tank as a necessity, it has been my most versatile equipment addition.

(pH METER). Although it is not a necessity, a pH meter will give you more insight into wine chemistry than any other piece of luxury equipment. You can quickly determine the effect on this all-important measurement of various procedures, such as the effect on pH of increasing or decreasing the acid level, cold stabilization and malolactic fermentation, and how much sulfite to add, to name a few. See page 189 for more on digital pH meters.

Chemicals Glossary

Some chemicals, most notably potassium metabisulfite and organic additives, have a limited shelf life. It is a good idea to mark new chemicals with the month and date of acquisition with a Sharpie pen and when its useful life will expire.

POTASSIUM METABISULFITE. Some people are allergic to sulfite and asthmatics are particularly sensitive to it. The fumes are highly caustic and care should always be taken to avoid breathing it or getting the solution in your mouth. Nevertheless, potassium metabisulfite, also referred to as "sulfite" or "meta," is the wine-maker's best friend! Its virtues are many and impressive. It kills unwanted bacteria and foreign yeast but not cultured yeast. It kills natural malolactic bacteria and yeasts present in the vineyard. It inhibits enzymatic browning of white wines. It promotes

> **POTASSIUM METABISULFITE**
> *Symbol:* $K_2S_2O_5$
> *Preparation:* dissolve in a little warm water and stir to dissolve thoroughly.
> *Weight:* 1 tsp. = 6.3g.
> *Shelf life:* 6 to 12 months. It will be less than full strength when purchased and never stops disintegrating. Store tightly closed and away from heat or light.

clarification after fermentation is over. It stabilizes a white wine with residual sugar and discourages renewed fermentation. It extends the shelf life of your wine, and at the right level, it actually improves the flavor. However, don't use it indiscriminately. Low levels will provide all the benefits.

There is universal agreement among vintners around the world that sulfite is needed after fermentation. It not only kills microbial bacteria and other would-be spoilers, but it is also an antioxidant. The shelf life of a wine with normal pH and no sulfite will not be much more than one year, depending on the pH. The principal controversy is about using sulfite before fermentation. Some wine-makers use no sulfite until after fermentation in the belief that a more flavorful wine results. These folks, comprising the "brown school," will accept a bit of browning in their white wines in exchange for the slightly greater complexity they believe the natural yeast produce early in fermentation. The browning will largely disappear during clarification. They hope for more complexity from the natural yeasts that would otherwise be killed by sulfite. And they also want to keep the acetaldehyde to an absolute minimum. Some acetaldehyde is always formed during fermentation, and sulfiting before fermentation will increase the level of acetaldehyde somewhat.

TIP

Keep last year's sulfite next to the kitchen sink for dipping chicken and salmon to kill possible salmonella. Hold your breath and drain immediately!

The "green school" counters that the natural yeast is killed by very low alcohol levels (5-6%), and there is no assurance that the by-products of wild yeast fermentation will benefit the wine anyway — they could be a negative. The green school wants to eliminate all forms of natural yeast and malolactic bacteria. They prefer to avoid all browning in favor of a clean fermentation with a predictable outcome. They don't care if the aldehyde level is marginally higher, since it is so low as to escape detection anyway.

Take your pick, but note that if sulfite is not used until after fermentation is complete, extra care should be taken in cleanliness before and during crushing, as the risk of spoilage goes up. Sulfite everything that comes in contact with the must or wine and then rinse the equipment with water. Discard overripe and spoiled clusters with greater care. I would never omit the sulfite with grapes having *botrytis,* mold, or high pH; in fact, more sulfite should be used.

Some winemakers use the potassium version of Campden tablets, which add about 65 ppm of sulfite at the rate of one tablet per gallon. They must be crushed with a mortar and pestle, and even then are difficult to completely dissolve. Granular potassium metabisulfite is easier to dissolve and less expensive.

Metabisulfite decomposes rather quickly and will not be at its full theoretical strength even when new. It should be tightly capped, stored it in a cool, dark place, and replaced at least once a year. Use last year's metabisulfite for making a cleaning solution.

See Appendix C for technical data on the exacting use of potassium metabisulfite in relation to pH and for use of a 10% stock solution.

TANNIN. Since white grapes have little or no tannin, some wine-makers like to add a very small quantity (¼-½ tsp. per 5 gallons) of tannin for astringency and as an aid in later fining with gelatin or isinglass. I seldom use tannin in white wines because I usually soak the grapes on the skins and stems overnight, which adds a little tannin.

PECTIC ENZYME. Pectic enzyme is commonly used in making fruit wines from apricots, peaches and other pit fruits. It can also be used for grape wines. It increases the yield of white grapes by breaking down the pulp and makes pressing more efficient. It aids in extracting flavors from the skins of red grapes by accelerating physical disintegration of the berry. Follow manufacturer's instructions for recommended dosage, shelf life and storage, which is usually refrigerated. Note that enzymes will be rendered ineffective if bentonite (or tannin) is added at the same time.

POTASSIUM BITARTRATE. Potassium bitartrate can be used as seed to hasten tartrate crystallization at the rate of 1 tsp. per gallon when cold stabilizing. Dissolve it in a quart of wine and stir it back into the carboy with a dowel when the wine is at its coldest.

POTASSIUM SORBATE. You will not need this chemical unless you plan to make wines having residual sugar, as it is not needed for dry table wines. Although it will not stop active fermentation, potassium sorbate will reduce the risk of renewed fermentation in wines which are bottled with higher levels of unfermented sugar. Add it at the rate of 1 gram per gallon (200 ppm) and use it in conjunction with potassium metabisulfite for maximum effectiveness. It has

POTASSIUM SORBATE
Dosage: 3/4 to 1-1/4 g per gal.
Weight: 1 tsp. = 3.3g.
Shelf life: 6 months.

a distinct flavor which some people dislike. Potassium sorbate will generate a disagreeable, geranium-like odor if it is present during malolactic fermentation. See notes at page 97 on stopping fermentation without use of potassium sorbate.

The Glossaries after several of the succeeding Chapters should also be consulted:

Yeasts and supplements	page 42
Fining agents	page 58
Bottling	page 83
Acids	page 89
Carbonates	page 92
Malolactic bacteria	page 127

Chapter Two

FERMENTING WHITE TABLE WINES

he basic process for making white table wines is as simple as it is universal. After the grapes are crushed and pressed, the juice is fermented in an enclosed container, free of air. Home winemakers typically ferment their white wines in partially filled carboys topped with an air lock. After most of the sugar has been fermented and the frothy stage of fermentation is past, the carboys are topped up and allowed to ferment to complete dryness. After it is dry, the wine is clarified, the residual sugar and total acid are corrected, and it is bottled. The commercial winery will filter at least once in addition to gravity fining, and may also age the wine in oak casks for a period of time. But the basic procedure is otherwise the same for both.

Sterilizing solution

The first step in the new fermenting season should be the preparation of a jug of sulfite solution. It is easier to always have a jug of sterilizing solution ready for cleaning equipment than having to mix a new solution every time. It will be used repeatedly throughout the season. The exact concentration is not critical, so start with 1 teaspoon of potassium metabisulfite and an optional tablespoon of citric acid dissolved in a gallon of water. I get fresh meta every year because it is below its theoretical strength when purchased and continues deteriorating, and I use last year's meta to make my cleaning solutions. The solution can be reused; after rinsing out a carboy, for instance, just funnel it back into the jug. When it gets low, top it up with more water and meta. If it picks up too much sediment, mix a new solution.

For treating newly crushed musts with sulfite, you might want to make a 10% solution of potassium metabisulfite. It's handier than measuring and dissolving fractional teaspoons for each addition, but it has a short shelf life. (See page 204.)

Cleanliness

Cleanliness is important, but not in the sense that a beginning winemaker might expect. Don't worry about a few earwigs and spiders! They'll settle out in the lees just like the dead yeast cells. Nor is a little dirt any cause for concern. My point is not to en-courage a disregard of cleanliness, but to emphasize the principal concern of a home winemaker — AIR. Without air as the catalyst, most dirt, bacteria and other potential sources of spoilage remain innocuous. If you want to be a fanatic about something, let it be air rather than dirt. Minimize air contact in making white wines, and you are not likely to experience spoilage problems.

Yes, the equipment should be clean, but it need not be surgically sterile. If the crusher and press were cleaned after the last use and show no signs of mold, it will suffice to hose them down. If they look dirty, they should be scrubbed and then sprayed with sulfite cleaning solution in a hand sprayer. Some winemakers religiously sulfite everything that comes into contact with their wine. But if my equipment is clean, I normally just hose it down and have had no problems with spoilage. That's probably because I sulfite the juice at crushing and am a fanatic about air.

Culling bad fruit

Before being crushed, the grapes should be examined carefully and any rotten clusters discarded. If a cluster is raisined and hard, discard it and proceed using only fruit that is of sound quality.

Over-ripe berries which have started to sour, in particular, should not be fermented. Sometimes there will not be a bad cluster in the whole lot; at other times, culling out the bad fruit can be tedious. But it is important with white wines. Resist the temptation to wash the fruit as it probably would not remove any residual sprays and would only set the stage for unwanted mold and infection.

Preparing a yeast starter solution

A yeast starter solution should be initiated as soon as the grapes or juice arrive. Spontaneous or "natural" fermentation — the process of crushing and pressing without sulfite and letting natural yeast on the grapes and in the air establish and do the fermenting — is fashionable with some commercial vintners. But it's not recommended for the home winemaker, particularly with white wines. It takes too long for natural yeast to multiply to the point where they start converting the sugar to alcohol, and the result is too uncertain. In addition, most strains of wild yeast will not ferment to complete dryness because they are killed off by low alcohol levels. You will get better results using one of the many strains of cultured wine yeast.

There are two steps involved in building a yeast starter solution, the first being to activate the packet of dry yeast. Start with ½ cup of warm water — about 90-100°F (32-38°C). Sprinkle the yeast granules over the surface, without stirring. It will be fully rehydrated in 20 minutes.

The second step is increasing the volume. This is best done by squeezing a cup of fresh grape juice and diluting it with a cup of water to lower the sugar level (diluted, because yeast multiply faster with medium sugar concentration than high). Add a pinch of yeast food, such as Superfood®, Fermaid K®, or diammonium phosphate ("D.A.P.") to stimulate multiplication. Mix the yeast cup and diluted grape juice together in a carafe or jar, plug it with cheesecloth or paper towels and set it atop the hot water heater or in a warm window sill. This should all be accomplished within 30 minutes after the yeast was initially hydrated. The starter solution will be actively fermenting in an hour or two, maybe sooner.

The 1½ pints of yeast starter solution thus concocted will be sufficient to inoculate 10 gallons of must at the optimum starter-to-must ratio of 2%. A larger volume of starter could be used, but that would needlessly dilute the wine. If you have more than 10 gallons of must to ferment and need more starter, start with 2 or 3 cups of fresh juice, dilute with an equal volume of water, and follow the same procedure. Always wait until the starter is fermenting actively before inoculating.

Normally, one prefers to work with dry yeasts as they are so convenient. However, some excellent yeast strains exist which are available only in liquid form. With yeast in foil pouches, such as Wyeast, or yeast in a vial, such as White Labs, just follow the instructions to activate it. Then you need to increase the volume to at least 2% of your must volume.

If your grapes have not arrived, start with ½ cup of freshly pressed juice from oranges, grapefruits or Thompson seedless grapes diluted with ½ cup of water. Don't use canned or pasteurized juices as they might contain preservatives which would inhibit yeast growth. Bring the diluted juice to a brief boil to kill the wild yeast. After it has cooled, add a pinch of yeast food or D.A.P. and the liquid yeast sample. Plug the carafe or jar with cheesecloth and set it in a warm place. It might take a day, but it will eventually become active. It speeds up the process to pour it back and forth between containers for aeration. Yeast like air during the multiplication stage (but when they reach maximum concentration and start converting the sugar to alcohol, air should be eliminated).

When the grapes arrive, add a cup of the freshly pressed grape juice plus a cup of water to increase the volume. Put it back in the warm spot until it is active again and ready to add to the must a few hours later.

Of course, if you already have wine actively fermenting and want to use the same strain of yeast for the next batch of grapes, it's even easier to get a starter. Just siphon a cup or two of the lees off the bottom of the fermenting must and add it to an equal volume of fresh grape juice diluted with water. It will be active shortly.

CRUSHER

Crushing

The grapes should be crushed as soon as possible after being picked and fermentation initiated with as little delay as possible. If they were picked late in the day and are warm, however, I would suggest letting them cool overnight and crushing in the morning. More flavor will be retained if the grapes are crushed cool. White grapes should be crushed on the stems as the stems stabilize the mass in the press, facilitate drainage of the juice and add a bit of tannin. A simple crusher with two rollers, mounted over a primary fermenter or other receptacle, is all that one needs for crushing white grapes. If you have a crusher-stemmer, remove the de-stemming trough.

After crushing, the grapes go into a large pail or primary fermenter of food grade quality. A small amount of potassium metabisulfite is carefully measured, dissolved in an ounce or two of water and thoroughly mixed in. The dosage will depend on the condition of the grapes. For grapes in good condition and having normal sugar, acid and pH, the recommended dosage of metabisulfite is ¼ tsp per 5 gallons of volume, which is roughly 45 parts per million (ppm). Or you could pulverize three Campden tablets per carboy with a mortar and pestle, which will be approximately 40ppm. If you mixed a 10% solution within the past two weeks (page 204),

Pawls

Reversing the pawls

ILLUSTRATION A

add 3.33 ml per U.S. gallon (.88 ml per liter) to get 45 ppm. If your grapes are high in sugar and low in acid, they presumably have a high pH, in which case the dosage should be increased to 100 ppm. Use of more than 120 ppm is not advisable unless the grapes are badly sunburned, have broken skins, bunchrot or are in extremely poor condition, which hopefully will not be the case.

Contrary to its current public image, metabisulfite is a great preservative and antioxidant and will help keep the must from browning. It kills natural yeast and bacteria but has little effect on cultured yeast at levels under 45 ppm. Don't hesitate to use it. On the other hand, never use more than necessary. Keep accurate records as to how much meta was added to each batch of wine and when. Be aware that an unfermented must will accommodate more meta than a finished wine. A new wine will handle larger doses of meta right after fermentation, when it still contains solids, than it will after clarification. In my experience judging at county fairs, excess meta is the most common mistake of home winemakers. They add too much, too late in the game. For a more complete discussion of potassium metabisulfite, please refer to page 23 and Appendix C.

Some winemakers also add pectic enzyme when the grapes are crushed as it will hasten maceration of the berries and increase the volume of liquid. I prefer not to use it because it also increases the volume of pulp, which should not be fermented. I question whether the yield is increased much at all after the pulp is settled and the juice racked off. Since I suspect that pectic enzyme makes clarification more difficult, I no longer use it on white wines.

Soak on the skins

If your schedule permits, let the crushed grapes soak on the skins for up to 12 hours to extract more varietal characteristic of the grape. You could add a couple of pounds of food-grade dry ice to the fermenter or frozen milk jugs (first sprayed with sulfite) before adding the crushed grapes to hasten the chill down. Then cover the mass with strips of plastic wrap to minimize air contact. But soaking is not always advisable — see Chapter 10.

Pressing

Dip the crushed grapes and juice out of the primary fermenter with a small pail and pour them into the press basket. It is not necessary to line the basket with cheesecloth or fiberglass mesh in pressing *vinifera* grapes, but one certainly could, as is commonly done in pressing the very slippery *labrusca* grapes. Compact the mass as much as possible by hand, then add more grapes and compress by hand again. When the basket is nearly full, place the wood blocks and screw in position and start ratcheting. When you meet stiff resistance and the flow diminishes to a trickle, take a break. Have another sip of last year's effort! The flow will stop completely in a few minutes, and then you can start cranking again. Repeat the cycle of pressing and waiting until it has been pressed to your satisfaction.

When it has been fully pressed, reverse the pawls (Illustration A inset, page 32), back off the ratchet assembly and remove the blocks. Discard the "cake," reassemble the basket, and repeat the process.

The grapes can actually be pressed two or three times to maximize the yield — open the basket, fluff them up and start over. Additional pressings are certainly worthwhile if you pressed whole clusters without first crushing in order to minimize skin contact, or if your press is inefficient due to its large capacity. The grapes in the center of the cake will still contain some juice. However, additional pressings will not increase the yield much if you crush the grapes, use pectic enzyme, soak on the skins and use a small press. You will get almost all of the fermentable juice with one hard pressing.

Set aside a cup or two of the must for later testing.

Settling out the solids

You will get a better wine by settling out the pulp and fermenting only the clear juice. Funnel the juice into carboys, let the pulp settle out overnight and siphon, or "rack," the clear juice off the pulp the next morning. This delay also gives the sulfite time to bond with the solids and sugars in the must so that it will no longer interfere with yeast multiplication.

You can add the yeast starter and nutrient as you press and transfer to carboys for settling of solids — it takes at least a day for fermentation to start. But if you get distracted and delay in racking off the pulp, the pulp and sediment will quickly get roiled up, ferment, and disintegrate. The other option is to add the yeast starter and nutrient the next morning when you rack the clear juice off the pulp.

Adjusting total acid and sugar

While the pulp is settling, the sugar and acidity of the must should be tested and preparations made to adjust them as necessary when the clear juice is racked off the pulp in the morning. A hydrometer is the only item needed to check the sugar level. For dry white table wines the sugar content should be in the range of 22–24°B. For wines destined to have some residual sugar, the initial sugar could be higher or lower because you have some flexibility. Note that if you test immediately after pressing, the reading will be a point or so high due to the suspended solids. So retest the clear juice the next morning to be sure.

An acid test kit for testing total acid is inexpensive and easy to use. The total titratable acid would ideally be between 6 and 9 grams/liter before fermentation. This book usually refers to acid readings as percentages, such as .6% or .9%, which is the same as 6 or 9 grams per liter. (See Appendix A for details on conducting titration tests.)

ACID. Hopefully, a titration test will reveal the acid level of the must to be within the desired range of .6-.9% and adjustments will not be needed. But sometimes, due to weather or timing of the pick, the acid level will be off. In hot climates, the sugar level can shoot past the desired level in one or two days, resulting in low acid. In any climate, rain or unseasonably cold weather can hamper ripening so that sugar and acid never do reach the desired levels. Humidity can cause mold and force premature harvesting. There are several ways to raise acidity (Chapter 8) and several ways to lower it (Chapter 9).

The acid level of a finished white wine should be a minimum of .55%, up to a maximum of .70%. For most grapes — i.e., those with pH between 3.2 and 3.4 — total acid in the .60–.65% range would be ideal. If the acid level of the juice is low, it should be raised right now. The lower the acid, the more important that it be raised before fermentation rather than after. If you fail to adjust before fermentation and end up having to raise it by more than .15–.20% afterward, the resulting wine could show a harshness after bottle aging, due to the artificial acid. If the acid is added before, it will integrate with the natural acids during fermentation and be less noticeable. In other words, you can make a much larger adjustment before fermentation. In addition, there is less tendency for bitartrate crystals to precipitate after bottling if the acid is added before. I have fermented many West Coast musts with good results where the acid was as low as .4%. But I always add the acid before fermentation. See Chapter 8 for a detailed discussion on raising acidity. Since acid drops somewhat during fermentation and cold stabilization, it wouldn't hurt to raise it to .65-.70% before fermentation, slightly above the goal of .60–.65% in the finished wine.

An excess of acid would also need to be corrected. Two of the options are the same — blending or chemicals. Another is use of a yeast strain that lowers acidity, such as Lalvin 71B. Malolactic fermentation is an excellent option for some types of white wines, such as Chardonnay and Sauvignon Blanc. The commentary in Chapter 9 will be helpful in deciding on which corrective action to take now. My rule of thumb is never to start fermentation of a white wine with acid in excess of 1.0%, even if MLF is planned. Lower it to 1.0% before fermentation with calcium carbonate.

SUGAR. If you are making a dry white table wine, such as Chardonnay, Sauvignon Blanc or Pinot Gris, the starting sugar level ideally should be 22-24°B. If it is low, plan to stir in some table sugar—1½ ounces of ordinary table sugar per gallon will raise the Brix by 1°. The practice of adding sugar, known as chaptalization, is common in Germany and other regions where grapes have difficulty ripening and sometimes have to be picked with sugar as low as 17°B. So if the sugar is much below 22°B, don't hesitate to raise it.

If are working with Riesling, Gewurztraminer and Semillon grapes, the starting sugar level is less critical. If the sugar is 18-20°B, you could consider a sparkling wine — Riesling makes a wonderful sparkling wine. Or, you could add sugar and make a dry wine, leaving some residual sugar to balance the higher acid that under-ripe grapes usually have. With late-harvest grapes, some residual sugar would definitely be in order.

White table wine grapes from the West Coast sometimes test at 26°B, in which case I add distilled or de-chlorinated water to lower the sugar to 24°B, acidified to .65% with either tartaric acid (or, if malolactic fermentation is not planned, with a 50-50 blend of tartaric and malic acids). Since the acid in grapes with high sugar is usually low, you should run another titration test after the water is added — more acid may be needed to raise it to at least .60%, pre-fermentation. Diluting the must with water will not affect the quality appreciably until you exceed 10% water, at which point it will start to diminish the depth of the finished wine.

How much water to add? The equation is:

$$\frac{\text{Brix}}{\text{desired Brix}} \times \text{gal. must} = \text{must vol.} + X \qquad \text{where } X \text{ is the gal. of water to add}$$

For example, you have 10 gallons of juice and you want to lower the Brix from 26° to 24°:

$$\frac{26}{24} \times 10 = 10 + X$$
$$1.08 \times 10 = 10 + X$$
$$10.8 - 10 = X$$
$$.8 = X$$

Here is a table for the more common sugar levels and volumes:

Orig. Brix	Gallons of Juice				
	5	10	15	20	
27°	.6	1.2	1.9	2.5	⎱ Gal. of water to
26°	.4	.8	1.2	1.7	⎰ get 24° Brix
25°	.2	.4	.6	.8	

If the Brix is above 27°, it would be better to use the equation above and ameliorate down to only 25°B to avoid excessive dilution.

Initiating fermentation

We are now at the point where you have pressed the grapes and let the pulp settle out for a few hours. The next step is to rack the juice off the solids into a primary fermenter, adjusting the acid or sugar in the process, as explained above. Use a racking stem so the pulp does not get drawn up along with the juice. Once the juice has been transferred you can add the yeast starter, which by now should have been built up to at least 2% of your juice volume.

Some winemakers let the must ferment a day or two in an open primary fermenter before transferring to carboys, which is acceptable practice as long as it is transferred to carboys as soon as fermentation starts to slow. I usually ferment in carboys from start to finish. The carboys should be filled ¾ full and plugged with cheesecloth or a paper towel to discourage fruit flies. The head space is needed to allow room for foaming. A certain amount of foaming always accompanies fermentation, but it can be quite dramatic with certain vigorous yeasts under warm conditions and in musts containing large amounts of pulp.

Temperature is a major consideration when attempting to initiate fermentation. Since yeast multiply faster under warm conditions, the temperature should be maintained at 65-70°F (18-21°C) until fermentation starts. As soon as you see signs of fermentation, add a teaspoon of a balanced yeast food or D.A.P. per 5 gallons of juice. The yeast food reduces the tendency to generate hydrogen sulfide, and it is good insurance against stuck fermentation toward the end of fermentation. Yeast food is particularly important if you had to ameliorate to lower the sugar and with certain strains of yeast. Once the fermentation starts, move the carboys outdoors or into the garage for cold fermentation.

You may notice some browning by this time. That's because the sulfite bonds to the sugar and other constituents in the must. With little or no free sulfite remaining to protect the must, it will start to brown at some point. But this is not a cause for concern because the browning will disappear later when the wine is clarified. It's not advisable to add more sulfite at this late date because it might interfere with fermentation and result in a higher level of volatile acids. If the browning bothers you, give the must an additional 25ppm of sulfite at pressing.

Fermentation should start 24 to 36 hours after inoculation. If fermentation is reluctant to start, it is almost always the result of too much sulfite, inoculating before the starter is fully active or low temperature rather than lack of nutrients. If it does not start, rack it into another carboy for aeration. If that doesn't work, see Appendix B.

Once fermentation starts, the must should be deprived of oxygen. In fact, avoidance of air contact should become your guiding principle from now until the wine is finally bottled and corked in six or eight months. Substitute an air lock for the cheesecloth. Pour a sulfite solution in the reservoir of the air lock to help discourage the fruit flies.

Cold fermentation

After fermentation starts, the goal changes. Whereas the initial goal was to get fermentation initiated as quickly as possible, now the goal is to avoid "runaway" fermentation. If a vigorous yeast is used under warm fermenting conditions, it could ferment to complete dryness in 3 or 4 days. That's much too fast to get a great wine — too much of the bouquet and complexity is lost. Overly vigorous fermentation can be avoided by using a slower yeast and, most importantly, by lowering the temperature of the must.

The ideal temperature range for fermenting most white wines is 50-60°F (10-16°C). In this range, it will take ten days or more for the sugar to ferment down to 10°B. At this slower rate, the loss of bouquet is minimized and more of the fruit flavor is retained.

When deciding where to ferment, look for the coolest place you can find. If you don't have an old refrigerator or access to a walk-in cooler, a small room where you can crank down the air conditioner would be great, as would a corner of the basement. Garages are often used but they can get hot in the fall. Late in the fall you can ferment white wines outside on the north side of the house and out of the direct sunlight. If your falls are hot and you ferment a lot of white wines (or beers), you might want to invest in a stainless steel immersion coil to run tap water through and then out into the garden.

Fermentation will start rather slowly, but will quickly gather momentum. The most vigorous phase of fermentation will occur when the sugar is dropping from 20°B to 10°B. Fermentation should be monitored at least twice daily during this stage. Lift a sample out of the carboy with a wine thief. If the sugar level appears to be falling by more than 2 or 3°B per day, find a way to cool it. If you don't have an immersion coil, you could make a cold water bath by setting the carboys in a tub or wading pool with running tap water, and covering them with a T-shirt or pillow case to wick water up for cooling by evaporation. If your tap water is too warm, drop in a block of ice or milk jugs with frozen water to cool it.

Once the sugar level drops to 10°B., the frothy, tumultuous stage is over. You can let it ferment to dryness at room temperature. (The wine will be marginally better if you have the patience to let it cold ferment until it stops, which could take weeks, depending on the temperature, and even then might have to be warmed to room temperature to get it to go to complete dryness.) With the higher alcohol content and lowered sugar level, fermentation will slow no matter what the temperature or what the yeast type. If you are shooting for a dry white table wine, it is good practice to add another ½ tsp. of yeast food per 5 gallons when the sugar level has dropped to 10-12°B as insurance against a stuck fermentation later. (But don't add D.A.P. or yeast food below 5°B.)

Be alert to possible "rotten egg" smell during or after fermentation, which indicates hydrogen sulfide. Immediate corrective action should be taken if it is encountered (see Appendix B). Note, however, that some yeasts, most notably Montrachet, will generate a mild hydrogen sulfide odor. This problem with Montrachet yeast will usually disappear after one or two rackings. It is a pronounced and unmistakable rotten egg odor that is cause for concern.

Combining carboys

When the hydrometer indicates that unfermented sugar is approaching 0°B, the carboys should be combined and filled to the top. There will still be around 2% unfermented sugar when the hydrometer reads 0°B. You want the carboys to be full when the wine falls still and CO_2 is no longer being produced to dispel air. If the unsightly muck on the neck and shoulders of the carboy doesn't bother you, just top up — the muck might look gross but will not affect wine quality. It would be equally acceptable to rack into clean carboys.

Unless hydrogen sulfide was encountered, you can use the "mud" and pulp on the bottom if more liquid is needed to fill the last carboy. It's also acceptable to top up with a similar wine of good quality. Or drop in some marbles. There will seldom be any defects in a wine, but note that you should always taste each carboy before two different lots are blended or combined. If one happened to have flaws, both batches might be ruined by blending.

Juggle the volumes as needed to fill a lesser number of carboys. As a result of combining carboys, three fermenting carboys will become two, or four will become three, as the case may be. This is where it becomes convenient to have carboys in a variety of sizes, such as 2.8, 3, 5, 6 and 7 gallon sizes. A few jugs and larger bottles — 1 gallon, 3 liter, 4 liter, 1.5 liter — should also have been located ahead of time to accommodate the excess volume. Top the jugs with an air lock and allow them to ferment to dryness along with the carboys. Very small air lock stoppers are made which will even allow you to ferment in wine bottles. Every container should be as full as possible so as to minimize air contact. The smallest container can be topped with water if necessary. The point is to take no chances with air.

If you crushed and pressed without de-stemming or plan to add oak chips of some type, the wine will have sufficient tannin. If not, this would be a good time to add ¼-½ tsp. of tannin per 5 gallons, first dissolved in an ounce or two of water. This small amount will add a bit of astringency to the wine and will be helpful in later clarification efforts involving isinglass or gelatin.

After the carboys have been combined, the wine should be allowed to ferment to dryness. Since this might take several weeks at temperatures below 60°F (16°C), I normally finish fermentation of dry white table wines at room temperature. This not only assures uninterrupted and complete fermentation but saves several weeks of fermenting time and allows for earlier clarification and bottling. A warmer temperature is also needed to support malolactic fermentation — if that is desired, add the starter and nutrient after the wine has warmed up. Unfortunately, if you have been cold fermenting outside, this means moving the carboys.

Raising the temperature is not a necessity as the wine will usually ferment to dryness but over a longer period. But note that a nearly finished wine should not be subjected to temperatures below 50°F (10°C) for an extended period of time. It might get "stuck" with a few points of unfermented sugar, and it could be difficult to re-initiate fermentation weeks later.

The wine will normally be dry when the bubbles stop, but confirm it with Clinitest® (see Appendix A). Clinitest® tablets are the only practical way to check residual sugar; hydrometers with a 0-35° scale will not accurately measure unfermented sugar because the alcohol level has altered the density of the liquid. And you cannot rely on your palate right after fermentation as the wine is still too yeasty. So Clinitest® is the answer. As long as the residual sugar is below .3% or .4% (dark blue-green on the chart), consider it dry, even though trace amounts of various unfermented sugars will always remain. Often, the RS will be less than .1%.

Settling the gross lees

After fermentation is complete, the carboys should be topped up again as necessary and left undisturbed for three or four weeks in a cool corner of the garage or basement while the dead yeast cells, pectins and various by-products of fermentation, called the "gross lees," settle out. The wine will be racked and fined several times over the next six or eight months to promote clarification. But first, the gross lees should be allowed to settle out. If this is done at temperatures under 50°F, the wine will also be cold stabilized in a month. Tartrate crystals seem to form and precipitate more readily if cold stabilization occurs before the first racking.

After the carboys have been combined and all effervescence has stopped, replace the air lock with a solid rubber stopper. Although not mandatory, it is a good practice to wrap the stopper with sticky plastic wrap of the type delicatessens use to wrap sandwiches. This helps hold the stopper firmly in place. If the wine is bone dry and the stopper keeps popping out, this is a signal that microbes may be busy converting hydrogen sulfide into mercaptans and disulfides. The minute volume of gas produced by this process cannot be detected with an air lock, but it will often force a stopper out. See Appendix B. After a month, the gross lees will have settled and clarification will have come to a standstill, and the wine will be ready for the first racking.

Of course, if you are attempting to put the wine through malolactic fermentation, you would use an air lock rather than a stopper and try to hold the temperature at 70°F (21°C) until MLF is complete, rather than cold stabilizing at this juncture.

Yeast Glossary

Many different strains of yeast are readily available to the home winemaker. Lallemand, Laffort, Wyeast, Enoferm, Uvaferm, White Laboratories, Red Star and Vierka are the most common lines. Note that some yeasts are not identified beyond the marketing name, such as "Sauternes." Although they are undoubtedly dependable, the nomenclature could be misleading to someone inclined to assume that the yeast type will determine the wine type. Nothing could be further from the truth. Neither should you assume that your wine will be ruined if you pick a strain not recommended for your grape variety, as the differences are marginal at best.

Much has been written about the different flavor characteristics that various strains of yeasts impart. Differences undoubtedly exist immediately after fermentation, and they matter greatly to a commercial winery not wanting to tie up its fermentation capacity too long and wanting its wines to be marketable as soon as possible. But the differences seem insignificant to this home winemaker's palate. Two years after a wine has been bottled, I have been unable to detect any difference based on yeast strain. Commercial vintners all have their favorites and swear to long-term differences between them, so I defer to them.

Anyway, selection of yeast strain is a lot of fun! Always keep in mind the physical conditions to which they will be exposed. If, for instance, the Brix of the must is abnormally high, and you want a dry wine, pick a strain that is tolerant of high alcohol, such as Prise de Mousse or Pasteur Champagne. Do not use Epernay II as it is not very tolerant of high alcohol. If the grapes have *botrytis cinerea*, higher levels of sulfite should be used. Since the Brix will probably be higher, use one which is tolerant of high sulfite and high alcohol, like Prise de Mousse. If you want to cold ferment a white wine, use a cold-tolerant yeast, such as Epernay II, Prise de Mousse or, my favorite, Steinberg. If you want to stop fermentation with some residual sugar, use a less vigorous strain, which would point to Steinberg or Epernay II, and deprive it of nutrients as well. If you suspect that the grapes have residual sulfur on them, do not use Montrachet as it is particularly prone to converting the sulfur into hydrogen sulfide. If the acid is high, use Lalvin 71-B, which will help lower the acid. If you plan to initiate malolactic fermentation later, do not use Prise de Mousse as it produces higher levels of SO_2.

Here is a brief description of the more common strains, including marketing names.

PRISE DE MOUSSE (Red Star Premier *Cuvée*; Lalvin EC-1118). This vigorous dry yeast is good for either reds or whites, including cooler fermenting temperatures. It is very popular with commercial wineries due to its willingness to ferment to completion with few problems. It has little effect on the varietal characteristic of the grape, which can be either a positive or negative, depending on the result desired. It settles well, making it a good choice for barrel fermentation. Prise de Mousse is one option for re-initiating a stuck fermentation and for *tirage* fermentation of sparkling wines because it is tolerant of alcohol and sulfite. Its tolerance for high alcohol levels makes it a good choice for late harvest and ice wines. It is a very low foamer and does not have the tendency of Montrachet to generate hydrogen sulfide. However, Prise de Mousse is not advised if you plan to initiate malolactic fermentation as it generates high levels of hydrogen sulfide and also competes with the ML bacteria for some of the same nutrients.

MONTRACHET (UCD #522) is quite vigorous and produces a finished wine, red or white, with excellent complexity. It remains one of my favorites for red wines, Chardonnay and even Gewurztraminer. However, it would not be a good choice for high sugar musts, over 25°B, and is prone to produce hydrogen sulfide, particularly if the grapes had residual sulfur on them. So be alert.

PASTEUR RED. This is a good general purpose yeast for full-bodied red wines, such as Cabernet Sauvignon, Zinfandel, Merlot and red Rhone varieties. It produces full-bodied, complex wines and has been a standard of some commercial vintners for many years.

PASTEUR CHAMPAGNE (UCD #595). This is an all-purpose yeast commonly used for white wines. It is not used to make sparkling wines, however. It has good vigor, is quite tolerant of sulfite and leaves a pleasant yeasty flavor. It generates moderate foam.

PASTEUR WHITE (Red Star, French White). This yeast is used to make austere, complex white wines. It is a high foamer, so be sure to leave plenty of head space in the carboy. It is not recommended for barrel fermentation due to foaming.

EPERNAY II (Red Star Côtes de Blanc). This medium-speed yeast emphasizes the fruit in either reds or whites. Epernay is sometimes used to ferment Rieslings or Gewurztraminers intended to have some residual sugar as it tends not to ferment all the way to dryness at cool temperatures (i.e., it tends to get stuck late in fermentation). It is not very tolerant of high alcohol levels. Add 1 tsp. per 5 U.S. gallons of diammonium phosphate if you want to ferment to complete dryness. It often leaves a "soapy" taste shortly after fermentation which will eventually dissipate.

STEINBERG (Geisenheim Inst.). This yeast ferments slowly and is ideal for cold fermenting a white wine over a long period of time. It produces a wine with good complexity, structure and aromas. It is my favorite for cool fermentation of white wines, such as Riesling, Gewurztraminer, Pinot Gris, Viognier and Muscats. It slows but does not completely stop at temperatures below 50°F (10°C). One disadvantage, if you want to leave some residual sugar, is that it takes a couple of rackings and perhaps a fining to get it to stop fermenting. Add 45 ppm at the second racking, when it should be almost still. It is not widely available but White Laboratories has it in pouch form.

LALLEMAND (http://www.lallemand.com) markets five of its popular Lalvin yeasts in 5-gram packets:

LALVIN EC 1118. Same as Prise de Mousse above.

LALVIN ICV D-47. Used primarily for Chardonnay and other dry white wines. Very vigorous, produces wines with good mouth feel.

LALVIN RC212. Classic strain for Pinot Noir and Zinfandel, as it provides good color extraction and emphasizes the fruit and spicy quality of the grape. Needs generous additions of yeast food.

LALVIN 71-B. This is an interesting yeast because it neutralizes up to 30% of the malic acid. It is a low foaming strain, which is often used to emphasize aroma and fruitiness in blush and semi-sweet wines, such as Riesling, Gewurztraminer and Pinot Gris. Use with Fermaid K® or SuperFerment®.

LALVIN ICV K-1. Recommended for Sauvignon Blanc, Semillon, French hybrid whites and light reds. It is claimed to retain fresh fruit aromas longer than standard yeasts and perhaps for that reason is used to ferment sparkling wine bases.

WYEAST LABS (http://www.wyeastlab.com) of Mt. Hood, Oregon has a line of liquid yeasts in foil pouches ("Vintners Choice") that are easy to activate. The line includes 12 strains at last count, including Rudisheimer and Assmanhausen.

Many other excellent strains of yeast have been isolated, but are generally available only in larger packages. Enoferm had 42 strains at last count! In addition to the 5 strains available in 5-gram packets, Lallemand has at least 26 other strains in its Laffort, Lalvin and Uvaferm lines. Gist-brocades (http://www.dsm.nl) markets about 12 different yeast strains, including the popular Fermirouge, Fermiblanc and Fermivin strains. Many "boutique" yeasts are available in small packets from http://www.morewinemaking.com or http://thebeveragepeople.com. Morewinemaking.com also has encapsulated yeasts in smaller quantities.

Note that "dry" does not mean freeze-dried, so don't put your yeasts in the freezer as you would freeze-dried malolactic packets. Dry yeasts store best at cool temperatures, such as the wine cellar.

For additional details on wine yeasts, check out these websites:

http://winemaking.jackkeller.net/strains.asp
http://www.lallemandwine.us/products/yeast_chart.php
http://www.scottlaboratories.com/home.asp

Yeast Supplements Glossary

DIAMMONIUM PHOSPHATE (D.A.P.).
The legal limit of this nitrogen
source is 3.6 g. per gallon (.95 g/L),
but much less will suffice. It is not
absolutely necessary as stuck fer-

DIAMMONIUM PHOSPHATE
Dosage: ½ - ¾ g/gal. .13-.20 g/L. **Weight:** 1 tsp. = 4.3g.

mentations are the exception rather than the rule. But after you
get a stuck fermentation, you will become a believer! It is good
for making yeast starter solutions and in musts that are nutrient
deficient, such as musts that have been pre-fined with bentonite or
settled before fermentation. A dose of D.A.P. at peak fermentation
adds a bit of insurance against hydrogen sulfide if the grapes had
residual sulfur on the skins. Malolactic bacteria cannot use D.A.P.
as a nutrient source.

BALANCED YEAST FOODS. Various proprietary brands, such as Fermaid K™, Su-
perFerment® and GO-FERM®, are blends
of D.A.P., yeast hulls, yeast extract and

FERMAID K™
Dosage: 1 g/gal.;.26g/L **Weight:** 1 tsp. = 4.8g.

vitamins, such as thiamin, B-1 and H. They are more expensive than
plain D.A.P. but undoubtedly better. In particular, they should be
used if you need to reinoculate a stuck fermentation or know the
vineyard to be deficient in nitrogen.

YEAST EXTRACT. This is a very good source of nitrogen for budding yeast cells. Malolactic bacteria like yeast extract as well.

YEAST HULLS or "ghosts." This is the
cell membranes of yeast — the innards
became yeast extract. The hulls promote
fermentation by absorbing some of the

YEAST HULLS
Dosage: 1.3 g/gal.; .34 g/L **Weight:** 1 tsp. = 2.8g.

fatty acids, which reduces any tendency toward hydrogen sulfide
production and higher volatile acidity. Yeast hulls also promote
malolactic fermentation and are helpful in re-starting a stuck primary fermentation.

Chapter Three

BULK AGING

he wine will be "bulk aged" for several months until it is clarified and bottled in late spring or early summer. In the meantime, it will be racked occasionally and fined with clarifying agents. Bulk aging is an important phase in the life cycle of a wine because it allows the vintner to check and re-check the total acid, pH and residual sugar readings and to make repeated taste evaluations. Increasingly smaller adjustments to the residual sugar and/or acid levels will be made to nudge the wine closer to the desired objective. Several months are needed to make these evaluations and adjustments because right after fermentation, the yeast and tannins are so overwhelming as to interfere with taste evaluation. In a few months, however, the yeast flavor will start to subside and the tannins to soften. By bottling time you will have a good sense of the wine you are working with. This is the principal benefit of bulk aging — a chance to get to know your product better and improve it!

Here is an overview of a racking and fining sequence that I have used with excellent results in clarifying white wines. It assumes bulk aging in glass or stainless steel vessels, not in oak barrels.

- **Cold Stabilization.** The wine falls still and the gross lees and tartrate crystals are allowed to precipitate for 4 to 6 weeks, preferably at temperatures under 50°F.

- **First racking.** The wine is racked off the gross lees, given 45 ppm of potassium metabisulfite and fined with Kieselsol-chitin.

- **Second racking.** Two months or so later, the wine is racked again and fined with isinglass. The acid-residual sugar balance is evaluated and adjusted as needed.

- **Third racking.** Two months later, the wine is racked, sulfited, and the acid-sugar balance fine-tuned in anticipation of bottling.

- **Bottling.** A month or two later the wine is bottled.

These intervals are not set in stone, but you do need to maintain a minimum level of sulfite.

Cold stabilization

After the wine falls still, it should be cold stabilized for a month or so. I move the carboys under the deck or along the north side of the house, out of direct sunlight. The temperature usually gets down into the 40s, which is sufficient cold stabilization to prevent tartrate formation after bottling. Wine won't freeze until its temperature drops below 27°F (-3°C). Cap the necks with fruit jars to keep the rain out and check occasionally for popped stoppers. When the wine is fully chilled, draw out a few cups of wine and dissolve some potassium bitartrate (cream of tartar) at the rate of 1 tsp. per gallon (1 g/L) and stir it back in. This will hasten the crystallization process.

What if you are not fermenting in the fall or winter or don't have cold enough winters to rely on Mother Nature? You wouldn't want to wait until the following winter to do the first racking, of course. The first thing to remember is that cold stabilization is not mandatory! Skipping this step would only mean that tartrate crystals might form during bottle aging. Although that would be bad news for a commercial winery trying to sell its wine to consumers who believe them to be glass shards, the crystals are as harmless as the cream of tartar sitting on the spice rack. Which is exactly what they are! The crystals are strictly a visual flaw, to uninformed consumers. Since I'm not commercial, I don't worry much about a few tartrate crystals a few years after bottling.

If you have a spare refrigerator or access to a walk-in cooler, chill the wine down for three weeks and then rack and sulfite. Seed with cream of tartar early during the chill.

Acid-sugar balance

In addition to cold stabilization, bulk aging gives you time to adjust the acid and residual sugar, add oak, etc. At each racking — and perhaps in between — you will be doing taste evaluations and titration tests to determine the acid level. Hopefully, with the corrections made before fermentation, the acid will be within the desired range, which can run from a low of .55% for a dry white table wine to a high of .70%. I consider .60-.65% to be optimum. If the acid is clearly high or low, you should start the correction process at the first or second racking and make increasingly smaller adjustments later.

It's not just the acid level, because acid is closely related to unfermented sugar in the final wine. You want to get the right balance between total acid and residual sugar before bottling. Most people like red table wines totally dry but not necessarily white table wines. A bone-dry white wine having residual sugar of less than .1% might seem well balanced at a very young age. This is because the fruitiness in a new wine has the same effect on the palate as sugar — it counters the acidity. But as the fruitiness diminishes over time, a bone-dry white wine will become too astringent for some people. A bit of residual sugar will keep it softer and fruitier and will be appreciated after the wine has aged a while. It also enhances the bouquet and brings out more of the varietal characteristic of the grape.

The optimum amount of residual sugar will vary with the level of acid, the mix of acids, the pH, the grape type, and — most importantly — your personal preference. Titration readings, while helpful, do not tell the whole story. A wine with lower pH, for instance, will require slightly more residual sugar to balance it than one having the same total acid but higher pH. Similarly, some wines with acidity of .65%, for example, will taste tarter than others having the same acidity (and the same residual sugar). This is because the ratio of the various acids differs from wine to wine, and some acids taste more sour than others. In addition, a varying portion of the total acidity will be attributable to tartrate salts, which are less sour than tartaric acid itself. These variables make the residual sugar decision as much a matter of art as science, even for a commercial vintner. Rely on your tastes buds as much as the titration readings when deciding on the level of residual sugar. The closer to bottling, the less the numbers count and the more your palate counts. And always remember: the wine will begin to taste tarter as the fruitiness diminishes with age.

Here are some very general parameters to keep in mind when balancing residual sugar (RS) and total acid. With a finished white table wine having total acidity in the .60–.70% range, few people could distinguish between .1% RS and .4% RS; both would taste "dry" to most people. Unless you know that you like your white table wines bone dry, a good level of residual sugar to aim for would probably be around .3 or .4%, assuming normal acid and pH. But again, it will depend on the grape type. Chardonnay, Sauvignon Blanc and Semillon, for instance, are often bottled drier than other varieties. If you like your wines with noticeable sweetness, you might want a residual sugar of .75–1.00%, and quite possibly higher. This would be very appropriate for a Gewurztraminer, Riesling or Viognier.

Given the absence of any hard and fast rules for balancing residual sugar and total acidity, I highly recommend the routine testing of the various commercial wines that you like, as well as your own. Test residual sugar with Clinitest®, total acid by titration and pH if you have a meter. Keep notes for future reference as they will help you define your palate and facilitate a better guess as to how much residual sugar a particular wine should have.

Chapter Four

First Racking

oward the end of fermentation, the partially filled carboys were combined and topped up. After fermentation stopped, the gross lees were allowed to settle for 4 to 6 weeks. The wine is now much clearer but is still visibly hazy and has ceased to clarify further. Having been stored cool/cold, it is sufficiently cold stabilized, as evidenced by crystals of potassium bitartrate which are probably visible in the carboy. This means that no crystals should form after bottling (unless you later deem it necessary to lower the acid using potassium carbonate). It is time for the first racking! The first racking is somewhat of a landmark event because it is your first opportunity to speculate on the wine's ultimate quality. Although it will still be very yeasty and its flavor will not peak until two years or so after bottling, you will get a sense of the depth of the flavor and the acid-sugar balance.

The exact timing of the first racking is not highly critical. But the longer the wine is left on the fermentation lees, the greater the risk that residual hydrogen sulfide compounds in the lees will be converted into mercaptans. I seldom delay the first racking more than six weeks after fermentation ceases, and I check regularly for off odors or flavors or popped stoppers, in which case I immediately rack and sulfite. But if you got by for six weeks without problems, you could probably leave it for a few more weeks without problems.

The purpose of racking a white wine is to hasten clarification so it can be bottled in the spring or early summer. With each racking some of the impurities will be left behind, either settled on the bottom or clinging to the glass. As a result, there will be less sediment to go back into suspension when the barometric pressure falls, when the temperature rises or when the carboy gets disturbed. After two or three rackings and adjusting the acid-sugar balance, the wine should be crystal clear and ready for bottling.

The concern when racking a white wine is AIR. Until now, air has not been a factor because the wine has been protected in a carboy and capped with either an air lock or a stopper. It has also been saturated with carbon dioxide, which makes it less sensitive to air. But from now on, air will be your number one enemy. White wines are particularly delicate and suffer from any air contact. Each racking exposes the wine to more air and deprives it of a bit of its potential. This is the reason I always sparge the empty carboy with argon prior to racking — to minimize air contact. You can make good wines without an argon tank, but someone devoted to making the very best wines possible will eventually want to invest $100 in a small tank of argon. It can be used in many different ways to enhance the quality of your wines and make your job easier in the process. Carbon dioxide could also be used, but argon is better because it is heavier and less readily absorbed by the wine. Nitrogen would be a poor third choice.

The number of rackings is kept to a minimum by combining as many treatments and adjustments as possible at each racking. Add meta, oak beans or chips, fining agents, adjust the acid, adjust the residual sugar, etc., all at the same racking, to the maximum extent possible. In addition to minimizing rackings and sparging the carboys with an inert gas, the rackings should take place as early as possible in the life of the wine. That's because a wine will recover from a racking more quickly when it is very young than when it is a year old, by which time it will be considerably more delicate.

Treatments at first racking

The first racking will have the following objectives:

• Fining for protein stability and clarity

• Making an adjustment to total acid if it is much outside the desired range

• Adding 45 ppm of potassium metabisulfite

Some winemakers add about 25 ppm at each racking, which is also acceptable protocol, as long as the number of rackings is limited. The important thing in bulk aging is to maintain 20-30 ppm of free sulfite at all times.

Testing and adjusting acidity

The acid, of course, should have been tested when the grapes were crushed and pressed and a correction made then. Since acidity changes somewhat during fermentation and the cold stabilization just ended, another titration test should be done now. The residual sugar level will not change, so there is no need to re-check it.

If it tastes like the acid level is within range, and the titration numbers show it to be in the ballpark, I usually wait until the next racking to fine-tune the acid level. The wine still contains a lot of saturated carbon dioxide, which forms carbonic acid. Although carbonic acid is a weak acid and will eventually break down, it can produce an artificially high titration reading. As a result, I don't place too much confidence in my titration readings at this early stage of bulk aging, even after boiling the specimen wine sample for twenty seconds to dispel trapped carbon dioxide. But if a re-test confirms the acid to be above .7% or below .55% and the acid-residual sugar tastes out of balance, make an adjustment at this racking. Don't forget that whether you are raising the acidity or lowering it, blending is always a good way to adjust the acid if you have other wine of the right acidity on hand.

INCREASING ACIDITY. When adjusting acid, bear in mind that increasing total acid after fermentation by more than a total of approximately .15% using an artificial acid could result in noticeable

harshness a year or two after bottling. That's why it is important
to adjust any major acid deficiency before fermentation — so you
won't have to raise it much after fermentation. Considerably more
acid can be added before fermentation than after without affecting
the ultimate quality of a wine. At this juncture, of course, you have
to live with whatever you did or did not do before fermentation.
If you erred in adjusting the acid before fermentation and it is still
low after the first racking, add as much tartaric acid as needed to
raise total acid to at least .55%. See Chapter 8 for a more complete
discussion on raising acidity.

LOWERING ACIDITY. A slight excess of acid can always be counter-
balanced with a higher level of residual sugar. And assuming you
have not yet sulfited, it's still not too late to use the best method
— malolactic fermentation! Although MLF will be a little harder to
initiate now than at the tail end of fermentation, it should still be
doable if you are careful to avoid the adverse conditions discussed
on page 122. If the acid is considerably high and MLF is not on your
agenda, you can lower it chemically with potassium carbonate. See
Chapter 9 for further reference.

Fining for protein stability

There are numerous fining agents for clarifying white wines,
each having advantages and disadvantages. (See Fining Agents
Glossary, p. 58.) I previously used bentonite extensively because it
is benign, effective and inexpensive. It attracts protein by-products
of fermentation and other positively charge particles. After fining
with a negatively charged agent, such as bentonite, a wine said to
be "protein stable," meaning that it will not be subject to microbial
spoilage or clouding if stored too warm after bottling.

I now use a Kieselsol-chitin combination most of the time because
it is easier and even more effective. In addition, it works at cellar
temperatures, unlike bentonite. If there is such a thing as a "magic
bullet" in clarifying white wines, it would have to be Kieselsol-
chitin. (See page 59.)

But bentonite is a good and less expensive fining agent, and some
of it in the prilled form (Vitaben or KWK) should always be kept on
hand. To make a bentonite slurry with an agglomerated or prilled
form, such as Vitaben or KWK, measure 3 teaspoons into 1½ cups

of warm water and let it soak overnight. It will be fully hydrated the next day and sufficient to fine 5 U.S. gallons (19 liters). If you are using regular bentonite, you will need to make a hot slurry. This is done by gradually adding 2 teaspoons to 1½ cups of boiling water. (Don't use wine as it will scorch.) Boil it for about 20 minutes, stirring regularly and adding water as necessary to maintain the original volume. After 20 minutes it will be fully hydrated, and you will be ready to proceed with racking.

Basic racking procedure

If fining with regular bentonite (as opposed to Kieselsol-chitin, since you shouldn't use both), get everything set up and ready for racking first, because the slurry should be blended in while hot, or at least warm. After making sure the receiving carboys are clean and (optionally) sparged with argon, dissolve your tartaric acid or carbonate, as the case may be, in a little water or wine and add it to the empty carboys. Add 45 parts per million (ppm) of potassium metabisulfite at this racking. This amounts to 17 ml of freshly mixed 10% sulfite solution for 5 U.S. gallons, or ¼ tsp of granular meta, first dissolved in water.

← TAPE—helps prevent movement of racking stem

Illustration B: Racking with no aeration—for white wines

If the full carboys have not been resting on a bench or counter, carefully move them to an elevated position. The move will disturb the lees, but the debris will quickly settle again. Gently tip the

← TAPE

ILLUSTRATION C:
Racking with aeration—for first racking of red wines

carboy back and insert a stick under it to create a deep spot. Position the racking stem at the deepest point in the full carboy, hose attached, and tape the hose to the side of the carboy to stabilize it. Draw up enough wine to fill the hose. Quickly cover the hose with your thumb and lower it into the empty carboy below and let it flow. Check the connection between the hose and racking stem to be sure air is not leaking in.

With white wines the bottom of the hose should be submerged so as to minimize splashing and aeration. (Illustration B.) If you are using Kieselsol-chitosan, follow the directions — Kieselsol first, followed by stirring in chitosan a few hours later. With a bentonite slurry, add it piping hot, in small doses at several times while racking. A small funnel helps. Rock and swirl the carboy to mix it in or stir it with a dowel to mix it in and help release trapped carbon dioxide. Watch the upper carboy and when it gets down to the lees, lift the racking stem to avoid siphoning sediment along with the wine. You lose a little wine with each racking.

One caveat if you have small carboys, jugs or bottles full of wine — these containers must be rotated into the main wine at each racking because the wine might not store safely in them until the next racking. Smaller containers should be racked into the new carboy before the larger container is racked.

With a little experience you will become quite adept at estimating volumes to get all containers full. In general, fill the largest carboy or container first and use progressively smaller containers for the excess. Top the smallest one with comparable wine or water to displace all air. You could also drop marbles in as a filler. Or displace the air with argon (but not carbon dioxide or nitrogen).

Needless to say, the carboys should be kept full at all times after fermentation is complete. This seems too fundamental to mention, but I have seen many otherwise good wines ruined by long-term aging with too much air space in the carboy. It is even more critical that smaller containers, such as jugs, be kept full and tightly stoppered, as wine cannot be safely kept in them for more than a few weeks under the best of conditions.

Trapped carbon dioxide will continue to effervesce for a few minutes after the racking. Stir it with a dowel to speed up the de-gassing — you want the trapped gas to escape before bottling. After the bubbles stop, plug the carboy once again with a solid rubber stopper wrapped with sticky plastic wrap and cap it with a fruit jar.

Bentonite precipitates in less than two weeks at room temperature, but it takes much longer at cellar temperature. If you are bulk aging in stainless steel tanks or glass containers that are too large to be moved and you cannot heat your room, plan to rack again in three or four weeks. By then, most of it will have precipitated, and the rest will gradually precipitate as the weather warms.

Oak additives

On the rare occasions when I use oak in a white wine, I usually add it a few days after the first racking, when wine is clear. A 5-gallon carboy of dry white table wine will accommodate about ¾ cup (85 beans) of Stavin beans for one to two months. Just stuff them in and start tasting it weekly to follow the progression. (I use a disposable 1-ml pipet as a straw – works great.) They will float at first and gradually sink. As soon as you think you have a bit too much oak, go on to the second racking. The oak flavor will recede over time. The beans can be rinsed off and dried on a towel for future use, as they have several more months of life left in them.

With oak chips, splinters, shavings or granular oak, just follow the directions and taste it regularly. The oak flavors will be extracted from chips or splinters in about two weeks. Make sure you buy toasted oak of high quality.

Fining Agents Glossary

Many different fining agents have been used over the centuries to clarify white and rosé wines. They all carry an electrical charge, positive or negative, and work by attracting impurities of the opposite charge as they precipitate. The more common fining agents described below are all Generally Recognized As Safe (GRAS) by the U.S. Food and Drug Administration, meaning that there is no upper limit on dosage — from a safety point of view. They cause little or no loss in wine quality if used judiciously. The degree of effectiveness depends on unknown variables because what works magically one year might not work so well the next year on the same grapes from the same vineyard. The (+) or (–) below indicates whether the fining agent is positively charged or negatively charged. You will usually need to use one fining agent of each electrical charge in order to achieve total clarity, but not necessarily at the same time. The information within the brackets [ ] indicates the temperature at which the fining agent is most effective. As a rule, a fining agent should not be pre-mixed with another fining agent or with tannin.

CHITIN, a.k.a. Chitosan. (+) [Cellar temp.] Chitin is a protein-base fining agent made from the exoskeletons of shellfish and crustaceans. Used in lieu of gelatin for counterfining Kieselsol, it can produce astounding results in just a day or two, even with difficult varieties, such as Sauvignon Blanc. The wine should be completely clear in a few days.

Two-part kits of chitosan and Kieselsol are marketed under brand names such as Claro-KC and Super-Kleer KC. Just follow the directions. If you are fermenting larger volumes, it might pay to find a source that sells chitin and Kieselsol in 16-ounce bottles. These additives have a limited shelf life.

BENTONITE. Bentonite is an excellent fining agent that is both effective and benign. Being negatively charged, it attracts positively charged particles in suspension and drags them to the bottom as it precipitates. Seldom can a white wine be fully clarified without using bentonite or some other negatively charged fining agent, such as Kieselsol. Even if a white wine appears to be clear, it should not be bottled without being fined with bentonite or Kieselsol. It needs exposure to negatively charged particles in order to strip out the positively-charged residual proteins and render it protein stable.

BENTONITE
Charge: -
Use at room temp.
Weight: 1 tsp. = 5.4

My usual dose is 2 teaspoons per 5 U. S. gallons, done at the first racking. But if the wine looks clear, 1 tsp. will suffice. See page 55 for making a hot slurry.

AGGLOMERATED BENTONITE. Making a slurry is easier with bentonite in agglomerated or prilled form, such as KWK or Vitaben. Add 3 teaspoons to 1½ cups of warm water, let it soak overnight, and it will be fully hydrated the next day — no need to boil and stir. The agglomerated form is also preferable because it compacts more after precipitating, so less wine is sacrificed.

AGGLOM. BENTONITE
Charge: -
Use at room temp.
Weight: 1 tsp. = 3.7g

Bentonite is not commonly used on red wines, as it takes out a bit of the color. It has a very high affinity for proteins and will strip out glucolytic enzymes, lysozyme, Scott color enzymes, etc., added at the same time. Wine treated with AR2000 or lysozyme should be lightly fined with bentonite at the rate of ½ tsp per carboy two or three weeks later to remove the enzyme before bottling.

KIESELSOL. Kieselsol enhances the negative charge of suspended particles, making them more negative. As a result, larger particles are formed and precipitation by gelatin or chitin is more complete. Commercial wineries have abandoned tannin in favor of Kieselsol as an adjunct for counterfining gelatin because Kieselsol-gelatin is a very effective +/− combination and doesn't run the risk of affecting flavor as tannin does.

KIESELSOL
Charge: -
Use at cellar temp.
Weight: 1ml/U.S. gal.
.26 ml/L

If you decide in favor of Kieselsol-gelatin at the first racking, skip the bentonite. Dissolve about ¼ tsp (~ 1 g) of gelatin in warm water and stir into 5 U.S. gallons (19 liters). A few hours after racking and adding the gelatin, stir in Kieselsol at the rate of 1 ml of per gallon. Kieselsol is quite heavy and will quickly sink to the bottom unless the wine is stirred vigorously. A slender wood dowel is indispensable when fining wines in carboys.

Some manufacturers recommend adding the Kieselsol first for best results, and others recommend adding the gelatin first. Winemakers are similarly divided, with some contending that the sequence results in a subtle difference in flavor.

A Kieselsol-gelatin combination might help in diminishing the bitter aftertaste that Gewurztraminers and Rieslings tend to have, but don't expect a miracle. Kieselsol has a limited shelf life and should be replaced when it turns gelatinous. Store it in a cool, unrefrigerated place and never let it freeze. Numerous brands of 30% Kieselsol solution are marketed, such as Nalco 1072, Klebosol and Neosol.

ISINGLASS. This protein is also effective and benign. Bentonite followed by isinglass is a good combination because they function independently of each other and bench trials are not needed to establish an optimum ratio of one to the other, as is advisable with tannin-gelatin.

ISINGLASS
Charge: +
Use at cellar temp.
Liquid: 1 oz. or 45 ml packet per carboy
Biofine - per instr.

I usually fine with Kieselsol-chitin at the first racking, followed by isinglass at the second racking, with 1 ounce usually being about right for 5 U. S. gallons (19 liters) of essentially clear wine. It serves as a polishing agent and seems to improve the mouthfeel.

Isinglass is available in both liquid form and granular form (Biofine). The liquid form seems to clarify faster, and you don't have to dissolve it. Small bottles and packets of liquid beermaker's isinglass are available at most brew shops, Note that isinglass will help remove a slight residual haze, but it will not clarify a cloudy wine.

GELATIN. Like isinglass, gelatin has a protein base and attracts negatively charged particles. However, gelatin is harsher on the wine and more difficult to work with because it requires tannin to flocculate. If you have too much gelatin relative to tannin, the residual gelatin will stay in suspension. If you have too much tannin, the flavor of the wine could be affected for quite some time, not to mention some cloudiness. Kieselsol-gelatin is normally a better combination to work with than tannin-gelatin.

GELATIN
Charge: +
Use at cellar temp.
Dosage: ⅛–¼ tsp./gal
U.S. (.03-.13g/L)
Weight: 1 t. = 3 g

Special grades of gelatin are available for winemaking, graded by molecule size, such as 100 bloom, 75 bloom, etc. In my experience, Knox unflavored gelatin works just as well. Granular gelatin is readied for fining by adding it to a small volume of warm water and letting it soak a few hours. Always keep notes on the amounts added. If cloudiness persists, it is usually the result of too much tannin relative to the gelatin, or vice versa. Finding the right ratio is the difficult part of a gelatin-tannin fining regimen. Bench tests should be conducted before fining the whole lot. If you are not set up to run bench trials to determine the right gelatin-to-tannin ratio for the white wine in question, stir in an equal weight of tannin right before or right after the gelatin.

Gelatin can also be used at the rate of ½ to 1 teaspoon per 5 U. S. gallons (19 liters) to soften astringent red wines by removing excess tannin. Don't do frequent sequential finings with gelatin because the full sensory effect of a fining might not be apparent for several weeks. Egg white is used for the same purpose and is gentler.

EGG WHITES. (+) [Cellar temp.] 1 egg white per 15-30 gallons. Egg white is an excellent fining agent for reducing astringency in red wines as well as stabilizing the color. It used in France for fining red Burgundies, as it is gentler than gelatin. Separate and discard <u>all</u> of the yolk. Dissolve a pinch of salt in a cup of warm water — the salt helps liquefy the egg white. Mix in the egg white, whisk to liquefy and skim off the foam. In addition to reducing astringency, egg white can be used to increase the brilliance of a finished wine, red or white. Like isinglass, it is not effective to clarify a cloudy white wine. Be sure to rack off the lees in about 10 days, before the egg white decomposes.

SPARKOLLOID™. This proprietary product marketed by Scott Laboratories is used extensively by commercial wineries prior to filtration as it is extremely effective in removing haze and pectins as well as being gentle. Its biggest drawback for home winemakers is that it will not precipitate completely by gravity. The only way

SPARKOLLOID™
Charge: +
Use at room temp.
Dosage: Up to 1 tsp. (1.2 g)
per gallon
Shelf life: 4 years, sealed
and stored dry.

to completely eliminate the residual microscopic Sparkolloid™ haze that otherwise settles out after bottling is by filtration. The post-bottling fluff is harmless but distracting, so I now use hot-mix Sparkolloid™ only when other fining agents fall short. (Cold-mix Sparkolloid is used only at crushing.) Another drawback of Sparkolloid™ is that the lees are very fluffy and a disappointing volume of wine is lost. The loss can be reduced somewhat by very gently stirring in an ounce or two of isinglass a month after the Sparkolloid™ has settled.

POTASSIUM CASEINATE. (+) [Cellar temp.] Consider fining with casein if your wine has excess astringency, greenness, excess oak, off flavors or colors, or slight oxidation. It is relatively harsh and should be used sparingly. It will coagulate as soon as it is mixed into warm water and will dissolve in a couple hours with occasional stirring. For maximum effectiveness, it should be forced into the wine in a fine stream while racking and be stirred vigorously to disperse it and minimize clumping. A long syringe with a fine tip would be ideal. Very little should be needed — try .14-.26 g/5 U.S. gallons (.007-.014 g/L).

PVPP. [Cellar temp.] Polyvinylpolypyrrolidone is an inert, insoluble plastic powder that can help in removing browning, off flavors and odors, protein haze and excess bitterness in Gewurztraminer and Riesling wines. It can also be used to counter the tendency of some blush and rosé wines to turn brown after bottling. If you do not have a pump and filter, use the brand sold as "Polyclar VT" or "Polyclar AT" rather than Polyclar V. The latter will not clear by gravity alone, whereas Polyclar VT or AT might, because the particles are larger. Bench trials are recommended to see if it will be effective —try it at the rate of 2 grams per gallon (½ g per liter) as a starting point. Like potassium caseinate, this fining agent is more appropriate for dealing with a specific problem than for general clarification.

Chapter Five

SUBSEQUENT RACKINGS

 f you fined with Kieselsol-chitin at the first racking, further fining probably shouldn't be necessary — it's that effective! If you fined with bentonite, it will have fully precipitated in two weeks if the wine was held at room temperature. But the wine may still be slightly cloudy, and a second fining agent will probably be needed to achieve clarity. The second racking should be done 30 to 60 days after the first racking, or at such time as the oak flavor, if oak was added, becomes sufficiently pronounced that racking is needed. The purpose of the second racking is to separate the wine from the lees of the first racking and to treat it as follows:

- adjust the acid slightly as needed.
- fine with isinglass (or gelatin)
- stir again to release trapped carbon dioxide.
- remove any oak beans previously added.

Acid adjustment

Do another titration test to check the acid level, first boiling the specimen for twenty seconds to dispel trapped carbon dioxide. Is the acid within the range of .60-.65%, plus or minus .05%? The most important test is: does it taste about right? If it is still too low, add more tartaric acid (or a combination of tartaric acid and malic acids unless you initiated malolactic fermentation). How much did you add at the first racking, and how much did it move the reading? Use the result of the first racking as a guide for this addition.

If the acid is still too high, it can be countered with a bit of table sugar or lowered chemically with potassium carbonate. See Chapter 8 for more details on raising acidity and Chapter 9 for lowering it.

Second clarifying agent

Regardless of whether you fined with Kieselsol-chitin, with Kieselsol-gelatin or with bentonite at the first racking, isinglass is a good follow-up fining agent. It is gentle and adds a bit of mouthfeel to the wine. Use about one ounce of liquid beermaker's isinglass or a packet per carboy. If you are using a granular version, such as Biofine, use it according to instructions.

Potassium metabisulfite

If you added 45 ppm of meta at the first racking, you can wait until the next racking to add more. Free sulfite diminishes over time by bonding with aldehydes, oxygen, sugars and other solids, but the 45 ppm added at the first racking should tide you over until the next racking. The reason for caution in adding sulfite is that too much total sulfite will tie up some of the esters and diminish flavor and bouquet, even if none of it remains as free sulfite.

If you added only 25 ppm at the first racking, add another 25 ppm now to replace what is lost through bulk aging and racking. Please be reminded that these sulfite figures pertain to bulk aging in glass or stainless steel. See Chapter 14 if you are using oak barrels because free sulfite drops much faster in wood and needs to be closely monitored.

Racking procedure

The procedure is the same as the first racking. Sparge your carboys with inert gas if you have a tank. Add everything to the carboy, including the isinglass, and proceed to rack. Stir it with a dowel after racking to help release the remaining trapped carbon dioxide, of which there will still be some. Don't forget to add the small jugs and bottles first! Leave it undisturbed for another month or two.

Third racking

The wine should be brilliant by now. One final racking is needed in anticipation of bottling to:

- Fine tune the acid-residual sugar balance, if necessary.
- Boost the level of potassium metabisulfite.

Run another titration test to check the acid level. Does it taste about right? The acid should be close enough by now that you can rely on taste more than the numbers. Note that this racking may not even be necessary. If the clarity, acid level and residual sugar are acceptable, you can dissolve ¼ tsp. of potassium metabisulfite in 25 ml of water and dispense 1 ml into each 750-ml bottle with a 1-ml pipet. This is 45 ppm. Or dispense .65 ml of a

TIP

If you run out of backup wine for topping up, don't run out and buy a bottle of the same wine. Top up with one of last year's wines: white into white and red into red, of course. Use a sweet one if this year's wine needs more RS. Use up one that has too much sulfite or oak but is otherwise sound.

freshly made 10% solution per 750ml bottle, which is also 45 ppm. Then, you can bottle directly out of the carboy and eliminate the third racking. This is not to say that a third racking would appreciably reduce the quality of the wine, it's just that you want to minimize racking and air exposure any time you can.

If the acid is still low, raise it to at least .55%, and preferably to .60-.65%, if you can do so without violating the cumulative, post-fermentation rule-of-thumb maximum of .15%. When the acid is getting close to optimum, I often add half the calculated dose and stir in a little more a week later if my palate so suggests.

If you started out with too much acidity and the prior addition of carbonate did not lower it below .70%, you could lower it chemically with potassium carbonate. But a better option might be to mask a slight excess of acid with a bit of table sugar.

Additional rackings and fining agents

Occasionally, a wine will not fall brilliantly clear using the regimen discussed above. Some winemakers complain about Gewurztraminer, but I have had the most trouble with Sauvignon Blanc. Residual haze leaves you with the decision of whether to live with a little sediment after bottling or whether to venture off into unknown territory by using a third fining agent. Using a third fining agent might set you back in your quest for clarity. If you decide in favor of a third fining agent, bench trials are very important, both to find out which third agent is most effective and also to establish the minimum dose to get maximum benefit. If you don't run bench trials, you will have no way of knowing whether a poor result is due to use of too much or too little of the third agent.

If my wine still contained considerable visible haze at this point and I were intent on eliminating it, I would probably use a light dose of Sparkolloid™. It is all but guaranteed to produce a wine that is free of visible haze. However, unless you have the capacity to filter, there will inevitably be some microscopic Sparkolloid™ remaining in suspension that will precipitate as white fluff after bottling. It gets down to a matter of tradeoffs. You lose a little quality each time you rack and fine, so it's usually better to live with a little sediment. You can stand the bottles upright for a few months before opening and decant into a carafe.

Chapter Six

FERMENTING RED WINES

he procedure for making red wine is less involved in some respects than for white wines. Clarification is not the challenge it can be with whites, and red wines are not as sensitive to air contact. In this sense, the process is easier for red wines than whites. But it's not necessarily easier to make a great red wine than white, it's just that the process is a little easier. It still takes great fruit to make a great wine!

The general procedure is as follows:

- The stems are separated and discarded at crushing.
- The crushed grapes are fermented on the skins in a primary fermenter for several days before being pressed. The "cap" of emaciated skins is punched down at least twice daily.
- When unfermented sugar has dropped to approximately 0°B, the wine is pressed and fermentation is completed in a carboy topped with an air lock.
- Red wines are fermented warmer than whites to extract more flavor and complexity. The preferred ambient temperature range is 70-75°F (21–24°C).

A workshop or spare room with temperature control is an ideal place to ferment red wines.

Preparatory

Follow the procedures in Chapter 2 for culling out bad fruit, cleanliness and preparing a yeast starter. Hard and raisined berries are not a problem as much as overripe but juicy berries, which usually have an abnormally high sugar content and may even have started to sour. If there are many of these berries on the clusters, I would suggest discarding the worst clusters or at least picking off the bad berries. They could boost the sugar level too high for a first class red wine.

Crushing and de-stemming

Since the stems must be separated before fermentation to avoid extreme astringency in the finished wine, it is a near necessity to own or have access to a crusher-stemmer. A crusher-stemmer automatically separates the stems while it crushes. Without a crusher-stemmer, at least 90% of the stems would have to be raked out by hand after crushing and the remaining grapes stripped off. This

STEMMER-CRUSHER

can be done, but it becomes extremely tedious with even as little as 100 pounds. If you don't own a crusher-stemmer, try your best to borrow or rent one for a few hours. At a minimum, get a milk crate from a distributor and put together a makeshift device to separate the stems. (See below.)

After the grapes are crushed and de-stemmed, the mass goes into a primary fermenter, which for most home winemakers will consist of a large food-grade, plastic garbage can with a lid. I have several different sizes of the Rubbermaid Brute® containers and find them to be quite satisfactory. The primary fermenter should be filled to no more than ¾ capacity to allow room for the cap of grape skins, or chapeau, which will rise to the surface as fermentation starts.

A normal dose of potassium metabisulfite (45 ppm) should be added when crushing. Some winemakers omit meta at this stage, reasoning that red grapes have an abundance of tannin, which by itself is a good preservative. However, meta is desirable in my opinion because it kills the malolactic bacteria which might otherwise multiply and establish. There are three strains of malolactic bacteria, two of which are undesirable. Although malolactic fermentation is desirable, the better regimen is to kill all natural bacteria with meta at the crush and add a cultured ML strain later.

I normally add pectic enzyme a few hours after crushing and sulfiting in the belief that it hastens the breakdown of the berry and extraction of color and flavors. You could add D.A.P. or a balanced yeast food now, but the yeast will make better use of it if you wait until fermentation is underway. The nutrients will diminish the chance of a stuck fermentation or problems with hydrogen sulfide toward the end of fermentation.

Be sure to get an accurate titration of total acid right after the crush when the juice is clear. It picks up pigment from the skins soon after fermentation starts, making it harder to read the endpoint when titrating with phenolphthalein (see Appendix A). Total acidity should be corrected before fermentation if it is outside the range of .65-1.0% at the time of the crush, as further discussed below.

Testing sugar

Fermentable sugar is usually a little higher in red grapes than white grapes, probably 24 to 27°B on the hydrometer. If the sugar level is low, add table sugar to raise it to 23 or 24°B. The rule of thumb is that 1½ ounces of sugar per U.S. gallon will raise the Brix by 1°. This adjustment should be made in terms of the amount of wine that you estimate that you will end up with, not the volume in your fermenter, which contains skins, etc. Since 30% of 100 pounds of grapes will consists of skins, stems, pulp and seeds, you will have about 70 pounds of wine for every 100 pounds of grapes, which translates roughly to 7 gallons of finished wine.

If the sugar is high, I suggest adding water to lower the Brix to 25°B or even 24°B to avoid an excessively high alcohol level. The formula is the same as for white grapes, but you have to use the estimated final volume of wine, which will be approximately 7 gallons per 100 pounds in the case of red grapes:

Here is a helpful table for lowering sugar to 24°B:

Orig. Brix	Gallons of Juice				
	5	10	15	20	
27°	.6	1.2	1.9	2.5	} Gal. of water to
26°	.4	.8	1.2	1.7	} get 24° Brix
25°	.2	.4	.6	.8	

If the Brix is above 27°, use the equation on page 36 and lower it to only 25°B to avoid excessive dilution. Water additions should be acidified with tartaric acid to .6%, and you will want to re-check the acidity of the must after adding the acidified water. Five teaspoons of tartaric acid per gallon of water will raise the acid level to about 0.6%.

Adjusting acidity

The desired acid range for a finished red wine is a little lower than for a white wine. Total acid in a finished red wine should be approximately .55%-65%. It will decrease somewhat during fermentation and cold stabilization, probably in the range of .05%. So if total acid of the must is around .65%, it need not be corrected before fermentation. If it ends up too low after fermentation and clarification, it will need only a small increase.

Major acid corrections should always be made before fermentation. If the total acid is less than .60% after crushing, raise it to .60% or .65% before fermentation by the addition of tartaric acid. Again, do your calculations in terms of volume of wine, using the rule of thumb that 100 pounds of red grapes will yield about 7 gallons of finished wine. Don't use malic acid or an acid blend, either of which would add a flavor that is not desirable in a red wine.

If the acidity of your must is much above .65%, you will want put the wine through malolactic fermentation after primary fermentation. Malolactic fermentation will lower total acid by .15-.40%, depending on how much of the total acid was originally comprised of malic acid. If malolactic fermentation pushes the acidity below .55%, it can be raised later by adding tartaric acid. I invariably put all of my red wines through MLF, even if total acid is low—it's a good practice to do so with red wines because malic acid gives red wines an undesirable flavor. See Chapter 12 for a more complete discussion of malolactic fermentation.

Note that when a must is extremely acidic, the pH is likely to be too low to support MLF. Total acid should be lowered chemically with calcium carbonate to 1.0% before fermentation, which usually raises the pH to the minimum level needed to get a malolactic fermentation going (about 3.2 for most strains

Winemakers always want to know the pH of their red wine musts. And for good reason, as it exceeds acidity in importance. The pH, or power hydrogen ion, is a measure of the concentration of hydrogen ions in solution and is basically a measure of the strength of the acidity. The pH of red wine musts should be between 3.4 and 3.8, with the lower figure being more acidic and sour. A pH of 3.6 or 3.7 would be preferable to 3.3 for a finished red wine. Wines with a pH much higher than 3.8 tend to be unstable and have a shorter shelf life because they are more prone to microbial activity and oxidation. A red wine with a pH below 3.3 would be too tart.

Important as the pH of a red wine may be, it is somewhat academic for the home winemaker, who usually has no control over when the grapes are picked. And although acid corrections will also affect pH, corrections are normally based on total acid, not pH. So if you do not have access to a pH meter, proceed on the assumption that if the acidity is in the right range, the pH will be also.

See Chapter 8 for addressing the unusual situation of both high pH and high acid.

Inoculating and fermenting

The grapes have now been crushed, de-stemmed and sulfited. You have either tested the acid and sugar or set aside a sample for later testing. A few hours have passed since sulfiting, and the sulfite has bonded to the sugars, so that it will no longer interfere with yeast multiplication. The yeast starter, which you re-hydrated earlier (page 29), is foamy and active. It's time to inoculate!

Sprinkle the yeast starter over the surface of the must. Or pour it into one spot, but don't stir. If the ambient temperature is 70°-75°F (21-24°C), there should be some visible signs of fermentation in a day. A cap should have formed by the following day, and soon the cap will rise high and fermentation will be tumultuous. This is the time to add a balanced yeast food (or D.A.P.) at the rate of 1 tsp. per 100 pounds of grapes. It's also safe to add a malolactic starter and nutrient now (or you can wait until you press). It is important to punch down the cap twice a day and preferably three or four times a day when the sugar level is dropping from 20°B to 10°B.

There is little that can be done to slow the rate of fermentation of a red must being fermented at higher temperatures. Even a slower yeast, such as Epernay II, will naturally be very active in the desired temperature range of 70-75°F (21-24°C). No matter what the yeast strain, sugar Brix will drop very rapidly during this phase.

It would be counterproductive to ferment cooler in an attempt to prolong the fermentation and skin-contact period as less flavor would be extracted from the skins at lower temperatures. Cool fermentation is not done with red wines. If you want more skin contact, do a 3 or 4 day pre-fermentation cold soak (Chapter 11) and let it ferment as fast as it wants. A primary fermentation at higher temperatures will result in a wine with good structure and complexity but not one that will take years and years to mature. Plan to press when the sugar drops to 0°B (and add malolactic nutrient and starter if not previously done).

If your fermenting room is cool, wrap a blanket around the primary fermenter and set the fermenter on a piece of wood to keep it off the cold floor. If this doesn't work, use an electric blanket. It is important that a red wine be fermented warm in order to extract the maximum from the skins.

Punching down the cap

The cap has to be punched down during fermentation, i.e., pushed under the surface and covered with fermenting wine. The object of punching down is to prevent aerobic bacteria from developing on the cap, to promote contact between the juice and skins, to allow some heat to escape and to give the yeast a bit more oxygen. You also want to stir up the lees to get the nutrients back into circulation. Commercial wineries pump juice from the bottom of the tank and spray it over the cap. The home winemaker has to rely on the old-fashioned way of punching down. The cap should be punched down twice a day, except during peak fermentation, when it should be punched down three or four times a day.

Almost any flat surface can be used to push it down, such as a stainless steel pan or big spatula. Care should always be taken not to expose fermenting wines to metals other than stainless steel. Non-resinous wood, food-grade plastic and stainless steel are all acceptable. (If you get serious about making red wines, you will want to invest in a long-handled, stainless steel punch-down tool and a lees stirrer.) After punching down, the utensils should be removed from the room and rinsed to avoid attracting fruit flies.

Monitor the temperature in the cap during the most vigorous phase, which will occur as the Brix falls from 20° to 10°B. You want the temperature to spike up to 85-90°F (27-29°C). But if it exceeds 95°F (35°C), steps should be taken to lower it. If you have a stainless steel immersion coil, put it to use. Plastic milk jugs with ice (and a secure cap) are another way to cool it down. In an extreme case you could toss in some food-grade dry ice: 20 pounds will lower the temperature of twenty gallons of fermenting must by about 20°F.

If your grapes had a very high Brix and you are concerned that the level of alcohol might end up too high, the alcohol can be kept slightly lower by fermenting warmer and punching down more frequently and vigorously. This lets more of the alcohol evaporate.

Be alert throughout fermentation for potential problems with hydrogen sulfide. Rotten egg stink requires immediate remedial action. I mention this unpleasant possibility not because it is so common, but because it is so much easier to correct if dealt with promptly (see Appendix B).

Expect to encounter the ubiquitous fruit fly during fall fermentations. In addition to being a big nuisance, flies can lead to high volatile acidity in the wine. It's impossible to exclude them from the room, but an old sheet draped over the fermenter lid and held tight with bungie cords will help keep them out of the wine.

Pressing

When the hydrometer indicates that the unfermented sugar is around 0°B, fermentation will have slowed to nearly a standstill. This will usually occur 5 or 6 days after inoculation. The grapes will be quite emaciated, and the cap will not reform as quickly or rise as high. It's time to press! You could press sooner if the goal is a lighter wine, but the unfermented sugar level should not be allowed to drop much below 0°B because fermentation might stick if it is racked and pressed with too little unfermented sugar remaining. Even at 0°B, about 2% sugar remains. (A regular hydrometer with 0 to 35°B scale is no longer accurate because the high alcohol level has altered the specific density of the liquid, but one with a -5 to 5°B scale would be quite accurate.)

Add your malolactic nutrient and starter now if you did not add it earlier. These bacteria thrive on warm temperatures, skins and pulp, so sprinkle the nutrient over the cap, followed by the starter if you have not already done so. Then give it a good punch down to mix it well into the must. I try to do this at my last punch down before pressing, but you could do it after pressing as well. See Chapter 12 for more information on malolactic fermentation.

TĮP

If you like kits and are interested in making more wine, you could press only lightly and use the remaining must and skins to start fermentation on a concentrate kit. The resulting concentrate wine will be a little better.

Dip everything out of the primary fermenter, pour it into the press basket and press in the same manner as white grapes. The hard-pressed portion will have more tannin and be less fruity than the free run, so some winemakers keep the two portions separate and blend them later. Or not, as seems best.

Carboy fermentation

After pressing, the wine is funneled into clean carboys filled nearly full and topped with an air lock. The wine will ferment to total dryness in a few more days at 70°F (21°C). Excess volume can be fermented to dryness in gallon jugs or even in wine bottles if you have small stoppers that fit. The small containers will be blended in at the first racking. The wine should not be left on the pulp and lees any longer than necessary, so proceed with the first racking soon after it has fermented to total dryness.

First racking - with MLF

If you added malolactic starter, as is advised for red table wines, MLF might be finished by now. Most likely, it will take a few more weeks at 65-70°F for the process to go to completion. (See Chapter 12, page 124 to determine when MLF is complete.) Continue stirring up the lees once or twice a week to hasten the process, always being alert to off odors indicative of hydrogen sulfide. Immediately rack off the lees if you detect odors.

After MLF has run its course, as confirmed by a chromatography test, rack and sulfite and then store the carboys at a lower temperature. You could proceed to cold stabilize before MLF is finished, and it would probably resume in the spring. But it might have to be re-inoculated, and there is always some risk that will not restart. So I prefer to hasten the wine through malolactic fermentation right after primary fermentation at room temperature and then cold stabilize.

First racking - no MLF

Assuming that you sulfited when crushing and that malolactic fermentation has not been initiated, the wine will be ready for its first racking about a month after pressing. Dryness can be confirmed with Clinitest® as well as by taste. If the residual sugar is less than .3% and there are no bubbles in the carboy indicating activity, you can assume that the wine is dry and proceed with racking. Check total acid (first boiling the sample for 20 seconds in the microwave oven) and adjust it if it is below .55% or above .65%. If it is close to this range, I would wait until later to adjust it because acid readings at this early stage can be a little unreliable. Since it is assumed here that you have not inoculated with a malolactic starter, add 45 ppm of sulfite at this racking. If you experienced any problem with hydrogen sulfide to date, add 0.2 ppm of 1% copper sulfate (page 196). In that case I would also use a solid rubber stopper, rather than an air lock, as it will alert you more quickly to a continuing problem with hydrogen sulfide. If it pops out, that's a good sign that microbes might be converting residual sulfur compounds into mercaptans (see Appendix B).

Unlike white wines, which suffer from exposure to air, red wines will benefit from a little air contact during bulk aging. Trickle it down the sides of the carboy to give it some aeration on this first racking. (See Illustration C, page 56.) A little air during bulk aging of a red wine softens the tannins and lowers the fruit level to the point where the subtleties and nuances of the wine can be appreciated sooner. It also lowers the risk of hydrogen sulfide problems.

Subsequent rackings

After a couple of more months, the rest of the gross lees will have settled, and the wine should be racked again. This time, and at all future rackings, the end of the racking hose should be submerged to minimize aeration (Illustration B, page 55). Since the goal is to give it some exposure to air, not deprive it of air entirely, I do not sparge the carboys with inert gas. A little air is good.

Subsequent rackings should take place at increasingly longer intervals. Wait three or four months until the third racking, and plan to rack every six months or so thereafter. Add 25 ppm of sulfite at each racking.

The ideal bottling time, assuming that you are bulk aging in glass or stainless steel rather than oak barrels, is in the second year. The fruit level of a dry red table wine that is bottled six or eight months after fermentation will be too high, and it will taste "adolescent" for years to come if deprived of all exposure to air and bottled young.

Bulk aging through the warmer temperatures of summer will also precipitate more of the solids, which means less sediment in the bottle. If you need your carboys for the new crop, at least wait until fall to bottle. But it would be better, if you can, to wait a few more months before bottling. If the pH of the wine is much above 3.6, I treat it with lysozyme (1 gram/gal. U.S.) to enhance the effectiveness of the sulfite and increase microbial stability.

Final racking

About a month before bottling, the wine should be racked for the last time. Add ¼ tsp. of meta per 5 gallons (45 ppm). Meta is recommended to rule out malolactic fermentation after bottling and to prolong shelf life. You could fine with gelatin or egg white if the wine seems overly tannic and needs to be softened, giving it two weeks to settle out before bottling. See Chapter 7 for comments on bottling. See Appendix C for further discussion on the use of meta relative to pH.

Chapter Seven

BOTTLING

 bottling party can be a lot of fun, particularly if enlivened with samples of prior vintages. Bottling involves a great deal of preparation and tedious work, which is why the occasion should be made into a party. Bottles have to be rinsed and sulfited, wine racked into them and corked and everything cleaned up afterwards. This work is undoubtedly the reason home winemakers, including the author, tend to get behind schedule in their bottling.

April or May is a good time to bottle a white wine because it is as clear as you are likely to get it. The temperature will have warmed somewhat by then, so less air will be absorbed during bottling. But if the wine is fully clarified in March and you can get to it, why wait? There is no benefit in waiting to bottle a white wine once it is clarified and the acid-residual level is fine-tuned.

Red wines are ideally bulk aged through at least one summer before bottling. In fact, if you don't need the carboys for the new crop, a big red wine will be improved by holding it over into the second year before bottling. Another racking or two will expose it to a bit more oxygen and help soften the tannins and lower the fruit profile.

New bottles can be purchased at wine supply stores, but the cost mounts quickly if you have much wine. It's a question of how much wine you have and what your time is worth. If you have the time, it's easy to find used bottles at the recycle depot or to get a restaurant or wedding caterer to save them for you. Most labels can be soaked and scraped off in a hot solution of soap and trisodium phosphate. Laundry soaps containing a surfactant seem to soften the paper faster. A spray washer attached to an outdoor or laundry sink tap makes rinsing more convenient.

I usually bottle some out of each carboy in 375-ml bottles — these are for early consumption. I like one or two magnums for long-term aging and special occasions — wine truly does age more gracefully in larger bottles. Most of it, of course, goes into 750-ml bottles, which will be the standard for most wine makers.

Corks and closure devices

Closure devices affect the maturation rate of a wine. Crown caps and metal screw caps (but not plastic) do a superior job of retaining the fruit and freshness in a wine, as well as free sulfite. However, the wine will evolve faster with a natural cork. I have always assumed this to be result of the air that gets compressed into the bottle as the cork is rammed in and then reacts with the sulfite and tannins.

Another factor in the aging curve of a wine is the method of bulk aging. Wine that is bulk aged in oak barrels picks up minute amounts of oxygen as the barrel is opened, topped up and re-sealed. After a year in oak, it will be farther along the maturation path than the same wine bulked aged in glass or stainless steel. These considerations suggest that while screw caps or crown caps might be fine for a Chardonnay that spent considerable time in an oak barrel, for instance, one would probably not want to bulk age a Cabernet Sauvignon in glass or stainless steel, bottle it young and use metal closure devices. It would take too long to soften and reach its peak. Since red wines are inherently slow to mature, natural corks would seem to be the most logical choice for red wines.

My experience with synthetic and composite cork materials has been negative. At best, they have not been around long enough to be proved for long-term aging. At worst, they could place your wine in jeopardy. An Australian study found that synthetic corks, such as SupremeCorq™, are inferior at retaining free sulfite. My personal experience, as well as anecdotal feedback, confirms that

Steve Foisie of the Boeing Employees Winemaking Club evaluating one of his eastern Washington red wines just prior to bottling.

finding. Free sulfite can drop to zero in less than eighteen months. Altec corks, made of a composite material, retain the free sulfite but taint the wine. The Australian study referenced the taint as trichloroanisole, or TCA, the principal chemical in "corked" wine.

Given my own bad experiences with non-natural corks, I now use natural corks almost exclusively. I may bottle a few white wines destined for very long-term aging in sparkling cider bottles, filled nearly full and closed with crown caps, but most are protected with natural corks. I know that about 2% will be "corked," but this is an acceptable tradeoff, given my experience with the alternatives.

Good quality corks have are expensive. I use the less expensive "One-plus-One" or "Twin Caps" on my wines that I don't intend to age for more than five years. These closures have a core made of a composite cork material with a thin "coin" of natural cork on each end. They have been around for many years, are easy to insert and remove, and I have had no problems with them.

Sulfite

No chapter on bottling would be complete without a comment regarding sulfite. All wines should be bottled with a low level of free sulfite, added shortly before bottling. In most cases, it will be added at the third racking. You can get technical by measuring existing free sulfite and the pH of the wine and calculating how much more sulfite should be added to attain the right level (see Appendix C). If I were a commercial winery or had a very large batch of wine, I would be doing just that. But as a home winemaker who processes small lots, I usually take the easy way and, with white wines, add 45 ppm at the third racking and bottle two to four weeks later. If the pH is down close to 3.0, you would be over-sulfiting at 45 ppm, so cut the dose way down. On the other hand, if the pH is above 3.6 or 3.7, the wine will be subject to microbial instability and should be treated with lysozyme early in bulk aging as well as a higher dose of sulfite at the final racking.

Inserting corks

Dipping corks in warm water for a few seconds to lubricate them is optional. If you do soak them, use distilled water. If you dip your corks in city tap water, it should have been run through a carbon filter to remove the chlorine. A higher percentage of bottles will end up "corked" if the corks are exposed to chlorine. If soaked for more than a few seconds corks get spongy and tend to ooze back out of the bottle. It is preferable and works just as well to insert them dry. Stand the bottles upright for a few hours afterwards to let the air pressure equalize and then store them upside down or on their sides to keep the corks from drying out.

Finishing touches

If you plan to cellar your wine for several years, use of a sealing cap might help keep the cork from drying out. But this is disputed. The relative humidity of the cellar is far more important. Think of a cap and label as an aesthetic touch to something you are rightly proud of! A new Wine Writer® pen or Pilot silver marker will leave a permanent mark on glass if you want to add a personal note to gift bottles.

Cellaring

The ideal cellar has high humidity to keep the corks moist, a constant temperature of 55°F (13°C), and no light or vibrations. I store my wines under the house, where they are subject only to seasonal temperature changes. This works fairly well, even though the temperature gets warmer in the summer than I would like. The white wines are stored at ground level and the red wines higher.

After two months in the bottle, the wine will have recovered from "bottling shock," and you will have your best impression yet of your effort. A white wine with good structure will continue to improve for another two years and a red wine for at least three or four years. It is a gross understatement to say that most homemade wines are drunk too young! A good Cabernet Sauvignon bulk aged in glass does not become drinkable in my scheme of things until it is five years old, and it continues to improve after that. Even a wine that shows no promise will show surprising improvement after six to twelve months in the bottle. So if you have a questionable batch, don't give up hope. Bottle it anyway!

Bottling Glossary

PLASTIC BOTTLING WAND. Many home winemakers use a plastic bottling wand affixed to the end of the racking hose. It can be used with either 5/16" or 3/8" hoses. Wine flows when the valve on the bottom is pushed against the bottle. Top it up slightly so that only about 1/4" of air space remains after the cork is inserted.

BOTTLE WASHER. This is a faucet sprayer which screws onto an outdoor or laundry sink tap. It is convenient for rinsing a large number of bottles but is not a necessity. I've read that it can damage the water pipes under your house (the abrupt cutoff) but have never experienced that problem.

CORKS. The typical domestic 750ml bottle uses a no. 9 cork. Some imported bottles have a slightly narrower neck in which the less expensive no. 8's work better. The Australian study indicates that a 44 mm cork will preserve a wine slightly better than a 38 mm cork, but I certainly wouldn't be concerned about the difference unless the wine was destined for at least 10 years of aging. I would avoid corks shorter than 38 mm.

CORKER. If you are on a budget, a hand-held corker is adequate for small quantities. They are slow, difficult to use and scrape off bits of cork as the cork is forced through the orifice. Bench and floor models are prefer-able because, in addition to being faster and easier, they compress the entire length of the cork before it gets rammed into the bottle. Be sure to try the model in question if you intend to use composite or synthetic corks, which

Bench model corker

can be difficult to insert. I have been satisfied with both the Ferarri corker and the less expensive Portuguese corker.

RAISING ACIDITY

s grapes ripen, the sugar content rises and total acid falls. The amount of tartaric acid remains fairly constant throughout the life of the grape. It is other acids — principally malic — that decrease. Grapes grown in hot climates can quickly pass their peak and end up with too little acid and too much sugar. Corrective measures are sometimes needed to bring the acid up to the minimum desired pre-fermentation level of .60–.65%.

Blending

Blending should be one of the first options to consider. Natural acids are always to be preferred over manufactured acids, which will eventually taste harsh if added in any significant amount. If high-acid grapes are available, they can be blended with a low acid must. And vice versa. You could even blend in some of last year's high acid wine. Occasionally, I end up with a container of high acid wine. Rather than lowering the acid chemically, I might hold it for blending with a low-acid wine the next fall. The two could be blended after fermentation is complete. Better yet, blend last year's wine directly into the must at the peak of fermentation (when sugar is between 20° and 15°B).

Never hesitate to blend any high-acid wine or must into a low-acid one. Unusual blends of varieties can make delightful wines, and it's more fun to experiment than be stuck with a finished wine that is not balanced properly. One caveat in blending is that only wines of sound quality should be used. Never use a wine tainted with odors or off flavors for blending or, contrary to what you might expect, you will usually end up with an even larger batch of equally flawed wine. If the wine to be blended has too much acid or suffers from a slight overexposure to oak or sulfite, it will probably be acceptable for blending. But if it suffers from unpleasant organic flavors, such as ethyl acetate or acetaldehyde, even a small quantity will ruin a good wine. So always taste both lots before blending. See Chapter 16 for more on blending, including an equation for calculating the ratio of one wine or must to another.

Adding acid

Adding artificial acids is a common method of dealing with acid deficiency, used by commercial wineries as well as home winemakers. It's much better to add the acid before fermentation as it will marry better with the natural grape compounds and will be less inclined to precipitate as tartrate salts after bottling. In addition, a must with abnormally low acid is more inclined toward problems during fermentation. If total acid is less than .55%, an acid correction obviously will be needed. Raise it to at least .60% or .65% when you crush because it will drop slightly during fermentation and cold stabilization. Raising it to this level will not result in an overcorrection.

Tartaric acid is normally preferred for raising acidity. It is the dominant and most desirable of the three principal acids. It is also the safest acid to add in that some of it will precipitate as potassium bitartrate during cold stabilization in case you overcorrected. Adding 3.8 g per gallon (1 g per liter) will raise acidity by .1%, but follow-up additions might be needed after precipitation.

Hopefully, acidity will end up in the desired range after fermentation. But if it is much less than .55% after fermentation, it should be raised to that minimum threshold level. Otherwise, the wine will probably taste "flabby," even if bottled drier, and will have shorter shelf life. I always use tartaric acid in reds, but use a 50-50 blend of tartaric and malic acids for white musts that will not be put through malolactic fermentation.

Be cautious when adding acid, and never add more than necessary. Raising the acidity of a finished wine by more than .15% with artificial acids is a significant correction which should be exceeded only when necessary. A wine to which more has been added might taste fine initially, but the acid addition will become increasingly harsh and noticeable after bottling as the fruit diminishes over time. To avoid overcorrecting, I usually add half the calculated amount initially, taste and test it and add more at the next racking if necessary. It is also good practice to double check your titration reading before correcting.

High pH – high acid grapes

Most of the time, if grapes have a high pH, they will also have low acid, and the addition of tartaric acid to raise the acid will bring the pH down to an acceptable level. Sometimes, however, grapes have a high pH and high acid. These grapes are the most difficult to work with because you do not have much freedom to lower the pH by raising the acidity — it's already too high.

It is critical that a high pH high acid problem be addressed before fermentation. I always take pH and acid readings immediately after crushing, even if the grower gave me a number. The grower got his reading from a sampling, which is always subject to error. Crushing is the time to start addressing a pH problem because far more acid can be added before fermentation than after. If the pH of the must is high and acid is not added until after fermentation, the pH could easily end up so high as to be uncorrectable after fermentation, except at a self-defeating effect on taste. The problem of high pH is magnified further if you wait until after fermentation to address it because the pH tends to go up rather than down during cold stabilization, when the pH of the wine exceeds 3.65. The best solution is to add acid before fermentation.

One rule of thumb is to never start fermentation with the pH above 3.50. If the pH of your must is above 3.50, add enough tartaric acid to lower the pH to 3.50. This might require more tartaric acid than you feel comfortable adding. But remember that unless the must has been pressed and settled, you are testing what is basically free-run juice. The remaining juice to be released from the pulp and skins during fermentation will have an even higher pH. Since the pH will normally rise and TA fall slightly during fermentation, malolactic fermentation and clarification, there is a margin of error working in your favor here.

In my opinion, it is better to run the risk of raising total acidity too much before fermentation and having to lower it chemically afterward than to wait and risk having to make a big increase in acid after fermentation just to get the pH in line. A fermenting wine will accommodate a surprising amount of tartaric, compared with a finished wine. The tartaric acid will be much less harsh if given a chance to marry with the cocktail of natural ingredients during fermentation. In addition, it will be less inclined to precipitate as tartrate crystals if added before fermentation.

The pH of red grapes should be monitored closely during the first few days after crushing. The skins contain potassium which gets leached out and raises the pH by an unpredictable but sometimes significant amount. Most of the increase will occur during the first two days after crushing, whether cold soaking or fermenting. If the pH rises to unacceptable levels, consider adding more tartaric.

After fermentation is complete, check total acid, pH and residual sugar. (Remember that at this early point right after fermentation, the sample should be boiled for twenty seconds to dissipate the dissolved carbon dioxide before titrating.) Given the nature of problem grapes of this type, the pH may still be too high. Super-chilling the wine down to 25-30°F (-4 to -1°C) is one option. This is an excellent complement to acid addition because some of the tartaric acid will precipitate as potassium bitartrate crystals, which will lower pH. Finished wines with normal alcohol of 12% or more normally will not freeze until the temperature drops below 27°F (-3°C), and they will turn to slush before actually freezing and breaking the carboy. So 27°F (-3°C) is safe, if closely monitored. The precipitation process can be hastened by stirring in potassium bitartrate crystals after the wine has chilled (1 tsp per gal., 1gram/liter) — they act as "seeds" to start the crystals growing. The acid level will fall as the tartrate crystals precipitate and the pH will rise, but not by much. The lowered acidity will allow you to add a bit more tartaric acid and cold stabilize again, which will lower the pH further. Each time, some of the potassium combines with the salt anion, which frees up H+ ions and thereby lowers the pH.

After raising total acid as much as one dares and doing successive cold stabilizations, there is little more that can be done to correct a finished wine with a high pH. Some winemakers use phosphoric acid rather than tartaric because it lowers the pH relatively faster than it raises the total acid. However, phosphoric acid seems to leave a peculiar flavor if used in any significant amount. It also affects the aesthetic quality of the wine by reducing the body and making it "thinner."

Although it will not lower the pH of a wine, lysozyme will enhance the effectiveness of sulfite by killing potentially troublesome bacteria. Since it does not affect flavor, I routinely add 1 gram per gallon to high pH wines early in bulk aging.

Don't despair if you are forced to accept a higher pH than hoped. A wine with high pH will have a somewhat shorter shelf life, and it will be more prone to spoilage. However, it will last surprisingly well. I once tasted a low acid wine with a pH of 4.25, and was surprised that it had not gone off, even after two years in the bottle. It was flabby for lack of acid, but it had not started to spoil. I have also been surprised at the high pH readings on many premium California red wines, some above 3.8. If your wine still has a high pH after having been adjusted as much as possible, don't be numbers driven. Bottle it anyway. Use lysozyme and extra meta (see Appendix C), store it as cool as you can, drink it a little sooner and enjoy it a little more while your other wines continue to age.

Acids Glossary

TARTARIC ACID. When using tartaric acid, remember that some will settle out during cold stabilization as potassium tartrate. It might have to be added a second time as a result of cold stabilization. Tartaric acid is normally the best choice for treating acid-deficient grapes as it is the principal acid found in grapes as well as the most stable. A small quantity of

> **TARTARIC ACID**
> **Preparation:** dissolve in wine
> **Dosage:** 1 g. per liter (3.8 g./gal.) raises TA by .1%
> **Weight:** 1 tsp. = 4.8 g.

this basic supply should be kept on hand. Dissolve it in some of the wine rather than water.

MALIC ACID. As grapes ripen, the sugar goes up and acidity goes down; it is principally the malic acid that falls off. Malic acid is

MALIC ACID
Preparation: dissolve in wine
Dosage: .9 g. per liter
(3.4 g./gal.) raises TA by .1%
Weight: 1 tsp. = 4.5g.

acceptable for raising the acidity of white grapes of the fruity variety, such as Riesling, Gewurztraminer and Muscat varieties, but is not used to acidify red wines. It is slightly less sour and a little "fresher" than tartaric acid. When lowering pH is a prime consideration, use tartaric acid rather than malic acid.

Note that only half of the malic acid will be converted to lactic acid by malolactic fermentation; the other half remains as malic. This means that if any malic acid was added along the way, a chromatography test will no longer be valid. I never add malic acid if the wine has gone through malolactic fermentation or will go through it.

(CITRIC ACID). Citric acid is not an essential supply item. It can be safely added only after fermentation and only after malolactic fermentation. It should be avoided in red wines and used most sparingly in white wines. The overwhelming majority of the total acids in a wine consist of tartaric and malic; very little is citric and most wine drinkers would not appreciate a strong citric flavor in a wine. If you think a wine would benefit from a little citric acid, the better and safer choice would be an acid blend, which will contain 10-20% citric.

(ACID BLEND). This is a mixture of tartaric, malic and citric acids which is more commonly used in adjusting acidity in fruit wines. The ratio of acids probably varies somewhat depending on the packager. It is comparable in strength to pure tartaric, but due to the citric acid should be used only in white wines and only in red wines after fermentation and MLF are complete and the wine has been treated with lysozme to preclude renewed MLF. If the acid level needs a significant increase, tartaric acid is again preferable.

(PHOSPHORIC ACID). Some winemakers use phosphoric acid as a way to lower the pH relatively more than raising total acidity. It will do that. However, it affects the wine quality by decreasing the fruitiness and reducing its body or feel in the mouth. This tradeoff is something you will have to experiment with and decide for yourself whether the sacrifice in quality is worth the gain in numbers.

LOWERING ACIDITY

 owering acidity is not as straightforward as raising it. Ideally, only the malic or citric acid would be lowered and tartaric — the most stable and desirable of the principal acids — would not be affected. Unfortunately, most acid-reduction techniques neutralize all the tartaric acid before affecting any of the malic or citric acid. As a result, care must be taken not to eliminate too much of the tartaric, which would reduce the stability and shelf life of the wine and affect the flavor as well. Here are some options for correcting excess acidity:

Blending

This is again the safest and most conservative choice, if you have low-acid grapes or wine on hand. This will be the exception rather than the rule. You could hold a high-acid wine over until the next year in the hope that low-acid grapes will be plentiful then. Normally, you will decide on some other technique.

Amelioration

The addition of water, known as "amelioration," is more commonly used to lower sugar in an over-ripe must. But it can also be used to dilute the acid, a common practice in cool locales where the summers are not hot enough to fully ripen the grapes. One gallon of water added to 5 gallons of must reduces acidity by about 10%, taking into account the ability of an increased volume of liquid to hold more acid. Since it also dilutes the flavor, one to five is about as far as amelioration should be pushed.

It is usually a good idea to sweeten the water to about 20°B (about 2 pounds per gallon) before adding it. Grapes that are high in acid are probably low in sugar, and sweetening prevents the alcohol level from dropping too low. Although it is generally not a legal practice for commercial wineries in the United States, the practice of adding sugar (known as "chaptalization") is common in many countries where grapes have difficulty ripening.

Amelioration would not be my first choice as a means of lowering acid. But if the acid level of the must were well above the desired pre-fermentation maximum of 1.0% (10 g/L), cautious amelioration could be used in combination with some of the following alternatives.

Calcium carbonate

Calcium carbonate ($CaCO_3$), or precipitated chalk, is often used to lower total acid. It does not require cold stabilization to force complete precipitation, as does potassium carbonate. (In fact, it will not precipitate at low temperatures.) However, calcium carbonate is more likely to affect the flavor than potassium carbonate and can take many months to precipitate. Due to these disadvantages, calcium carbonate is acceptable for reducing acidity in a must or perhaps in a very young wine but should not be used later in bulk aging. I use it most often at the crush and never use it after the first racking.

Use calcium carbonate sparingly because it preferentially reduces tartaric acid. Not until all the tartaric acid has been neutralized will it act on the malic or citric acid. Add too much and you run the risk of reducing all the tartaric acid. For this reason, total acid should not be lowered by more than .3% or .4% (3-4 g/L) using either calcium carbonate or potassium carbonate.

If acidity exceeds 1.0% (10 g/L), you can draw off one-fourth or one-third of the must and calculate the amount of calcium carbonate to neutralize all the acid in that portion. Use the formula on page 169 to make sure you will not be overcorrecting. Dissolve about 90-95% of the calculated amount in a bit of water, and stir it in. This will reduce all of the tartaric acid and most of the malic and citric acid in the smaller portion. As soon as the foaming is over, mix the treated must back into the main batch. This procedure will allow a greater overall acid correction and still leave ample tartaric acid.

Adding calcium carbonate at the rate of 2.5 g/gal (.66 g/L) will reduce acidity by roughly .1%, but this should be confirmed with bench trials as the effect can vary. It will also raise the pH but by an amount that will vary greatly depending on the chemistry of the must. Since weights per teaspoon of this very fluffy compound vary considerably, it should be weighed rather than measured by volume.

Potassium carbonate

Potassium carbonate (K_2CO_3) reduces acidity by converting tartaric acid to potassium bitartrate which can be precipitated out by chilling the wine for several weeks. Adding 3.8 g/gal (1 g/L) will reduce acidity by about .1%, although its effect cannot be predicted with great precision because you never know how completely it will precipitate. Sometimes it lowers acidity more than expected, apparently by initiating the tartrate precipitation process. To be conservative, add half of the estimated amount initially and test the acid level after two or three weeks of cold stabilization. If more is needed, the first addition serves as a guide for the next.

POTASSIUM CARBONATE
Preparation: Dissolve in water
Dosage: 3.8 g./gal. lowers acid by .1%
Weight: 1 tsp = 5.9 g.

Again, total acid should not be lowered by more than .3-.4% using K_2CO_3 to avoid the possibility of eliminating all the tartaric. And for that same reason, it should not be used in addition to calcium carbonate. Potassium carbonate will raise pH more than calcium carbonate.

Potassium bicarbonate ($KHCO_3$) is essentially the same as potassium carbonate. Use 3.4 grams per gallon to lower acidity by .1%.

Malolactic fermentation

As discussed in detail in Chapter 12, malolactic fermentation is a very effective way to lower acidity. The bacteria convert malic acid into lactic acid, which is half as acidic as malic acid, without affecting the tartaric acid. It is an excellent option if a large reduction in acidity is needed. The disadvantage of malolactic fermentation is that it reduces the fruitiness in the finished wine. On the other hand, it gives a buttery quality to white wines that many people like.

Cold fermenting

Fermenting over an extended period of time at 45-50°F (7-10°C) with a cold-tolerant yeast will cause some of the tartrates to settle out for the same reason as cold stabilization discussed below — tartrates are less soluble as the temperature falls and the alcohol level rises.

Carbonic maceration

Carbonic maceration (Chapter 11) is also an effective way to lower total acid. Not all of the malic acid will disappear, but there will be no lactic acid formed to replace it, as in the case of malolactic fermentation.

Yeast Choice

If you will be fermenting a white wine and know in advance that the acid level needs to be lowered, consider Lalvin 71-B yeast as it will metabolize some of the malic acid. It is recommended for semi-sweet, aromatic varieties but not for most red wines.

Chapter Ten

FERMENTING VARIATIONS – WHITE WINES

he urge to make a better wine runs high in wine-makers! You will soon find yourself contemplating techniques to improve your product. Here are some variations in the basic fermentation process which might improve your wine. Although a better wine can never be guaranteed, the following techniques should not diminish the quality of your wine.

Soak on the skins

White grapes are often cold soaked on the skins for a few hours after crushing and sulfiting in the belief that more flavor and varietal characteristic will be released from the skins. Despite the lack of any empirical evidence that it actually does enhance the wine, I often do it myself. Some of my finest white wines were soaked on the skins before fermentation, and I'd like to attribute the success to the soak but cannot in all honesty. On other occasions, I have presoaked Semillon and Sauvignon Blanc musts that picked up an overly grassy or herbaceous flavor that I suspect was amplified by the cold soak.

There are so many variables in making wines that one can never be sure of the reasons for differing results. Almost any generalization can be debated. And what is true for one year or one vineyard might not hold true for the next. So the following guidelines should be considered with the variables in mind.

First, if you suspect that the grapes are still coated with sulfur from late or excessive spraying, don't soak them. Press the clusters whole without crushing. If they were crushed and soaked, more sulfur would wash off the skins, end up in the must and be converted to hydrogen sulfide during fermentation. In addition, if you suspect residual sulfur on the grapes, be sure to add 1 teaspoon of balanced yeast food per 5 gallons to reduce the tendency to generate hydrogen sulfide and another ½ teaspoon when the sugar has fermented down to 10-12°B.

Grapes that are in poor condition should not be soaked on the skins; skin contact should be minimized. In fact, if the grapes have sunburned and broken skins, low acid, bunchrot or some other defect, consider pressing without first crushing in order to minimize skin contact. And give them the maximum of 100 ppm of sulfite. Pressing without crushing will result in a slightly higher acid level, since the free run juice near the outer surface of the grapes is higher in acid.

The high acid level in under-ripe grapes could be reduced slightly by soaking on the skins and pressing twice. The second pressing will extract more of the juice from the center of the grape, which will have slightly lower acidity. Soaking on the skins should also bring out more of the varietal characteristic since the flavors in under-ripe grapes will not yet be fully developed.

Grape type is another consideration. Chardonnay is commonly soaked on the skins as the varietal character is inherently low and can always stand to be enhanced. Sauvignon Blanc is often soaked. But Gewurztraminer, Semillon and the Muscat varieties usually are not. On the other hand, I have made some wonderful Gewurztraminer and Semillon wines which were soaked on the skins. The rules in this game are made to be broken!

Stop fermentation before completion

Many white wines are bottled with some residual sugar. Rather than letting the wine ferment to dryness and back sweetening with table sugar, you will get a better wine by stopping fermentation when unfermented sugar has dropped to the desired level. This technique is a natural complement to cold fermentation of Riesling, Gewurztraminer and late harvest style wines. It is accomplished by fermenting at a cooler temperature and by using a slower yeast strain, such as Steinberg or Epernay. It also helps to deprive the yeast of nutrients by racking the juice off the pulp before fermentation and fermenting only the supernatant juice. It would even be a good idea to pre-fine with bentonite. Obviously, you will add no D.A.P. or yeast food of any type. If these measures are not taken, the wine will quickly ferment right past the desired sugar level before you can intervene. Taking these steps will widen the time frame for intervention.

If you are making a dessert or late harvest wine, monitor the progress of fermentation with your hydrometer. If you are aiming for a nearly dry white wine, you will need a good supply of Clinitest® tablets because the hydrometer (unless it is scale -5 to +5°B) will not give an accurate reading at higher alcohol levels. When the unfermented sugar has dropped to the desired level, the slowly fermenting wine is racked, sulfited and further chilled if possible.

One way to stop fermentation would be to put the carboy in your freezer until the wine turns to slush, which will kill most of the yeast. Then rack, sulfite and fine with bentonite to strip out more of the yeast and proteins. Obviously, you will have to stay on task to avoid freezing the wine. Chilling it in a spare refrigerator for 2 or 3 weeks might be a better way to go.

The key to stopping fermentation with some residual sugar is to separate the wine from the lees by racking, sulfiting it and keeping it chilled until it is fully clarified — several months, if necessary. If it restarts right after the first racking (which is very possible), rack again and add 45 ppm of sulfite at this racking. The sulfite will normally suffice to prevent renewed fermentation, again provided that the wine is kept cold until it has been completely clarified. For a sweet wine or one with significant *botrytis cinerea*, the meta dosage can be safely increased to 100-150 ppm to avoid renewed fermentation.

If you do not have a spare refrigerator, move the carboys to the coldest spot you can find without running the risk of freezing. A wine will not freeze until its temperature gets below 27°F. Let the gross lees settle out for a month. Then rack again, sulfite and give it two more months to further clarify. At the next racking, fine with a Kieselsol-chitin combination and another dose of meta.

By this time the goal of clarification before spring should have been met. To be on the safe side, however, let it set through the summer — the last thing you want is renewed fermentation after bottling! You might notice a few bubbles rising during the summer, which could be trapped CO_2 being forced out of solution as the temperature rises. Or it could be very slow fermentation. In either case, wait it out and let the remaining yeast die through the winter to come. The residual sugar level will not drop appreciably.

The slickest and easiest way to stop fermentation with residual sugar is to use encapsulated yeast! Just pull the bags when residual sugar has dropped to the desired level. Clarification will also be easier.

Note that stopping fermentation also has the effect of keeping the alcohol level slightly lower. If your grapes had a high sugar content, such that you are concerned about a "hot" wine (i.e., where the alcohol detracts from aesthetics), stopping fermentation at 1% RS, for example, would keep the alcohol lower by about .5%.

Ferment the free-run must separately

Wineries and home winemakers alike often ferment the free-run juice separately. As the crushed grapes are poured into the press basket, about half of the total juice will flow through before pressing even begins. This is known as the "free run" must and will usually have slightly higher sugar and slightly higher acid than the pressed juice. The free-run must is widely believed to produce a higher quality white wine.

Pour the crushed grapes into the press basket and catch the free-run juice as it drains. Add the usual 45 ppm of meta and transfer the must to carboys to let the pulp settle out. Rack the clear juice off the pulp the next morning, but there might not be much pulp. Add some yeast food to encourage fermentation to complete dryness if a dry wine is the goal.

With 200 pounds of grapes, you will have approximately 6 gallons of free run juice, which will be enough for one carboy after fermentation is complete. Ferment the hard-pressed juice separately. If you do not detect enough difference between the free run wine and the pressed, the two can be blended after completion of fermentation. Note, however, that the difference between the two lots might not become apparent for six months or a year, when they are more delicate.

Although the free-run must is widely believed to produce a superior wine, I have not been able to confirm in my own mind that it is better than both halves being fermented together. I am, however, a firm believer in settling a must and discarding the pulp. I once fermented 4 gallons of pure pulp from three different varieties of white grapes. The pulp compacted during fermentation and the resulting 3 gallons of wine was initially very clean and delicate, although light bodied. After a year in the bottle, however it lost all its fruit and seemed quite acidic and alcoholic, even though both were lower than the wine from the clear juice. This gives credibility to the practice of commercial wineries of settling and discarding the pulp and fermenting only the clear juice.

Pre-fine with bentonite

Pre-fining with bentonite will remove protein impurities and solids from a must and is something to consider for grapes having too much *botrytis*. Since the bentonite will remove nitrogen, the fining will make it easier to stop fermentation with some residual sugar remaining, where that is desired. Pre-fining might also help reduce the "foxy" flavor in Concord and other *labrusca* grapes.

Crush, sulfite and press as usual. Then make a bentonite slurry (½ tsp. per gallon) and stir it in after pressing and while racking into carboys. Let it settle overnight and rack the supernatant juice off the pulp and finings the next morning. Some winemakers leave the bentonite in throughout fermentation. It sinks to the bottom initially but the fermentation activity will stir it back into suspension. Clarification should be easier.

Ferment the dregs and leftovers: Sur Lie

Aging *sur lie* is a recommended way to enhance the mouthfeel of a white wine and impart a slightly yeasty flavor. Leave it on the lees after it falls still. Stir up the lees with a dowel once or twice a week over the next several months. Then proceed with your normal fining and clarification regimen.

It takes eight or ten months of contact with the lees to get much effect. To simulate the result and save many months, you could try an enzyme, such as Sur-Lie. Use 2 grams per gallon for 3 or 4 weeks.

Similarly, you can combine the leftovers from several different fermentations together to make what I very loosely label as a *cuvée*. Keep adding the lees, sediment, yeast "mud" and excess volumes of the different varieties as you rack and consolidate carboys. Add the mud, even if it's all that remains from a racking! You might end up with 50% solids. It doesn't look very appealing, but after a few months on the lees with an occasional stirring, the wine will acquire a delicious, yeasty flavor. Make sure the container is fully topped up when the wine finishes fermenting, store it cool and stir up the lees occasionally with a heavy dowel. On more than one occasion, my *cuvée* was my best white wine of the year! A venture of this nature obviously assumes you encountered no hydrogen sulfide during fermentation. Start monitoring the sulfite level after two months— the lees are an effective antioxident for only a few weeks.

Malolactic fermentation

Malolactic fermentation adds a buttery flavor to Chardonnay and Sauvignon Blanc wines, which many people like. Although it diminishes the fruitiness, it is an excellent way to lower acidity. Add the ML starter and nutrient toward the end of fermentation. See Chapter 12.

Glucolytic enzyme

Rapidase AR 2000 enhances the bouquet of aromatic wines, such as Gewurztraminer, Riesling and the Muscat varieties. It does wonders in dry Gewurztraminer. The recommended dosage is 1 to 3 grams per hectoliter (100 liters, or 26.4 U.S. gallons), with 2 grams per hL being my personal standard. Dissolve 2 grams (⅝ tsp.) of the enzyme in 25 ml of water. This will inoculate 26 gallons at the rate of 2 grams per hL. The change in bouquet should be monitored regularly, and when the wine has sufficient aromas, it should be fined with bentonite (10 grams per hL, ½ tsp. per carboy). (Without the bentonite fining, the enzyme would continue working and could affect the flavor or shorten the shelf life of your wine.)

If you later decide to blend a treated wine with an untreated wine, the treated wine should first be fined with bentonite (½ tsp. per carboy). Otherwise, enzyme activity will continue after blending. The more sugar present, the less effective this enzyme is. So if you want to enhance the aromatics of a white wine and also have some residual sugar, the best way is to ferment to dryness, treat with AR 2000, fine with bentonite and then back sweeten.

Store your AR2000 in the refrigerator in a small, tightly sealed jelly jar with a dessicant pouch in the bottom, and it should be good for 2 years. Moisture diminishes its shelf life.

This enzyme can also be used to enhance the bouquet of red wines, such as Merlot, Pinot Noir, Syrah, Sangiovese and Zinfandel. Since it does not work well in the presence of sugar, wait until after fermentation to treat the wine. And since tannins stop the enzyme action, I usually add ½ tsp. of a finishing tannin per carboy, such as Tan Cor Grand Cru, rather than fining with bentonite.

Oak during fermentation

A barrel-fermented white wine will have a different — and in my opinion, better — character than one which is strictly barrel-aged. New barrels are often broken in by first fermenting a white wine and later used for longer term aging of either a white or a red wine. To simulate barrel fermentation, use about 2½ ounces (85 beans) of Stavin oak beans per carboy (or a small stave) during primary fermentation. Transfer the beans or staves from carboy to carboy as you rack, until enough oak flavor has been extracted.

Ice wine

The term "ice wine" does not have a universal definition, but in some wine regions the term is restricted by law to wines made from grapes that were left to hang into the winter and harvested at subzero temperatures—at least 19°F (-7°C), or even colder. After a prolonged hangtime, the berries lose a good deal of their original water content, the yield is greatly reduced, and the flavors are dramatically intensified. The grapes are picked and crushed while frozen solid, often at night. The water freezes but the sugar does not, so the press volume is further reduced at these low temperatures. The ice shards can be strained out to reduce the water content and intensify the flavor even further. The picking process is very labor intensive and the yield low, all of which combine to make ice wine exceedingly expensive.

MAKING A MUTÉ

Dip out 1 qt. of must before the ice core is fully thawed. Will be nearly 40°B. Dissolve ½ tsp. agglomerated bentonite in ½ cup hot water and stir it in a few hours later. Pour off the clear juice the next day and re-freeze it. Thaw and add back after clarification, when you back sweeten.

Historically, ice wine has come from Germany and Austria, but Ontario's Niagara Peninsula is probably the largest producer today. British Columbia is also a producer. Vidal and Riesling are the most common varieties used. The appellation regulations in these areas forbid the artificial freezing of grapes. To make true ice wine, all you have to do is go out some dark December night when it is appropriately cold and pick only those berries that are shriveled and dried out but not rotten. After a few hours, you might have enough grapes to make a gallon or two of wine! This assumes that you have access to grapes that have been left to hang.

If this approach looks too daunting, get late harvest grapes and try making a "false ice wine." Freeze them in your freezer or a locker plant, press them while still frozen and strain out the ice shards. As always, the quality of the grapes remains the paramount consideration, not whether they were frozen by Mother Nature and picked at night.

Rather than working with frozen grapes, I usually crush, press and then freeze the must in small containers or large Ziploc bags, which might take two or three days. The bags can be thawed one at a time in a plastic or stainless steel colander set atop a plastic pail or vitreous crock. After a few hours most of the sugar and juice will have dripped out, and a porous ice core will remain. Discard the ice core before it melts and dilutes the must. The sooner you toss the ice core, the higher the Brix will be. Repeat this tedious process with the remaining bags of frozen juice. Reserve about 5% of the must volume before fermenting to make a muté (see inset), hold it in the freezer and use it after fermentation for sweetening the final wine. Reserved must is better than adding sugar or honey because it gives more flavor.

Monitor the Brix of your must as the ice cores thaw. To make a sweet dessert wine you want to start fermentation with a sugar of approximately 35°B. If the Brix is higher, let more of the ice cores thaw. If you want to make a somewhat drier, Alsatian style of Gewurztraminer or Riesling, let more of the ice core melt and start fermentation at 28°B.

An ice wine or late-harvest wine will not ferment to complete dryness. After fermentation has slowed to a crawl, rack and sulfite. Let the gross lees settle out for 4 to 6 weeks, as with any other white wine. Then rack and sulfite at 100 ppm and add the muté. Continue holding it as cold as possible for further clarification.

Reducing the volume increases both the total acidity and the sugar level of the must, so the acid level in the final wine may have to be adjusted later to suit your taste.

Epernay II yeast is commonly used for ice wine because it is not very vigorous and tends to stop fermenting with a few points of residual sugar

Colander with thawing ice core

remaining, which is what you want. Encapsulated yeast (ProDessert BA11) is a great way to go if you don't mind the extra cost. Just pull the yeast bag out when the residual sugar is where you want it, and fermentation is over — no struggle to stop fermentation. It also makes clarification much easier.

Vidal, Riesling and Gewurztraminer all lend themselves nicely to this technique, as do late harvest Sauvignon Blanc and Semillon. Late harvest grapes are preferable to early season grapes as they will already have a higher sugar level, more flavor and hopefully some *botrytis cinerea*.

Fermentation notes – ice wine

DAY 1 – A 5 gal. bucket of Gewurztraminer arrives by air freight, fully thawed, but cold. Took readings (21.8° B., 0.7% TA; label says: 20.9°B., 0.8% TA, 3.15 pH, and 15 ppm sulfite). Diverted 3 qts. to restart a different batch of Gewurz. that is stuck and immediately refroze the rest in bowls and 1-gallon Ziploc bags. Held back 1 cup to make a yeast starter solution (Epernay II/ Cotes de Blanc). The must took about 36 hours to completely freeze.

DAY 3 – Rigged a plastic colander atop the 6-gal. bucket. Put a chunk of frozen must in the colander and the fermenting yeast starter solution in the bottom of the bucket. The juice drips into the yeast starter as it thaws. About 6-8 hrs. later (depending on temperature), the goodies had dripped out and only the ice core remained. Discarded the ice core.

Repeated the thawing procedure until all the frozen must containers were thawed, discarding the ice cores. The goal is a concentrated Gewurztraminer juice with more intense flavors. With less volume, both Brix and total acid will be higher. The sugar-acid balance will be adjusted during bulk aging.

TIP

If your pail of late harvest must is still frozen, you can let it thaw and drain into a larger vessel rather than refreezing it in small containers. Just drill some ½" holes near the bottom so the syrup can run out and throw away the ice core when the Brix has dropped into the desired range.

DAY 5 – The juice is all thawed, except that one is held back for sweetening after fermentation. Transferred the rest of the thawed juice to a small carboy and topped with an airlock. Freezing, thawing and discarding the ice core raised the Brix by about 5°B; it also raised the total acid; did not take measurements. Had to bring it inside to get fermentation started. Could have raised the Brix more by discarding the ice cores sooner.

Thereafter, I followed the procedure for making any white wine. After clarification it needed to be sweetened to balance the elevated acid level.

Sweetening with reserve must without causing renewed fermentation. This is not as tricky as it would seem, but it is imperative that the wine be totally clarified before adding the reserve must. The haze in white wines is a nutrient for yeast and has to be removed. I let the wine ferment to "dryness" and gave it about a month to clarify. By then, most of the gross lees had settled out. Racked and sulfited (30 ppm) after one month. Let it clarify for two more months, by which time it was very clear. Fined with bentonite — slurry of 1 tsp per 5 gal. Racked 3 or 4 weeks later, adding the reserve must and 45 ppm sulfite. You could also add potassium sorbate if you feel it is needed. Later added AR 2000 glucolytic enzyme to enhance the bouquet—at the rate of 2 g per 25 gal. Three weeks later, fined with ½ tsp. bentonite before bottling.

Chapter Eleven

FERMENTING VARIATIONS — RED WINES

here are fewer fermenting alternatives for red wines than whites. Red wines are typically fermented to complete dryness and bottled with no residual sugar. The principal variable is the length of time the grapes are in contact with the skins and seeds, which can greatly affect the outcome. Malolactic fermentation is covered separately in Chapter 12.

Cold Soaking: Early Pressing

Red grapes can be soaked on the skins for several days prior to fermentation. This increases the color and fruitiness of the wine and allows for earlier pressing, before the harsher, alcohol-soluble tannins are extracted from the seeds. It also gives the berries more time to disintegrate before pressing. Cold soaking is commonly done in conjunction with early pressing.

Here is how one might cold soak and ferment a batch of red grapes, such as Pinot Noir, Syrah, Grenache or Sangiovese, to get a fruit-forward, low-tannin red wine: Crush and de-stem as usual. Sulfite (45 ppm) is advisable. One ounce per 5 gallons of high quality, toasted oak chips can be added during the cold soak to enhance and stabilize the color. Tie the chips up in a food-grade nylon bag having some porosity. Weight the bag or bags with marbles to keep them continuously submerged during the soak.

To chill the juice below 60°F (°C), you can drop one or two well-cleaned, plastic milk jugs of ice into each fermenter. Lay strips of plastic wrap over the surface to minimize air contact, and wrap the fermenter with an old blanket or sleeping bag. Rotate fresh ice jugs out of the freezer each day, stirring the must and replacing the plastic strips. After three or four days, stop the chilling and let the temperature gradually rise. When the must has warmed to almost room temperature, sprinkle your re-hydrated yeast starter and nutrient over the surface. (The temperature difference between the yeast starter and the must should be less than 12°F to avoid excessive temperature shock to the yeast.) After fermentation has started, punch down three or four times a day during peak fermentation and twice a day after the peak.

The temperature in the cap during most of the fermentation time should be in the 75-80°F (24-27°C) range, but it is good practice to let the temperature spike up to 85-90°F (29-32°C) for a day or two in order to extract some of the phenols that would otherwise be left behind. This elevated temperature tends to occur naturally during peak fermentation — i.e., when the unfermented sugar level is dropping from 20°B down to 10°B.

Early pressing goes hand in hand with cold soaking: if the goal is to maximize the water-soluble tannins and minimize the alcohol-soluble tannins, it follows that you want to press early — right after the sugar has dropped to about 5°B. Keep the seeds out of the basket when you press. Transfer to carboys and maintain a 70-75°F (21-24°C) temperature after pressing. Add your ML starter and nutrient at pressing.

Rack and return. Another way to discard the seeds midway during fermentation has come to be known as "rack and return." Dip the cap and skins out with a plastic colander and dump them into a clean fermenter. Then either rack or pour the fermenting wine on top of the skins, being careful to keep most of the seeds in the old fermenter. I know winemakers who use this technique to keep the level of seed tannins (known as catchetins) down, but it makes more sense to me to simply press at 5°B.

Extended maceration

Extended maceration is the opposite of cold soaking/early pressing. The idea is to leave the still wine in contact with the skins and seeds after fermentation is complete in order to maximize the extraction of phenols and tannins, particularly catchetins. Commercial wineries working with high quality grapes and wanting to extract the maximum flavor sometimes do this with part of the crop and use it for blending. The still wine is held in airtight vats for a period of time ranging from several days to several weeks. The air space is kept flooded with an inert gas to minimize exposure to air and acetification. Note that the color will not get deeper during extended maceration; in fact at some point in time the skins will start reabsorbing pigments and the wine will lose some color. But extraction of seed tannins and phenols will increase as they are more soluble in alcohol than water.

Since the added complexity comes from the seeds, not the skins, extended maceration should be undertaken only with well-ripened fruit; you would not want to extract the tannins out of green seeds. Nor would it be advisable to extend maceration if you had off odors during primary fermentation. Ladle out some of the pulp and lees from the bottom of the fermenter and see what it smells like. Chew some seeds — do they taste green? And either a sluggish fermentation or hoards of fruit flies could mean high volatile acid and a disappointing result if you opt for extended maceration.

The secret in extended maceration is to catch the softening of the tannins at just the right point in time and press immediately. The wine will usually be completely dry after 12 or 13 days of fermentation, and several days later the cap will sink. The vintner tastes the wine on a daily basis, awaiting a change in the chemical makeup of the tannins. One day the wine will taste dramatically softer, as though it has aged much longer than it really has. The wine is quickly pressed within a day. If pressing is delayed, the wine quickly becomes more tannic. So pressing takes place during this short window of opportunity.

Few home winemakers will own the ideal equipment for extended maceration (a stainless steel tank with a floating lid) because this equipment is expensive. Nevertheless, it is possible to do extended maceration using a Rubbermaid Brute® or comparable primary fermenter with a lid. The most important thing is to protect the wine from air after fermentation ceases and CO_2 is no longer being produced.

Here is how you can successfully extend maceration using an ordinary fermenter and inert gas, such as argon or carbon dioxide: Crush, ferment and punch down as usual for red grapes. Once the sugar level has dropped to approximately 0°B on the hydrometer (assuming the pulp and lees meet the taste test above!), start laying strips of plastic wrap directly on top of the diminishing cap. This will trap the slight CO_2 that is still being produced and keep air out. Maintain an ambient temperature in the range of 75°F (24°C). (The cap will sink if the temperature is allowed to drop.) The effervescence from fermentation of the remaining sugar will help maintain a cap. Continue punching down, but once a day will suffice from now on. Replace the plastic wrap and fermenter lid each time. After fermentation is complete (as confirmed by Clinitest®, not a hydrometer), the risk of spoilage goes up. So the head space should be sparged with argon or carbon dioxide to minimize the formation of volatile acids and acetification.

The wine should be tasted every day from this point forward. It might get harsher at first, but will mellow dramatically one day soon, indicating that it is time to press! All this time the head space should have been religiously sparged with carbon dioxide or argon.

Some home winemakers (and wineries as well) like to wait until the cap has sunk before pressing. This will occur when most of the trapped carbon dioxide has escaped or when the temperature falls. However, I am not aware that the sinking of the cap has any particular significance in terms of the polymerization of tannins that occurs during extended maceration. By arbitrarily pressing when the cap sinks, you might miss the window of opportunity, when the tannins soften. The better practice is to go by taste.

In most cases the softening will be so dramatic as to leave no doubt. A wine that one day is totally undrinkable will be glorious beyond description the next day. It will be mellow and have overwhelming fruit and flavor. This is the time to press. Pressing could wait a couple more days without permanently damage to the wine, but the longer you wait, the longer it will take to age. What you want to avoid is extended skin contact after the softening. So get it off the seeds right away.

Note that although the softening will normally occur between two and three weeks after crushing, it is somewhat temperature dependent and could take longer at lower temperatures. Extended maceration is not recommended for high pH wines due to the risk of spoilage.

Make a rosé

Good rosés are not appreciated in the United States to the extent that a winery can afford to divert quality red grapes, such as Sangiovese, Cabernet Sauvignon, Merlot or Zinfandel. This is not a consideration for the home winemaker because revenue is not the goal! In fact, by drawing off part of a red grape must that has soaked for several hours, you might end up with the best of both worlds — a delicious rosé and a highly extracted red wine of better quality than it otherwise would be.

Crush and de-stem the grapes as though a red table wine were to be made, using 45 ppm of meta, and let it soak overnight. Then dip out part of the must (no skins) and transfer 10-20% to carboys. Treat it with ½ tsp. of lysozyme per 5 gallons, if you have it, to discourage malolactic fermentation later.

The question of when the rosé portion should be drawn off is a decision that is largely personal to your goal. The longer it is left on the skins, of course, the more color and complexity it will acquire. And the longer it will take to mature. Check the color every hour or two, and when the color looks right to you, make the transfer to carboys. Let it get a little darker than you think you would like because the color will lighten somewhat as the solids precipitate and the wine clears.

Inoculate and ferment the rosé portion separately, in a carboy, as though it were a white wine. Use a slow fermenting yeast that will give the wine a floral quality, such as 71B, Cotes de Blanc (Epernay II), ICV GRE or Rhone 4600. The procedure for fermenting and clarifying white wines should be followed from this point forward.

Since most people expect a touch of sweetness in a rosé, you want some residual sugar in the wine. After the wine has been clarified, add some table sugar to raise residual sugar to the desired level, say .5% RS. Or you could stop fermentation at the desired point by racking, sulfiting and chilling.

Continue fermenting the main portion of the original must as you would for a normal red table wine. Punch the cap down twice daily and press when the unfermented sugar reaches 0°B, etc. Since all of the skins are concentrated in a smaller volume of wine, the extraction of phenols and intensity of flavors should be higher. Add the ML starter and nutrient when you press.

Alternatively, you could make the whole batch into a rosé. Crush, sulfite and soak the entire crushing on the skins until the desired color is attained. Then press and finish in carboys as above.

In cold, wet years when red grapes don't ripen and will not make a premium dry red table wine due to high acidity, it will be easier to get desirable red *vinifera* grapes. The higher acidity can be countered with higher residual sugar.

If your grapes have a high level of sugar — more than 25°B — you will want to dilute it with water down to about 23½ or 24°B and will probably have to add acid to get the acid up to 0.6-0.7%, pre-fermentation.

The pinkness in rosés sometimes turns brown after bottling, diminishing the wine's appeal, but not ruining it. To minimize this possibility, beyond minimizing exposure to oxygen as much as possible, you could do two things: (1) add no meta until after fermentation; and (2) fine with Polyclar VT after fermentation.

Carbonic maceration

Carbonic maceration is a good way to lower total acidity and end up with a unique red wine in the process. The grapes are not even crushed; they are placed in an air-free atmosphere at 80°-90°F. for two or three weeks. It is the natural enzymes within the berry, not yeast, that convert the sugar to alcohol. The resulting wine is relatively low in tannin, very dark in color and has an unusual fruity quality akin to volatile acidity or malic acid that you will either like or dislike.

Carbonic maceration is often used to enhance wine made from

under-ripe, high-acid grapes of lesser quality. It can be used with premium fruit as well but captures less of the complexity from the skins than conventional fermentation. Regardless of the fruit, the challenge is keeping air out until the enzyme process starts and begins generating its own CO_2 as the grapes would spoil quickly if exposed to air at the higher temperatures necessary to initiate the enzyme process.

The ideal procedure would consist of completely filling an airtight container with whole clusters of red grapes, displacing the air with argon or CO_2, sealing it against air penetration and pressing after about three weeks at 85°F (29°C). A stainless steel vat with floating lid would be an ideal piece of equipment for carbonic maceration, since it is air tight and has an air lock. But let's assume you do not have a vat and want to try carbonic maceration using only a Rubbermaid Brute® primary fermenter and lid. Here's one way it can be done:

As soon as the grapes arrive, crush and de-stem about 10% of the batch. Initiate fermentation in this portion with a dependable wine yeast, such as Prise de Mousse, before adding the grape clusters. The purpose of fermenting this small batch of ordinary red grape must is to generate sufficient CO_2 to displace the air in the container and protect the grapes until the enzyme process starts a few days later.

Once fermentation has started in this small batch, dump it into the primary fermenter. Now add the remaining 90% of the grapes, which will be whole clusters on the stems. Ideally, the container would be full to the top. Give it a good dose of argon or CO_2 if you have a tank, with the gas being discharged at the bottom of the fermenter. Put the lid in place and tape it with duct tape. You probably will not be able to totally seal the container, so tape it as best you can.

Since you will not know for sure how fast the sugar is being converted to alcohol or when it slows down or stops, plan to press two to three weeks after the container is sealed. If you cannot keep the room temperature at 85°F (29°C), wrap the container with an electric blanket set on high.

When the container is opened in two or three weeks, the grapes will look almost the same as the day they were added. But they will have lost all their structure and firmness and will collapse with the slightest pressure. There will be a considerable amount of wine accumulated at the bottom of the container, consisting of the original fermented portion plus additional juice that dripped out of the clusters during maceration. This can be racked out before pressing and kept separate as it will have less carbonic flavor than the wine remaining in the clusters.

The pressed and "free-run" portions will both still have several points of unfermented sugar and should be fermented to dryness in carboys with the protection of air locks. The two lots can be combined at pressing. Or they can be fermented to dryness separately and blended later. Or not, as appeals to you. The pressed portion will have more carbonic flavor than the other.

Here is a variation that can be used to add a touch of the carbonic flavor to a traditional fermentation of Pinot Noir, for example. Set aside a small part of the grape clusters before crushing and de-stemming, at most 10%. After the main portion has been crushed and de-stemmed, add the whole clusters back and ferment normally in an open primary fermenter at 80-85°F (27-29°C), punch down, etc. The carbonic process will take place within the whole berries and become part of the overall wine when everything is pressed. But the carbonic quality will be less pronounced.

Pinot Noir and Gamay grapes are the classic grapes for carbonic maceration. In my opinion, the flavor of these grape types is highly compatible with the carbonic flavor that results. Since these two varieties are low in tannin, it is better to use whole clusters with stems; the resulting wine will still be low in tannin. If you are using higher tannin grapes, such as Cabernet Sauvignon or Zinfandel, the grapes could be stripped off the stems to keep the tannin level lower. Even with Cabernet Sauvignon, I have found the tannin level to be high, but not ruinously so as a result of using whole clusters.

Notes on Tannins and Enzymes

Enological tannins and enzymes are widely used by commercial winemakers all over the world — France, Italy, Australia, the United States, you name it. There are numerous producers with products promising many different benefits, such as enhanced mouthfeel, more bouquet, fruitier wine, improved color stability and improved filterability. No additive can ever be guaranteed to give the result hoped for, but if you experiment first with bench trials, you should not get a badly disappointing outcome. In most cases, the right dosage will improve your wine, and no one will know the difference. Then your dilemma becomes whether to reference it on your label! In the minds of some people, these additives are different in character than sulfite, tartaric acid, potassium carbonate, bentonite and the other traditional additives.

The sequence in which tannins and enzymes are used is important. Although enzymes are inhibited only slightly by low levels of free sulfite in solution, they nevertheless should not be added at the same time as sulfite. Add them a few minutes or hours after sulfiting, by which time the sulfite will be thoroughly dispersed and bonded.

Enzymes are inhibited far more by either bentonite or tannins than by sulfite. When using both an enzyme and tannin, the usual sequence is to wait an hour or two after crushing and sulfiting before adding enzymes. Then wait about four hours before adding the tannin to give the enzyme time to do most of its work.

When preparing your solutions, be sure to use chlorine-free water. Distilled or deionized water would be best, but tap water is acceptable if it has first been run through a carbon filter and then boiled to drive off any residual chlorine.

Get more information on tannins and enzymes by downloading Scott's Fermentation Handbook at www.scottlaboratories.com.

Scottzyme Color Pro - liquid - This pectinase helps to extract more color and tannin out of the grape skins and to improve clarity and reduce herbaceous character in the finished wine. You would want to consider using this enzyme, pre-fermentation, with Pinot Noir, Sangiovese, Grenache or other light-colored red grapes. Give it about 3 or 4 hours to work before adding an optional fermentation tannin.

Dosage – crushed red grapes: 3-5 ml per 100 pounds. Use the lower dosage for underripe fruit and the higher dosage to make a big red from ripe fruit.

Dosage – white juice: Although white grapes have no color, some wineries use Color Pro, at the rate of 0.75-1ml per 100 pounds, to improve filtration and clarification.

Preparation and use: For easier and more uniform dispersion, dilute your dosage with ten times its volume of distilled water. Sprinkle this over the grapes before crushing or mix it into the must (but 1 to 2 hours after sulfiting).

Duration of treatment: At temperatures above 60°F (16°C), give it 2 to 3 days to fully react before adding any tannins. At lower temperatures, give it 4 to 7 days and stir it up daily as the enzyme tends to settle at the bottom.

Shelf life: 1 to 2 years if refrigerated and tightly sealed.

Laffort Tanin VR Supra - powder - This tannin was developed for use during fermentation of red wines. Some natural tannins are always lost by precipitation during fermentation. VR Supra retains more of the natural tannins by allowing them to bind with anthocyanins and renders the wine more color stable. Add it during or right after crushing for maximum effect. (Or, if you used Color Pro right after crushing, add it 3 or 4 hours later to help preserve the tannins and colors extracted by Color Pro.)

Since bench trials are impractical, Laffort recommends starting with 20g/hL at the crush. If a taste test indicates that more is needed, then add more in increments of 6.3g/hL during the first 3 or 4 days of fermentation.

Dosage: Red vinifera must, 30-50g/hL (6-10 g/5 gal.)

Dosage: Non-vinifera red musts, 40-60g/hL (8-12 g/5 gal.)

Preparation and use: Dissolve the dosage in 10 times its weight of warm water (95°F/35°C). Stir it in thoroughly.

Shelf life: 4 years stored at 65°F (18°C), tightly sealed and dry.

Laffort Tanin VR Supra NF - powder - This fermentation tannin is similar to VR Supra, except that it contains no chestnut tannins, which can leave a detectible bitterness in the aftertaste. Use it at the rate 300 ppm for the more delicate red wines, such as Pinot Noir, Sangiovese and Grenache. The preparation, use and recommended dosage rates are the same as for VR Supra, above.

Laffort Filtrozym - powder – As the name suggests, this enzyme was developed to improve the fining, clarification and filtration of wines that are high in pectins and colloids — whites, reds and rosés. It is particularly recommended for *botrytised* wines, which are frequently difficult to clarify and filter due to excessive glucans. Use it post-fermentation after the gross lees have been settled out and give it six weeks to work at temperatures between 55 and 65°F (13-18°C). It should not be used at temperatures under 50°F (10°C).

Dosage:	white wines	2-3g/hL (.4-.6 g/5-gal.)
	rosés	3-4g/hL (.6-.8 g/5-gal.)
	red wines	4-5g/hL (.8-1.0 g/5-gal.)

Preparation and use: Dissolve the dosage in ten times its weight of distilled water and stir it into the wine a few minutes later during racking. Should be used immediately — don't store a mixed solution after rehydration.

Weight: 1 tsp. = 3.2 grams

Shelf life: 3 years at room temperature, stored dry; 6 months after opening.

Scottzyme KS - liquid – This enzyme should be reserved for special situations; namely, wines that are extremely difficult to settle or hard to filter. It would be a good choice for late harvest and ice wines, which are likely to be difficult to clarify. ***Never use it before pressing.*** It is most effective in white wines if used after pressing but before fermentation.

Dosage, white juice: 2.6 – 3.9ml/hL   (0.5-0.75 ml/5-gal.)

Dosage, red and white wine: 5 - 7.8ml/hL   (1 -1.5 ml/5-gal.)

Preparation and use: For better dispersion dilute the dosage in cool water to make about a 10% solution. Blend in during racking. Stir daily if the wine's temperature is less than 60°F as it takes several days to react.

Bench trials recommended before use in wines - Make a 2.5% solution (2.5ml plus water to 100ml total) and try at various rates:

Rate	2.5% soln./375-ml btl.
2.6ml/hL	0.36ml
3.9ml/hL	0.54ml
5.0ml/hL	0.72ml
6.5ml/hL	0.90ml
7.8ml/hL	1.08ml

Shelf life: Loses about 5% per year if kept tightly closed and stored cool.

Laffort Tan' Cor Grand Cru – powder – This is an aging tannin to add structure to and enhance the mid-palate of premium red wines without adding harshness or excessive oakiness. It would be a good choice for wines to be aged in used oak barrels, but can also be used 6 weeks before bottling. Try it in Syrah or Zinfandel for starters!

Dosage:

Before barrel aging:

carboys & used barrels	10-30 g/hL (2-6 g/5 gal.)
new barrels	5-15 g/hL (1-3 g/5 gal.)
6 weeks before bottling:	5-10 g/hL (1-2 g/5 gal.)

Preparation and use: Dissolve the dosage in 10 times its weight of warm water (95°F/35°C). Blend in during racking. Can be used during the first two or three rackings but be sure to evaluate in between. Err on the low side as the tannin does not integrate as readily as some of the oak tannins.

Weight: 1 tsp. = 1.9 grams

Shelf life: 4 years stored tightly sealed and dry.

Rapidase AR2000 – powder – This enzyme is discussed on pages 100 to 101. Unlike tannins and most other enzymes, it affects the bouquet and aroma.

Bench Trials

The manufacturers generally recommend bench trials for most tannins and enzymes to determine what, within the range, the dose should be. But bench trials are impractical if the tannin or enzyme is being used before fermentation. In addition it is hard to evaluate the outcome so early in the wine's life because tannins and enzymes are intended to improve the wine qualitatively rather than quantitatively; i.e., to improve the color or the mid-palate, or the bouquet, etc. I usually give the must a dose somewhere in the lower half of the recommended range and live with the result. Or, in the case of VR Supra, give it the minimum dose initially and add more a day or two later if my taste buds suggest that more would be helpful. As a result, I seldom run bench trials for treatments being made before fermentation.

Bench trials make more sense for post-fermentation treatments because you can evaluate the result with more confidence. With Tan' Cor Grand Cru, for instance, it would be advisable to test it in the range of 50ppm to 125ppm. Make a 5% solution (below) and dispense it with a 1-ml pipet into 375-ml bottles. Cork the bottles, wait one to two weeks and then evaluate. In the meantime, of course, keep the carboy or barrel sparged with argon!

With Rapidase AR 2000, I usually treat the wine at the rate of 2 grams per hectoliter. Rather than doing bench trials, as recommended by Rapidase, I monitor the progress and fine with bentonite when the bouquet has been enhanced to my satisfaction. This may not be the equivalent of bench trials from 1 to 3 grams per hL, but it seems to work because this enzyme is keeps working to some extent until removed from the wine.

To make a 5% solution – any 5% solution -- dissolve 5 g. (powder) or 5ml (liquid) in 80ml of distilled water (95°F / 35°C). Bring total volume to 100ml after it is dissolved. A 1-ml Class A pipet is almost a necessity for dealing with fractions of a milliliter because it gives you much better ability to stop the flow at the right time.

Rate		5% soln./375ml btl.
5g/hL	(50 ppm)	0.37 ml
7.5g/hL	(75 ppm)	0.56 ml
10g/hL	(100 ppm)	0.75 ml
12.5g/hL	(125 ppm)	0.94 ml
15g/hL	(150 ppm)	1.12 ml
20 g/hL	(200 ppm)	1.50 ml
30g/hL	(300 ppm)	2.25 ml

Chapter Twelve

MALOLATIC FERMENTATION

 alolactic fermentation (MLF) imparts a unique flavor which is particularly noticeable in white wines. It takes some of the sharpness off the acid as it is perceived around the edge of the tongue and "rounds out" a wine. MLF is commonly sought in dry red table wines. It is also used for some dry white wines, such as Chardonnay, Sauvignon Blanc, and sometimes Semillon, but is generally avoided for fruity white wines, such as Riesling, Gewurztraminer, Muscats and Chenin Blanc. The diacetyl produced by malolactic bacteria is the principal source of the "buttery" quality in white wines such as Chardonnay.

Malolactic bacteria break down the malic acid into lactic acid, producing water and carbon dioxide in the process. Since lactic acid is only half as acidic as malic acid, total acidity is lowered by half the amount of malic acid converted. For example, if the original malic acid content happened to be .4% and all were converted to lactic, total acidity would drop by .2%. MLF is the only practical way for the home winemaker to selectively reduce malic acid without first neutralizing all of the tartaric acid, which is the desirable acid.

Malolactic bacteria occur naturally in the air and on the grapes.

If potassium metabisulfite is omitted, the malolactic bacteria often multiply to the point where they will do their job. However it might not happen until the following spring or summer, if at all, and the wrong strain might develop. Since two of the three strains of malolactic bacteria are undesirable, the better practice is to kill all malolactic bacteria by sulfiting at crushing and then to inoculate after fermentation with a pure strain of the desired bacteria, *leuconostoc oenos*. The outcome is more certain this way.

Note that potassium sorbate should not be used if you seek malolactic fermentation because it is a nutrient to the bacteria which results in an objectionable "geranium" flavor.

Adverse conditions

Malolactic bacteria are finicky critters. They thrive only under certain conditions and even then, nothing is guaranteed. The following are the conditions in which they struggle. If you want MLF, do your best to *avoid* these conditions:

HIGH ALCOHOL. Malolactic bacteria are not very tolerant of high alcohol levels, which is why it is more difficult to initiate MLF in still wines. If my grapes had high sugar and I did not want to add water to lower the sugar level, I would be concerned about the inhibitory effect of high alcohol. I would add the ML nutrient and starter when fermentation peaks (about 18°B), before much sugar has been converted to alcohol. However, ML should not be added at the same time as the yeast because that would be an invitation to an unacceptably high level of volatile acids in the finished wine.

HIGH SULFITE. Malolactic bacteria are much more sensitive to sulfite than yeast are. Even a modest level such as 25 ppm of free sulfite is likely to kill malolactic bacteria. It is best in my opinion to use ¼ tsp. per 5 gallons (= 45 ppm) of sulfite at the crush. This kills all natural malolactic bacteria, including the bad strains. If you want MLF, inoculate later with a cultured strain. Note that total sulfite in excess of 100 ppm is also likely to inhibit MLF, even if none of it is in free state.

LOW TEMPERATURES. Most strains of *leuconostoc oenos* are barely active at 65°F (18°C). The "OSU" strain will work at lower temperatures, but all strains are more active in the desired temperature range of 70-75°F (21-24°C).

LOW pH. If your grapes have high acid, the pH might be too low to cultivate malolactic bacteria. Most strains of malolactic bacteria will work in red wines having a pH of 3.3 or higher and in white wines having a pH of 3.1 or higher. If you do not know the pH of the must, but know that total acid is high and want malolactic fermentation to reduce acidity, use calcium carbonate to lower the total acidity to 1.0% before adding the malolactic starter.

Malolactic bacteria might tolerate one adverse condition, but not two or three. It is quite easy to avoid MLF — just use sulfite, keep the temperature down, and clarify the wine before allowing the temperature to rise, and it would be most unusual to experience any MLF.

It's more complicated if you want MLF. Great care should be taken to make the conditions as ideal as possible before adding the starter — no free SO_2, temperature at 70-75°F (21-24°C) and proper acidity and pH. It also helps to use yeast extract or a malolactic nutrient at the rate of ½ g/gal and to stir up the lees and nutrients with a slender dowel once or twice a week.

Note that although yeast love diammonium phosphate, malolactic bacteria are indifferent to it.

When to inoculate

It is somewhat more difficult to get MLF started after fermentation is over, due to high alcohol, reduced nutrients and absence of heat from fermentation. In addition, the malolactic bacteria very much like the presence of skins. Many winemakers add the malolactic starter and yeast extract as soon as fermentation reaches its peak, which is usually about two or three days after the yeast starter was added. This is a surefire way to get it started, due to the presence of skins and fermentation heat. And it has the advantage of getting the wine through MLF sooner.

Other winemakers, the author included, wait until pressing to add the ML starter and nutrient. Or, they inoculate at the last punch down or even after the wine is still. Freeze-dried, direct-add strains of ML bacteria are very dependable, and this gives you some latitude.

The one thing you do *not* want to do is to inoculate before the wine is fermenting vigorously. ML bacteria and yeast compete for some of the same nutrients, which is an invitation to high volatile acids in the end. Another caveat is not to use Prise de Mousse yeast, which gobbles up a lot of the same nutrients the ML bacteria need. Use a different yeast or at least wait until primary fermentation is over and add extra ML nutrient if using Prise de Mousse.

Malolactic fermentation is not as easily induced in white wines since they are fermented cooler than reds, have fewer nutrients and are not fermented on the skins. White wines are most successfully inoculated as soon as they are still. Do not rack off the lees as the lees are an important source of nutrients for the bacteria. Raise the temperature of the wine to 70-75°F (21-24°C), add ¼ teaspoon per gallon of yeast extract or proprietary MLF nutrient, such as Leucofood®, and then stir in the MLF starter. A small packet of Chr. Hansen *Vinaflora oenos* will treat up to 60 gallons, which is approximately ⅛ teaspoon per 5 gallons. However, with a still white wine, it wouldn't hurt to double the dosage. Keep the wine at 70-75°F (21-24°C), stir up the lees every week with a slender dowel, and you will eventually get it to start and go to completion. Note that if you add the ML starter during primary fermentation, you will end up with less diacetyl (the buttery quality) because the yeast will consume some of it.

TIP

Freeze-dried, direct-add MLF starter has a short life span after being opened. The smallest packages will treat 60 gallons. If you don't need the whole package for the present inoculation(s), dip out your ¼ tsp. and inoculate your wine. Quickly insert the packet of remaining ML powder into a FoodSaver bag, seal it and put it back in the freezer. It will still be good several months later. The cell count might be down, but it will still work!

A low pH wine will take longer to complete MLF than a high pH wine. This is due to the low pH and also due to the fact that underripe grapes usually have more malic acid to be converted.

When is MLF complete?

It is important to know when MLF is complete because the temperature should be lowered as soon afterward as possible. The higher temperatures and lack of meta create a risk of undesirable side reactions. This risk is drastically reduced when the temperature is lowered and meta added. You also want to know whether or not the conversion is complete before bottling as renewed malolactic activity in the bottle could ruin the wine.

There are several ways to determine when all the malic acid has been converted to lactic acid, the simplest being to watch the bubble activity closely. MLF generates tiny bubbles of CO_2. Give the carboy a quick twist — a rush of small bubbles is a good indication of malolactic activity, particularly if Clinitest® indicates that the wine is bone dry. If the conditions have been right, and it appears to have MLF started, and the temperature has been constantly maintained at 65°F (18°C) or more, the conversion will probably be complete when the bubbles slow noticeably and then stop. This is an acceptable method of monitoring MLF, although not the most reliable.

You could supplement bubble watching with periodic titration tests, which will indicate reductions in total acidity. When total acid stops falling and the bubbles stop, MLF is presumably complete, again assuming proper conditions and a temperature continuously above 65°F (18°C).

Paper chromatography is the best way of testing for completion of MLF. A test kit is not prohibitively expensive or difficult to use (see Appendix A). With red wines, a test could be run as soon as the wine falls still. If the MLF starter was added at the peak of fermentation, MLF might be complete by then, in which case the wine can be racked, sulfited and chilled to reduce the risk of spoilage. More likely, you will need to hold the temperature at 70-75°F (21-24°C) a few more weeks until it finishes.

Once you have malolactic fermentation underway, do your utmost to keep it going without interruption. Keep the temperature up and stir up the lees every week or two with a slender dowel. It's not only a matter of wanting to finish MLF so that the wine can be cold stabilized during the depth of winter — you want to avoid the risk of renewed MLF after bottling. If you let the temperature fall or cold stabilize, for instance, malolactic fermentation would stop, but the bacteria will not die, even if you sulfite. Activity might or might not resume the following summer. If it does not, you would want to reinoculate. If a chromatography test indicates that some malic acid remains, get the temperature up to 75°F (24°C) with a healthy dose of fresh starter and nutrient.

If a wine has gone through MLF and the acid drops so low that it has to be increased, be sure to use tartaric acid rather than malic. Malic acid would be an invitation to renewed activity. Don't use acid blend because they almost always contain some malic acid.

Stuck MLF

If malolactic fermentation appears to have stopped but a chromatography test reveals the process to be only partially complete, it may have stuck. This usually occurs when conditions are or have become adverse:

- Temperature below 65°F
- High alcohol
- High level of free sulfite
- pH below 3.2

One option, if the acid level seems fine and the malic flavor is not objectionable, is to treat it with lysozyme (1½ g. per gallon) to rule out the possibility of renewed activity after bottling. This is where you are sure the malic acid level is acceptable to your palate.

If you want to finish MLF, the next step is to re-inoculate. Raise the temperature to 70-75°F (21-24°C), add another ½ teaspoon of yeast MLF nutrient, such as Bactiv-aid® or Leucofood®, and add double the amount of starter. With Viniflora® Oenos, that would be ¼ tsp. per 5 gallons. If the wine has low pH, high alcohol, low temperature and/or high sulfite, use a different strain of ML starter, one that is more tolerant of these conditions. Stir up the lees with your dowel twice weekly, and it should start again.

If you have tried everything and cannot get MLF to go to completion, go ahead and bottle anyway. The wine itself will not be inferior if most of the malic acid has been converted. The risk of post-bottling MLF can be eliminated by first treating it with lysozyme at the rate 1½ grams per gallon.

If you do not have lysozyme, the risk of post-bottling MLF can be reduced by racking off the lees, sulfiting at 75 ppm and chilling the wine down to 25°F (-4°C) for a week or two, which will kill a lot of the bacteria.

Precautions

The absence of meta in combination with higher temperatures greatly increases the risk of spoilage problems. The carboy should be kept full, and the wine should not be exposed to air during this time of vulnerability. The bit of CO_2 generated by MLF will protect it from air and acetobacter. Acetobacter, which cannot form without oxygen, is indicated by a white film or crust on the surface in the neck of the carboy. It is a precursor to vinegar and even trace amounts are objectionable. The risk can be lowered by occasionally sprinkling a few grains of sulfite over the surface of the wine in the neck of the carboy.

Anytime a white crust does appears in the neck of the carboy, the best remedy is to insert a small tube into the wine, add a bit of water or sound wine and "float" the scum out of the carboy, as it is almost impossible to spoon or siphon it out. A tiny burette funnel and small tube make this procedure easier. Then rack, sulfite at 45 ppm and cool. If a surface film does develop, just hope the wine is not already ruined. A heavy dose of meta might help deal with an off flavor but there is no actual cure.

The risk of acetobacter can be reduced by occasionally adding a tablespoon of brandy in the neck of the carboy. Better yet, spray a mist of Everclear over the surface, as wineries do. The alcohol kills the bacteria.

Ultimately, you will want to put all of your red table wines through malolactic fermentation. In addition to lowering total acidity, it eliminates the "bright, fruity" taste of malic acid, which most people find objectionable in red wines. As to white wines, the choice is less clear because MLF takes away some of the fruitiness. On the other hand, MLF adds a buttery flavor that is generally regarded as a plus.

Malolactic Bacteria Glossary

Several different strains of cultured malolactic bacteria have been isolated and developed commercially. Most wine supply stores will carry one or two different strains. Some strains produce more diacetyl than others. Some work at lower pH than others, and some at lower temperatures. Here are some notes on those that are often available.

VINIFLORA® OENOS by Chr. Hansen (Denmark). This direct-add strain is a very good choice to inoculate a still wine. It can be added directly to the wine without the nuisance of having to make a starter solution several days before inoculating. It is freeze-dried and will keep a season or two in the freezer, as long as the foil packet has not been opened. Once opened, it should be used promptly as it is very sensitive to humidity. Freeze-dried ML starters are the best choice to induce malolactic fermentation.

UVAFERM MVR. Lallemand markets several freeze-dried, direct-add cultures in packets sufficient for 66 gallons (227 liters).

OREGON STATE UNIVERSITY STRAIN. This strain was isolated for use on the low pH Pinot Noirs from Oregon's Willamette Valley. I like it not so much because it is said to work as low as 2.9 pH, but because it is more active in the 65-70°F (18-21°C) range. It is easier to maintain this temperature during winter months than 70-75°F (21-24°C), as required by the other strains. This strain is marketed by Lallemand as "OSU" and by Wyeast Laboratories, Mt. Hood, Oregon, as "Vintner's Choice." The latter is in liquid form in foil packets which can be added directly without making a starter solution.

LALLEMAND X-3. This is a good combination of four different strains. It comes in dried form (not freeze-dried), but making a starter solution is easy. Lallemand markets several other strains as well.

TWO-PART STARTERS. The traditional two-part, wet malolactic starter is the least expensive, but it must be activated a week before inoculating and given time to completely convert all malic acid in the starter sample to lactic acid. Ideally, this would be confirmed by chromatography before inoculating because MLF is not likely to start unless the conversion is complete.

LYSOZYME. This casein derivative works by dissolving the cell walls of gram-positive bacteria and can be used to stop or delay the malolactic fermentation process.

• If you were not able to get your wine fully through malolactic fermentation, lysozyme at the rate of 1½ gram per U.S. gallon will prevent renewed MLF after bottling.

• Similarly, if you wanted to put a Chardonnay or Pinot Noir only partially through malolactic fermentation, you could stop the process at the desired point.

• Some wine makers routinely use lysozyme before barrel aging because it increases the stability of the finished wine.

• It can be used instead of sulfite to kill natural malolactic bacteria in red-grape musts. I use it in high-pH wines to augment the sulfite.

• If you are struggling with a stuck primary fermentation, lysozyme will keep the volatile acid level from creeping up while you get the primary fermentation restarted at warmer temperatures.

• If you want to re-inoculate with a ML starter after using lysozyme, fine first with bentonite to remove the excess.

It is critical that white wines be fined with bentonite (½ t. per 5 gal.) after lysozyme. Otherwise, a haze will develop when chilled, even if clear before. Other negatively-charged fining agents do not seem to strip it out, so use bentonite.

To prepare lysozyme, mix it into a bit of warm water and wait until it is no longer cloudy. Then gently stir it into the wine. Stored dry and cool, lysozyme has a shelf life of five years.

Here are the recommended dosages:

For sluggish or stuck primary fermentation:
Red – 1 g. per gal.
White – 1½ g. per gal.

For all other uses, such as stability during
barrel aging (after MLF is over), for blending a partially
complete ML wine with another and to block MLF:
1½ g. per gal.

Chapter Thirteen

SpArkLiNG WiNES

parkling wines from the Champagne area of France are the only ones which can rightfully be called "Champagne." However, fine sparkling wines come from many other parts of the world, and there is no reason your cellar could not be added to the list! The home winemaker can in fact make first class sparkling wines — far better than you ever expect. But you have to start with good fruit. And it takes a lot of work and patience. The technique described below — known to the French as *méthode champenoise* — is the best process there is for making sparkling wines, whether it be with Pinot Noir, Chardonnay, Riesling, peaches or apricots. The discussion that follows is in terms of white grape juice, but the same technique would work for peaches or apricots as long as the acid level is raised to .7% or more.

Méthode champenoise

The goal initially is to make a sound dry white table wine having alcohol in the range of 10 to 11%. The first fermentation is known as the *cuvée* fermentation and is done by home winemakers in carboys in essentially the same manner as set forth in Chapter 2 for regular white table wines, except that the grapes are picked when the sugar level is 18-20°B. After the *cuvée* has been fermented, racked and clarified, a measured amount of sugar and fresh yeast starter are added, and the wine is bottled and capped. The sugar ferments slowly in the bottle; it is this *tirage* fermentation that gives the wine its effervescence.

After the *tirage* fermentation, the wine is aged on the lees in the bottle for a period of time ranging from several months to many years. Then the bottles are "riddled." Riddling, or *remuage* to the French, is the process of manipulating the lees into the neck of the bottle with sharp twists of the bottle. The bottles are held at an angle in a rack, and the angle is gradually increased until the rack is flat and the bottles vertical.

Next, an ice plug is frozen in the neck of the bottle to hold the lees in place when the bottle is tipped up. When the bottle is tipped to a 45° angle and the cap removed, the lees are blown out along with the ice plug. The wine is now "disgorged." A measured amount of sugar syrup — the *dosage* — is quickly added to sweeten the remaining wine. The bottle is then permanently closed. This is the essence of *méthode champenoise*, used by makers of fine sparkling wines throughout the world.

Grapes for sparkling wines

Although Pinot Noir and Chardonnay are the classic grape types for French champagnes, other varieties also work well, including Semillon, Sauvignon Blanc and Riesling or blends thereof. Grapes for sparkling wines are picked at an earlier stage of ripeness — typically between 18 and 20°B — in order to produce a still wine with only 10-11% alcohol before bottle fermentation. A lower level of alcohol is desired because sugar will be added for bottle fermentation, and that will raise the alcohol level to the desired level of 13% or so. If you started with grapes having a Brix of 24°, the wine would have 13% alcohol after the *cuvée* fermentation. It would be difficult to initiate bottle fermentation with 13% alcohol; and even if successful, the finished wine would have alcohol of 14.5% after bottle fermentation. That is too high. So it works best to use grapes having a Brix of 18 to 20°.

Ideally, total acid of the grapes would be .75-.80%, but the acid usually will not have dropped to that level when the sugar is still below 20°B. So an acid level of 1% or more is to be expected when grapes are picked at 18-20°B. Higher acid can be countered with a higher level of residual sugar when the dosage is added.

Crushing and pressing

White grapes, such as Chardonnay, are crushed, pressed and processed as though you were setting out to make a typical dry white table wine, per Chapter 2. However, if you are processing red grapes, such as Pinot Noir, you will need to decide before crushing whether you want a sparkling white wine, a blush or a rosé. Although Pinot Noir grapes are red, the juice is white. But if crushed and left on the skins, the juice will absorb pigment from the skins. Coloration can be completely avoided if the grapes are pressed without first being crushed. The resulting white wine is known and marketed as *blanc de noirs* to distinguish it from a *blanc de blancs* made from white grapes. You could use half Chardonnay for up-front fruit and half Pinot Noir for a longer aftertaste.

On the other hand, if you want enough color that a blush wine will result, the grapes should be crushed and soaked on the skins for a few hours and then pressed and fermented. If you want an even darker, rosé-type sparkling wine, crush, de-stem and cold soak on the skins for up to a day before pressing and fermenting.

Whether processing red grapes or white grapes, meta should be carefully limited to 45 ppm at pressing. This will be sufficient to discourage malolactic fermentation, which most producers avoid in their sparkling wines (one notable exception being Dom Pérignon). Since grapes of this type are typically low in tannin, I like to add ¼-½ tsp. of tannin per 5 gallons at pressing as an aid in clarifying.

Although almost any strain of yeast could be used for the *cuvée* fermentation, I am partial to cold fermenting with Steinberg yeast when working with Pinot Noir or Chardonnay to preserve as much of the fruit and bouquet as possible. But Prise de Mousse also works well.

Cuvée fermentation

The *cuvée* fermentation takes place in carboys filled to about ¾ capacity and topped with air locks. When unfermented sugar is nearing 0°B., the carboys are combined or topped up and the temperature raised to about 70°F to encourage complete fermentation. When Clinitest® confirms that the wine is dry, the carboys should be topped up again if necessary and the wine cold stabilized for a month or two.

Racking, fining and clarifying

The challenge of clarifying is the same as it is with any white wine. Follow the procedures in Chapter 2, with one exception: since you want no free SO_2 in solution when the *tirage* yeast is added for bottle fermentation, meta should be omitted entirely at the last racking. This is when the wine is reinoculated with a fresh yeast starter, bottled and *tirage* fermentation initiated. Everything else is the same.

You want the wine to be crystal clear before the sugar is added for bottle fermentation because if it isn't clear by then, you'll never be able to clear it in the bottle. If the second fining attempt is not a total success and the wine has been cold stabilized for several months, proceed with bottle fermentation anyway. The haze will be an aesthetic negative but will not affect the flavor.

Choice of bottles

Whether you plan to purchase new bottles or soak labels off used bottles and clean them up, they should be heavy sparkling wine bottles of U.S. origin, free of chips or flaws. Avoid sparkling cider bottles and any that are not heavy enough to withstand the high pressure that will build up after bottle fermentation. Bottles made in the U.S. are preferable because the neck is the right diameter to accommodate a standard crown cap such as is used for beer or soda pop. Rather than inserting a mushroom cork or plastic cap, it's better to cap the bottles with a crown cap for the *tirage* fermentation – it's much easier to pop off when disgorging and adding the dosage. Bottles from Spain, France and Italy have a larger neck diameter which U.S. crown caps will not fit.

Bottles having any stain or mold in them should also be discarded — they're not worth the effort. It is important that bottles for sparkling wines be carefully cleaned with a brush to remove any stain or film they may contain. The cleaner the glass, the more freely the sediment will slip down into the neck of the bottle when it is riddled.

Bottling and *tirage* fermentation

After several months of cold stabilization and two or perhaps three rackings, the *cuvée* wine will be totally dry and hopefully crystal clear. It will be either white or blush as planned and will have alcohol in the 10 to 11% range. Total acid will have dropped slightly from its pre-fermentation level. Other types of wine might have been blended in along the way if you had them on hand and felt experimental.

The procedure for making sparkling wines now departs from that for dry white table wines: it is time to add a measured amount of sugar, inoculate with a fresh yeast starter and bottle the wine for the *tirage* fermentation. The more sugar you add, the more carbonated the wine will be. Add too much, and you'll have bottles exploding all over the place! So the amount of sugar has to be carefully measured to stay within the limits of the bottle strength.

Although champagne bottles will withstand pressures of 8 or 10 atmospheres, commercial winemakers seldom exceed 6 atmospheres of bottle pressure. It is better for the home winemaker to limit it to 4 atmospheres. This will provide an abundance of carbonation without running the risk of exploding bottles. In fact, there would be nothing wrong with adding only enough sugar to produce two atmospheres of pressure and ending up with a creamy, spritzy wine known in France as a *crémant*. The amount of carbonation and the alcohol level are far less important in the case of sparkling wines than is the quality of the grapes and the time spent on the lees.

Four grams of sugar per liter will generate one atmosphere of pressure after bottle fermentation. To produce four atmospheres, therefore, you will need 16 grams of sugar per liter. This is the equivalent of 2⅛ ounces per gallon. Before doing the calculations, do another Clinitest® just to make sure there is no unfermented sugar left in the wine. If there is, convert the percentage to grams or ounces and deduct it from your calculated additions.

It will be more difficult to initiate the *tirage* fermentation than the initial fermentation. In addition to 10 or 11% alcohol, the wine has been clarified and has a low nutrient level compared to the original must. This combination of factors creates a rather hostile atmosphere in which to re-initiate fermentation. So it has to be done with some care. Here is how to handle this critical stage:

Choice of yeast is important for bottle fermentation. You want a yeast which is vigorous and alcohol-tolerant, making Prise de Mousse or Uvaferm 43 a good choice. Surprisingly, Pasteur Champagne is not recommended. To eliminate the riddling step (below), you can dispense 1-1½ grams of an encapsulated yeast (ProElif®) into each bottle—it doesn't generate much sediment.

Before activating the yeast, a sugar syrup should be made by dissolving a carefully calculated and weighed amount of cane or beet sugar (10½ ounces per 5 U.S. gallons / 19 liters of wine) in an equal volume of warm water or wine. Heat it gently in the microwave if necessary to dissolve it. Set the syrup aside to cool.

Now activate two packets of the dry yeast in four ounces of warm water as explained in Chapter 2. After the yeast is rehydrated, rack the *cuvée* into a large pail or primary fermenter and add the sugar syrup and activated yeast plus ½ tsp. of Fermaid K® or D.A.P. per 5 gallons. If using ProElif®, put 1-1½ grams of yeast beads in each 750-ml bottle. Also add about one ounce of liquid beermaker's isinglass. The isinglass will help clarification after bottle fermentation by coagulating with the yeast hulls. You can also add another ¼ to ½ tsp. of tannin at this time, dissolved in water, because most of the tannin that was previously added will have precipitated during clarification of the *cuvée* fermentation. And some of the tannin being added now will precipitate with the additional isinglass being added. Any excess will oxidize during the time it spends on the lees.

After everything is mixed up in the pail and stirred a bit for aeration, the wine should be immediately racked into your washed-and-rinsed champagne bottles. Use your dowel to stir up the yeast in the pail occasionally while racking — solids tend to settle rather quickly and you want some yeast in each bottle. Leave about an inch of air space in each bottle. Use a bottle capper to seal the bottles with crown caps.

The bottles should be stored at 55-60°F (13-16°C), not over 65°F (18°C), for two or three months while bottle fermentation takes place. Shake each bottle once a week during the first month to disperse the yeast. (It is always advisable to wear protective goggles and gloves while shaking bottles in case one is cracked or has a flaw.) After three months, bottle fermentation should be complete, but the time can vary. Test a bottle to be sure it is bone dry.

The natural desire is to get on with the process so you can start drinking your wine! But you will be well rewarded by waiting. A goodly portion of the high price tag on vintage champagnes from France is attributable to the many years spent on the lees. During this period of time the yeast cells die and decompose, which imparts a pleasing flavor. A distinct change in character is said to occur after two years on the lees and another after four or five years. I recently disgorged and sweetened some *blanc de noirs* that spent fourteen years on the lees.

In any event the wine should spend at least one year on the lees before being riddled and disgorged, simply to allow ample time for all the yeast cells to die and settle out. The bottles should be shaken two or three times a year during this time.

Riddling

Aside from a bottle capper, the only additional equipment needed for making sparkling wines is a riddling rack (See Illustration E, next page, for hole diameters and spacing using a standard two–by–two and ½" plywood for the frame.) The type of rack or method of construction is not important, but it should be designed with a pivot point so that the angle can be changed as riddling progresses. A small rack sufficient for 12 bottles should suffice. I built a huge one capable of holding 48 bottles and later discovered that I could riddle and disgorge only a case at a time. The longer it takes to get around to building your rack, the more time the wine will have on the lees, so there's no great rush on this project!

TIP

The need for a riddling rack can be eliminated by using ProElif® for the tirage fermentation as it produces very little sediment. The yeast beads will drop to the bottom of the neck when the bottles are inverted for disgorging, as discussed next.

When riddling is started, the bottles will be almost horizontal. By the end of riddling, the board will be horizontal and the bottles standing vertically, neck down, with the lees accumulated on the crown cap. Start the riddling process by vigorously shaking each

ILLUSTRATION E: Riddling Rack   end view

bottle to loosen the lees and stain that accumulated during aging. Place the bottles, stain now dissolved, in the rack, with the rack positioned so that the bottles rest at about 30° above horizontal.

After a few days the lees will have settled again — it's time for the first riddling installment. Give each bottle a sharp twist 90° in one direction, immediately followed by a sharp twist 45° back toward the original position. Drop it back in the slot with a small jolt which will help break the lees loose from the glass.

This process should be repeated every few days until the bottles have been rotated a full 360°. Then change the angle of the rack so that the bottles are closer to upright. Increase the bottle angle to perhaps 45° and repeat the process until they have been rotated another full 360°. Then increase the bottle angle another notch. As the angle gets steeper, the lees will slide toward the neck more willingly, and you can rotate them more than +90°/-45° each time. There will ultimately be about one teaspoon of yeast lees and isinglass resting in the neck of each bottle. Once riddled, the bottles can be stored indefinitely, neck down, or you can proceed at once with disgorging.

Disgorging, adding the dosage and recapping

The object in disgorging is to freeze an ice plug in the neck of the bottle, pop the cap to blow it out, add a measured quantity of sugar syrup to sweeten the wine and recap the bottle. The method I ultimately settled upon for freezing the ice plug is a plywood rack in the freezer. A piece of ½-inch plywood with holes (about

1⅜-1½" diameter) drilled on six inch centers works well; you might even be able to use the board from your riddling rack. Devise legs as needed to prop up the board in the freezer after it has been loaded with several bottles of wine.

If the freezer is full, chill the wine in a refrigerator for a day. Then get a hefty supply of crushed ice and sprinkle a generous quantity of calcium chloride on the ice to lower the freezing point and stick the necks of the bottles in. I have not tried this, but it would probably work if done on a cold winter day.

I suggest freezing only one bottle initially. Some of this bottle will be used to make the sugar syrup, or dosage, and the rest to top up the remaining bottles after the dosage is added. Check regularly to determine approximately how long it will take for an ice plug about 1-1½ inches long to form. If the ice plug is much longer, you will lose too much wine when the cap is popped off.

After the ice plug has formed, cradle the bottle in the crook of your arm at a 45° angle and pop the cap off. The lees in the ice plug will disappear instantly when the cap is popped off, and you will end up with almost 750 ml of clear sparkling wine which is bone dry. Cap this first bottle with a stopper to retain the sparkle and store it in the refrigerator for later use in topping up.

While the other 11 bottles are in the freezer, make the dosage. How much sugar to add? This takes us back to the topic of residual sugar/total acid discussed in Chapter 3! It's a matter of acid level and preference. A "brut" champagne of French origin might have residual sugar of up to 1.5%, a "sec" up to 2.5% and a "demi-sec" up to 4 or 5%. So ultimately it depends on your palate and the acidity.

TIP

Use a good quality brandy or cognac as a base for the sugar syrup rather than your sparkling wine. It makes a noticeable improvement.

Assuming that a Clinitest® confirms the wine to be totally dry, that you want residual sugar of 1%, and that you will be disgorging 11 bottles, you will need to add about 3 ounces of sugar per 11 bottles (750 ml x 11 x .01 = 82.5 g. = 2.9 ounces). Weigh out the needed amount of sugar and add it to a slightly smaller volume of wine from the first bottle. My container of choice is a measuring cup or beaker marked in milliliters. Now gently warm the sugar solution in the microwave as necessary to dissolve the sugar, stir, warm again, stir, etc.

Having been exposed to air, the wine will now need some protection in the form of SO_2. When the sugar has dissolved and the syrup cooled, dissolve ⅛ tsp. of potassium metabisulfite in 11 ml of water. One ml per bottle will raise the level of free SO_2 to about 45 parts per million. This is a bit on the high side and might be detectable right after adding the dosage and recorking, particularly since the effervescence will lift it right into your nostrils. However, the free SO_2 will quickly bond to the sugar and will not be noticeable after a few months. It is needed to give your sparkling wine a little protection against oxidation. If no sulfite is added at this stage, madeirization will probably be noticeable in less than a year.

Divide the total volume of sugar syrup in the beaker or measuring cup by 11 to determine the amount of syrup to be added to each bottle. First, using a pipet, dispense 1 ml of the sulfite solution into each bottle after it has been opened and disgorged. (Don't add it to the *dosage*.) Then use a 10-ml oral dispenser from the drug store to draw out the correct volume of syrup and dispense it into the bottle. Now the bottle should be topped up with dry sparkling wine from the first bottle and quickly corked or capped.

Corking

The classic mushroom-shaped cork is the best closure device but requires a special corker which is a relatively big expense for the limited use it will probably receive. Most home winemakers will be content to use a plastic closure, which can be driven in with a rubber mallet and held in place with a wire basket. Or you could use another crown cap — not very classy, but it will do a good job of retaining pressure and keeping air out. Crimp a foil capsule over the neck and the work is done—at last!

As you know by now, *méthode champenoise* is time consuming and labor intensive. If you are willing to make the commitment, consider doubling or tripling the quantity of grapes you normally process, particularly if high quality fruit at 18° to 19°B is available to you. That way, you can enjoy some of the wine while the rest continues to age on the lees. Larger quantities will also allow you to lightly press some of the grapes without crushing and to make a second wine from heavily pressed grapes. If you decide that the sugar level in the first batch to be disgorged and sweetened is either too high or too low, it can be corrected for the next batch. The key to premium champagne, once again, is starting with premium fruit and aging on the lees.

Chapter Fourteen

ALL ABOUT OAK

 ak has captured the fancy of winemakers and wine drinkers for many generations, and it continues to do so. It was once the only practical container material for fermenting and transporting wine but is now thought of as a way to enhance wine quality. An immense amount of research is being conducted on every imaginable aspect of the wood. This has led to greatly improved knowledge, better wines and more efficient use of a limited resource.

Oak, in my opinion, is a valuable asset in making all but the aromatic wines. Even someone who abhors highly-oaked wines should consider using it, but at a very low level, because oak does wonders to pull the acids, alcohol, tannins and glycerin into harmony. If you are concerned about the loss of delicate fruit flavors, then give the wine only a short exposure to oak. The oak bouquet and flavor will dissipate in a few months, resulting in a wine that is more balanced and cohesive, with little loss in fruit.

Oak affects a wine in a variety of ways. It adds another dimension to the bouquet and flavor; it increases volatile acidity and total acidity; it lowers the pH slightly; it releases tannins and other phenols into the wine; and it adds to the wine's overall complexity. The flavors and bouquet of caramel, coconut, vanilla, roasted nuts and cinnamon, for example, emanate from the wood, not the fruit. Although the ultimate effect depends on many factors, wood quality and toasting are the two most important variables, recognizing, of course, that nothing will ever compensate for inferior fruit quality.

The oak trees used for barrels are at least 100 years old and sometimes closer to 200 years old — it takes that long to reach the requisite 24-inch diameter. The tree is felled and allowed to dry in place for several months. Then it is transported to the mill, cut into usable size and stacked outside for drying. It is critical that the wood be air-dried. Air-dried wood has a denser cellular alignment and imparts better flavors than kiln-dried wood. The longer it is air-dried, the softer the tannins and the sweeter the flavors. It should be exposed to the elements for at least two winters and some wineries insist on three seasons, particularly for American oak, which has a more forward flavor than French oak. It even makes a difference where the oak is dried. Most American oak is dried in the Midwest, where the relative humidity is high enough to support the growth of mold and fungus on the wood. This consumes some of the harsh tannins and other phenols and sweetens the wood for purposes of aging wine.

Toasting technique is the most important of all the variables. Subjecting the oak to carefully controlled heat for limited period of time breaks down the cellulose and lignin. If the heat is too intense or held too long or if the heat source (usually scrap oak) is contaminated, the flavors and bouquet will suffer. Fortunately, American oak is now being toasted by skilled craftsmen. As more French firms have established subsidiaries in the U.S. and bought American firms, the French have lost the advantage in coopering they held a generation ago.

There are three general levels of toasting, and the wine will be different depending on which one is used. Which toast is to be used for which wine is completely the vintner's choice.

MEDIUM TOAST has a high concentration of vanilla which affects flavor more than bouquet. Less tannin is extracted with medium toast, so that a wine can be exposed to it for a longer period of time. Longer wood contact is beneficial in that it allows for better linking of tannin molecules, known as polymerization. The longer the exposure, the longer the chains of tannin molecules and the softer the effect. Medium toast has traditionally been used for heavy red wines because they seem to benefit from longer wood contact.

MEDIUM PLUS TOAST is darker brown in color and delivers the most complexity—aromas of coffee, caramel, butterscotch and roasted nuts. It is commonly used for Chardonnay and Pinot Noir as well as heavy red wines.

HEAVY TOAST is not as common, but it does exist and can be used. It imparts a pronounced toasty flavor very quickly, so you have to monitor the situation very carefully. I sometimes use it for a short while after extended aging in medium toast. After the wine has sufficient oak flavor, I add some heavily toasted cubes for a few days to give it a carbonized overlay. The wine picks up the toasty quality very quickly, so taste it daily and remove it before too much carbon flavor is added. This way, you get tannin polymerization from long-term contact with medium toast plus the toasty quality from a heavier toast. Overall, you sacrifice a lot of flexibility with heavy toast, so its use should be limited to special situations.

Oak species

French oak (*Quercus robur* and *Quercus sessiliflora*) is the most highly regarded source. It has been used in cooperage for many generations and is farmed in several forests in central France, most notably Allier, Nevers, Vosges, Troncais and Limousin. High worldwide demand has driven the price of French oak to prohibitive levels for ordinary wines, but it is highly sought after for use in making premium wines. French oak imparts a more subtle flavor than American oak and less oak bouquet. It adds more tannins, raises total acid more and lowers pH slightly more than American oak. The two species of French oak are interchangeable — the tightness of the grain is a bigger factor than which of the two species is used. Both species are grown in all of the French forests.

AMERICAN OAK (*Quercus alba*) is a tight-grained species of white oak that produces a more distinct aroma than French oak and imparts an oak flavor faster than French oak. But it usually softens more with age. Due to previous shortcomings in methods of drying, toasting and coopering, American oak developed a reputation for being inferior to French oak. However, methods of processing and coopering American oak have improved to the point where it can no longer be categorically said that French is better than American. Given extra air drying, American oak is every bit as good as French. The two are simply different, and the choice of one over the other depends on the vintner's preference. Many thousands of American oak barrels are now exported to France each year for use in making French wines.

American oak comes from the Midwest, as far south as Missouri and Kentucky, east to Virginia and as far north as Michigan. No matter what state or country, the colder the climate, the slower the tree will grow and the tighter the grain will be. Tighter-grained oak from Michigan, for example, can be expected to release flavors more slowly and allow for longer wine contact than a more porous wood from Kentucky.

HUNGARIAN OAK (*Quercus petraea, robur*) is is similar to French oak, but is less expensive. In my opinion, it is a better value than French oak. Both French oak and Hungarian oak add more structure to the wine than American oak, which adds more aromas.

OREGON OAK (*Quercus Garryana*) is gaining favor as wineries look for new and better species of oak, and hopefully less expensive ones. Some wineries use it almost exclusively. It delivers a floral quality that distinguishes it slightly from French oak, but the two are very similar in most respects.

French oak is widely used for aging Chardonnay, Pinot Noir and Cabernet Sauvignon. Try American oak with the fruitier varieties, such as Syrah, Zinfandel and Tempranillo.

Barrel alternatives

As you can see, the choices are many when it comes to oak. It's easy to get enthused about the various oak types and toasts and imagining how they will improve your wine. But if you want to learn the art of applying oak to wine, bear in mind that the quality of the wood and manner in which it is used count more than anything else. The species of oak makes some difference but it is only part of the equation. My suggestion, if you are a relative newcomer, is that you limit the variables until you have developed a good feel for the oak species you are using and what you like in the wine varieties that you tend to specialize in. The last thing a beginner needs is three or four different oak types in two or three toast levels. Buy one French oak and one American oak, both in medium or medium plus toast. Or, a medium toast and medium plus toast, both of the same species and source. Then do side-by-side carboys so that each time you can compare and add to your knowledge base. You will learn faster this way than with the very tempting "scatter-gun" approach.

It is difficult for a home winemaker to systematically add to his or her knowledge base by using barrels because the barrel cost and wine quantities are prohibitive. You need more side-by-side comparisons than one or two barrels would allow. In addition, the second wine through a barrel will not be the same as the first. It makes more sense to start out with barrel alternatives. Whether that be beans or staves or chips does not matter as long as the quality of the wood is high. Use the same product(s) for several seasons, and after you know what you like and don't like, then add a new variable, such as a new species or toast level.

This approach is not as confining as it might seem. There are enough different ways you can use two products to keep the learning process interesting. For instance, you could break in cubes or staves by using them during the primary fermentation of white wines, such as Chardonnay or Sauvignon Blanc. (Put the cubes in a nylon hose for easy removal.) Leave them in the primary fermentation for a few days. As soon as the oak flavor seems too strong, rack off or remove the oak.

This is essentially what wineries are doing when they break in new barrels by barrel fermenting white wines and then using the barrels for longer term aging of red wines. After the edge has been taken off a new barrel by fermenting white wine in it, oak-wine contact can be maintained longer in the wines to follow, hopefully for the 6 to 9 months required to get optimum polymerization of the tannins. The reason new

StaVin beans, about the size of a dime, add oak flavor to old barrels.

wood can be used this way without overwhelming a white wine is that the yeast metabolizes some of the oak elements. In addition, some of the oak tannins and flavors attach to the fermenting yeast cells and precipitate. But you still have to be careful. To avoid over-oaking their Chardonnay, some wineries will ferment a Semillon or Sauvignon Blanc in their new barrels for three or four days, then barrel ferment Chardonnay and finally use them for long-term aging of red wines.

There is no way to articulate when to stop oak contact in a wine, whether you are using cubes or barrels. In part, it depends on personal preference. It's something you learn by experience. There will be a pronounced flavor after a week, which will integrate and diminish. Then the flavor will come on quickly after several more weeks of contact. The process requires your weekly vigilance.

After bottling, the oak flavor will decrease markedly during the first year and somewhat during the second year. Note that the heavier the toast, the less the effect will diminish, due to the additional carbon. Until you develop a sense of how much the flavor will diminish over the course of one or two years, err on the short side to avoid over-oaking. American oak diminishes more than French oak.

When purchasing oak, always pay the premium price necessary to get quality oak. You are not going to get quality oak for a dollar a pound. The first time I used high quality oak, I tasted my wines a week later in amazement and said to myself, "It's the wood, stupid, not the barrels." I had always assumed that the distinct oak quality in commercial wines was the result of barrel aging. In reality, the quality of the oak and the toasting are more important than the form of the oak. In my case the staves and beans I used were distinctly superior to the various chips and splinters I had previously been using, some of which had not even been toasted and left a green taste. Since you have no choice but to trust the source, buy from a reputable one. Several reputable barrel manufacturers, listed in Appendix F, make their products available to wine supply shops and, in some cases, direct to home winemakers.

I am familiar with only two oak sources and have been impressed with the quality of both. StaVin has become a popular source of barrel alternatives for home as well as commercial winemakers. In addition to barrels, they have several products and systems for suspending the oak, such as food-grade stainless steel mesh sleeves filled with oak "beans," as StaVin calls them. The sleeves can be inserted through the bung and suspended in an older barrel which has lost all of its oak flavor or in larger stainless steel containers. The "beans" are cubes (approximately 7-8 mm, or ⅜ inch, thick) that have been toasted to one of the three standard degrees — medium, medium plus or heavy. They come in three different oak types— French, American and "European," which I assume is Hungarian. In general, medium plus toast imparts the most complexity.

If you bulk age in carboys, buy StaVin's beans, not the inserts or sleeves. The company recommends use of about 2½ oz. (85 beans) of new beans per 5 gallons. They also recommend leaving them in for two months. My preference is to start with less so that they can be left in longer. You can add a few more beans a few months later — then a few more, always monitoring the taste. Using less oak will allow for longer contact and better polymerization.

Innerstave has a high quality product called Chain-O-Oak™. Each package contains 17 staves, again about 7-8 mm thick. The staves can be linked together with nylon string, dropped into a barrel or

Staves are also used to boost oak flavor. One stave per 5 gallons is adequate.

tank and retrieved when the oak flavor starts getting too strong. As packaged, the staves are too wide to fit through the neck of a carboy. But they can be split down the middle.

Innerstave recommends 1½ staves per 5 gallons (.08 staves per liter). However, these staves have so much oak character that I would recommend using only one stave (2 halves) per 5 gallons. The cost of French oak is only slightly higher than American oak and works out to approximately 20¢ a bottle, which is comparable to StaVin beans. One advantage of staves is that a hole can be drilled in each stave after splitting so it can be suspended with fish line and easily pulled out and transferred to another carboy without having to rack. You can retain the same control with beans by suspending them in a small nylon sock.

These staves and beans are sized so that all of the oak character gets extracted. Wine penetrates oak about 3 to 4 mm. With exposure on both sides (6 sides in the case of cubes), the oak flavor and tannins will be extracted in 9 or 10 months.

The reason I suggest beans, staves or chips rather than jumping right into barrels is that these alternatives will deliver the oak flavor without the expense or contamination risk of barrels. If the lure of a barrel later becomes irresistible, then you will at least know the type of oak and toast that you prefer for your wine varieties and styles. In addition, the flavoring life of an oak barrel is limited. Almost all of the oak flavor will have been extracted from the standard 225-liter barrel by the end of three or four years of continuous use — yet, a barrel will last for 8 or 10 years as a container if properly cared for. The home winemaker faces the same dilemma as the commercial vintner — the oak flavor is gone before the barrel's utility as a storage container is gone. The obvious solution is to use alternative oak sources, such as staves or cubes. Wineries commonly do this in their older barrels, and I doubt that the quality is significantly diminished.

Selecting a barrel

If you want to make a world-class red wine, then you are talking about barrels. I have yet to encounter anyone who contends that staves, beans or other alternatives will equal a barrel of comparable quality wood. The wine picks up a little oxygen each time the bung is opened for tasting, testing or topping up. In addition to micro-oxidation, the fruit flavors get intensified from transpiration and repeated topping up. That is, the water and alcohol evaporate but the solids and flavors remain, and more get added with each topping up. In short, if you want the full potential of oak, then you will want to use barrels. Another shortcoming of glass or stainless steel compared to barrels is that the wine will be closed in and have less bouquet. To partially compensate for this lack of micro-oxygenation, I treat some red wines with AR-2000 to enhance the bouquet.

Aside from the type of oak and degree of toasting, barrel size is the biggest decision for the home winemaker. The optimum size for winemaking is the 225-liter size: the surface-to-volume ratio facilitates micro-oxygenation at just the right rate. The problem is that it takes close to 900 pounds of grapes to fill a 225-liter barrel one, including the 10% reserve that will be needed for topping up. That's a lot of wine for all but the wine clubs and groups. For that reason the 30 and 15 gallon sizes are more popular with home winemakers. The surface-to-volume ratio goes up as the barrel size decreases, but it is not prohibitive, even at the 15-gallon level. The increase in surface-to-volume ratio means that you have to be more alert to possible over-oaking and that the risk of oxidation will be a little higher.

Breaking in a barrel

First, make sure that your new barrel has a sweet oak aroma and that there are no construction flaws or problems, inside or out. A flashlight with a gooseneck head helps in examining the interior. The ends of all smaller barrels and many 55-gallon barrels will not be planed or toasted, which could influence your initiation of the barrel.

Although no two barrel manufacturers or wineries will have the same regimen for barrel treatment, they would all agree that a new barrel does not need to be cleaned with harsh chemicals. It was made with clean wood and then toasted to a high temperature, so there is no need for chemicals. Soap would only soften the wood; and soda ash, chemicals or even hot water would leach out some of the precious oak flavor and weaken the bung stave, which is the most vulnerable part of the barrel.

A new barrel should, however, be hydrated with care. If the wood is subjected to too much water too abruptly, it could swell abnormally and warp. The most conservative approach is to fill it ⅓ full with cold water and allow it to swell for four hours. Then fill it to the ⅔ level. After four more hours, fill it to the top and allow it to swell until it stops leaking. If it is still leaking after three days, empty it and refill it with fresh water. This is to guard against the growth of bacteria and microbes which could result using unsulfited, high-pH water. It is rare that a modern day barrel will still be leaking after three days of soaking, but it could happen. If so, I would take it back!

In general, stick with cold water unless there is some specific reason for doing otherwise. For example, if the ends have not been toasted, as will be the case with smaller barrels, you might want to give the ends a warm water soak, particularly if you plan to age white wines. Stand the barrel on end after the gradual hydration discussed above and use a warm water soak (90-100°F) of about 10% of the barrel volume. This will help reduce the harshness of the green oak. After a day or two of soaking, empty it, invert it and give the other end a soak. Similarly, if you are putting a used barrel back into circulation for the first time and are uncertain of its history, fill it with 90-100°F water. After the temperature has dropped to 65°F, drain it and immediately refill it with warm water, drain at 65°F, etc. If you detect any off odors after three or four repetitions, maybe it would be best to take it back to the prior owner rather than risking your wine.

Using the barrel

Barrels are best located in a cool, humid corner of the basement or cellar and the temperature kept under 60°F. Before filling the barrel, test the free sulfite in the wine and adjust it as necessary while racking. Free sulfite should be maintained at 20-30 parts per million throughout bulk aging. Some winemakers treat their wines with lysozyme (1½ g/gal.) before barrel aging to increase the stability of the wine and decrease its vulnerability to microbial spoilage during barrel aging.

Stay on task if you are using a new barrel, particularly if it is smaller than 60 gallons. Taste the wine every week during the first month and top up with some of your reserve wine each time. After the first month, it will suffice to taste and top up every two weeks. When the oak flavor seems right — maybe as soon as 1 or 2 months with a new barrel — rack it into an older barrel or into glass. Check and adjust the free sulfite level as necessary.

A new barrel soaks up a surprising amount of reserve wine when it is first placed into use. This is due to normal evaporation, plus it takes a considerable volume of wine to saturate the wood. The loss is less in a used barrel, which presumably was very recently emptied and is still saturated. After 2 or 3 years of use, a barrel will have lost most of its oak flavor, but it will still have great utility for

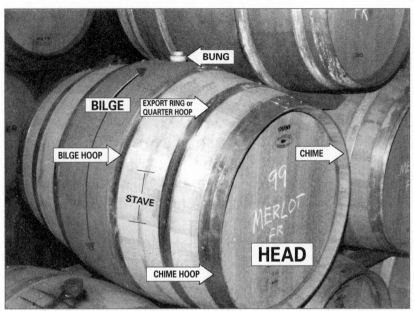

225 liter oak barrel.

micro-oxygenation and intensification of flavor. If the oak flavor is important to you, use staves or beans.

Wine aging in a used barrel should be racked two months after first being transferred, and every 2 or 3 months after that. At each racking the sulfite level should be checked and raised as indicated to about 25 ppm. Top it up every two weeks or so, and either sparge the gallon jug with argon or transfer the remaining wine into a smaller container. Red wines are usually aged one to two years in used 60-gallon barrels, but only a few months in small barrels, where it matures much faster.

The more frequently you top up, the faster the wine will age. If you want to slow down the aging process, top up less frequently. If the wine is through malolactic fermentation, replace the silicone plug firmly. When it is next removed, you should hear air rushing in to fill the vacuum. That little whoosh of air displacing the partial vacuum that built up will speed up aging. It's also reassurance that the barrel has been air tight. If the wine is still going through malolactic fermentation, you don't want an air-tight seal when you re-insert the plug.

Check the level of free sulfite each time you rack and raise it as necessary to the 20-30 ppm minimum. The level of free sulfite falls much faster in barrels than carboys and even faster in wines having a high pH. The level of free sulfite is so critical in barrel-aging that you should invest in a vacuum aspiration setup. You have invested a great deal of money in the barrel and even more in its contents, so don't risk the investment by cutting corners using the Ripper method or Titrets®, either of which always read high.

How long to oak?

There is no definitive answer to this question because it depends on many variables, such as the age of the barrel, whether it was previously used for barrel fermentation of white wines, whether red wine or white wine is to be aged, the type and toast of the oak, how frequently you top up and your fondness for oak flavor. Barrel size also has to be factored in because the surface-to-volume ratio of a 7½-gallon barrel is almost twice that of a 55-gallon barrel. My best advice is to taste every time you pull the bung to top up or test free sulfite, take notes, and realize that the oak flavor will go through cycles. The flavor will build up rapidly during the first week or two and then rather quickly integrate. It builds up again after several weeks or months — this is when you have to be alert and taste regularly. You can let the oak flavor develop a little further than you think you would like before racking or bottling because a significant amount will integrate during the next year or two, particularly with American oak. Your experience with chips and beans will help in this regard.

If you are breaking in a new barrel, you might want to barrel ferment a couple batches of white wine before deploying it for red wines. Wineries commonly barrel ferment Chardonnay wines first because it takes the harshness off the new oak, improves the white wine and facilitates longer oak contact for the red wines to follow. The resulting white wine is quite different than it would be if fermented in glass or stainless steel and then barrel aged. Taste at least weekly at the outset.

It is not mandatory that a barrel be broken in by first fermenting a white wine; but if you don't take the edge off the oak via barrel fermentation, you will have to monitor the oak flavor with extra vigilance. With a white table wine going into a new barrel for bulk aging, as opposed to barrel fermentation, you might want to taste it in as little as three days. At the opposite extreme, a very fruity red wine will handle many months in an oak barrel that has seen considerable use. That's because almost all of the tannins and flavors are extracted during the first three years of contact with wine.

Given the subjective nature of oak contact, you are likely to leave some wine in contact too long. The best solution for an over-oaked wine is blending with a reserve that has not been exposed to oak. If blending isn't an option, try fining with potassium caseinate, which will help remove some of the excess oak.

Cleaning the barrel

A barrel should be thoroughly washed and cleaned with cold water immediately after being emptied. If you cold fermented or cold stabilized in the barrel, removal of the tartrate crust can be a challenge. Again, avoid the temptation to use harsh chemicals. Before resorting to chemicals, try to dissolve the tartrates by filling the barrel with 90-100°F water. Empty it after the temperature has dropped to 70° and then refill it. Only after several repetitions should harsh chemicals or a pressure sprayer be considered. The point is that an oak barrel is a piece of craftsmanship to be treated as gently as possible.

Once the barrel is clean, the best strategy, by far, is to keep it full of wine at all times, never leaving it empty for more than a few hours. The wood continues to hold a lot a wine after it has been emptied, and acetobacter will immediately start converting that wine into vinegar if given a few hours of exposure to air. If you have no wine to refill it, maybe you could "borrow" some for a few months. Your friend's wine would benefit from the bit of oak flavor which you sacrifice, and your barrel will be safer filled with trouble-free wine.

Barrel storage: dry

Most home winemakers will not find it feasible to keep all barrels full all of the time, especially if working with larger barrels or if one is dedicated solely to white wines. If you find yourself with an empty barrel and several days or months until it will be filled again, clean it as discussed in the previous section. Set it outside to drain for an hour, bung down. Then rotate the bung straight up and burn a dripless sulfur pastille or wick. (This should always be done outdoors.) Suspend the pastille on a thin copper wire so that it will not come into contact with the wood. Half a pastille will suffice for a 30 or 15 gallon barrel. Stopper it with a silicone bung. Repeat this ritual every 30 days or more frequently if you smell an offodor or cannot detect sulfite.

If your barrels are located in your cellar, chances are the humidity will exceed 60%, and the procedure discussed above will suffice. High humidity is particularly common in the eastern half of the United States. However, if you are located in an arid climate, or if your barrels are stored in an air conditioned environment, the procedure for maintaining an empty barrel should be modified slightly so the barrel does not dry out and leak. You still need to burn sulfur once a month. But the barrel should be filled with warm water (90-100°F.) every other month before burning the sulfur pastille. Fill it with warm water and empty it when the temperature has dropped to 70°. After draining it, bung down, for an hour, burn the sulfur and stopper with a silicone bung. This approach repeated every two months (with an intervening sulfur pastille) is better than storing the barrel long-term with a sulfite-citric acid solution, which would take a toll on the oak flavors over time.

Before putting a stored barrel back into use, it should be thoroughly rinsed with cold water to remove any debris from the burned sulfur and then gradually re-hydrated. If left in, the sulfur would be converted to hydrogen sulfide during barrel fermentation and that would be the beginning of a major headache.

References for barrel break-in, maintenance and repair
See *Vineyard and Winery Management*, Jan./Feb, 1996, pp 27-30 and *Practical Winery & Vineyard*, March/April, 1990, pp 41-42. These websites will also be helpful:

http://www.bouchardcooperages.com/usa
http://www.seguin-moreau.fr/page_us.php?page
http://www.worldcooperage.com/pages/product_maintain.html
http://www.morebeer.com/public/pdf/wbarrel.pdf

Chapter Fifteen

CONCENTRATE KITS

 he market for concentrate kits is booming! Modern food processing equipment and techniques have become highly sophisticated in recent years, enabling musts to be condensed with minimal loss of flavor. Concentrate kits have little or none of the caramelized flavor associated with the canned concentrates of yore. The essence of the fruit is trapped as the juice is gently reduced to the desired volume and then the essence is added back. Since modern processing techniques allow more of the grape to be retained, it makes sense nowadays to use higher fruit quality. Home winemakers can make enjoyable wines with concentrate kits any time of the year, no matter where they live. Very little equipment is needed, and the cost is reasonable. So the boom in Canada is quite understandable, and it is just underway in the United States.

There are numerous brands of these bagged and boxed products, all marketed by Canadian companies as far as I am aware. The grapes come from all over the world — Italy, France, Italy, Chile, Argentina, Australia, California and Washington being the most common sources. Most are packaged to make 23 liters of finished wine, which is 5 Imperial gallons or 6 U.S. gallons. Those that have been concentrated the least are packaged in 15-liter boxes; you add 8 liters of water to bring the total to 23 liters. The next level down is packaged in 5 to 7 kilogram boxes to which considerably more water must be added to bring the total to 23 liters. A few companies still sell undiluted aseptic juice in 23-liter boxes, but some have dropped sterilized juices due to problems with shelf life. No water is added — just add yeast and ferment. Most concentrate companies also market a variety of exotic specialty wines packaged to make smaller quantities of finished wine.

Bear in mind that concentrate kits are subject to the same old rule: the better the grapes, the better the wine. These producers have to line up their sources of supply and make commitments early in the summer, the same as wineries. Sometimes the grapes will be great and sometimes they will be below average. With the grapes coming from all over the world at different times of the year and typically being blended as well, it becomes impossible to conclude that one brand is better than another. Each will have some good ones in the pipeline at any given time and some not so good. But the chemistry will be optimized in all of them before they are packaged and sold.

Once you understand the basic procedure of Chapter 2 for fermenting white wines and Chapter 6 for red wines, there is little more to be said about fermenting concentrate kits. All fermentations are basically the same. The kits come packaged with yeast and additives needed to ferment and clarify. You don't even need a crusher or press, just a primary fermenter, carboys, racking hose and stem, etc. Follow the enclosed instructions, minimize the exposure to air, and you can expect 30 bottles of enjoyable wine. Use meta very sparingly as these kits are heavily sulfited and will not accommodate as much meta as fresh fruit.

You might find white wines from kits to be more difficult to clarify than wines from fresh grapes. The kits all come with one or two fining agents and directions which have undoubtedly been carefully tested. If you are not completely successful in clarifying your wine, don't worry about it as the residual haze is innocuous and will not affect the flavor.

The more concentrated the juice, the faster the wine will age. The 7-kg. boxes are marketed as "28-day" wines, and the 15-liter boxes as "6-week" wines. The aseptic juices are marketed as "6-month" wines. Be aware that these are optimistic figures as all will improve with additional aging.

In my opinion the future for concentrate kits looks very bright for home winemakers. I say this because the processing technology and equipment will continue to improve. With the large number of brands on the market, competition should keep prices down.

Here are notes on several of my fermentations.

Six-Month Aseptic Juice Burgundy

LABEL: 23°B. sugar; 3.60 pH; 7.5 grams total acid; 78 parts per million sulfite. (My hydrometer read 23° also; my Titret® ampule showed something less than 70 ppm sulfite; and the pH of the finished wine was 3.52.)

DAY 1. Began a yeast starter by emptying a package of yeast in ½ cup of warm water. Fifteen minutes later, when it was fully hydrated, I added 1 tsp. of sugar and a pinch of diammonium phosphate and set it aside. Poured the entire 6 gallons, including pulp and sediment, into a 7-gallon carboy rather than using a primary fermenter. Two hours later, I added the yeast starter over the surface of the must and emptied another package of the same yeast (Red Star Premier Cuvee) for good measure.

DAY 2. Fermentation underway. No air lock.

DAY 4. Vigorous fermentation. Sugar down to 1° B.

DAY 5. Hydrometer indicates sugar is 1° B. Still fermenting actively but much slower. Racked from the large carboy into 5 gallon carboy plus 3 liter jug. Topped with air locks.

DAY 11. Fell still.

DAY 14. Racked and sulfited (25 ppm). Final volume was almost 6 U.S. gallons. Set it outside to cold stabilize. After a month in the cool spring air, most of the solids have settled out and the wine could be bottled. However, it has a sharp "bite" to the palate, as though a large amount of acid was added.

MONTH 2. Racked, adding 3 ounces of sugar to raise the residual sugar level to .5%. The sugar made the wine more mellow but a bit more is needed to balance the acid. Added another 1½ ounces of sugar, which seemed to give the desired balance.

MONTH 3. Bottled. The adjustments elevated this wine to what might be considered jug wine quality. The packaging did not indicate what is meant by "Burgundy," but I doubt that it contains any Pinot Noir.

MONTH 8. Quite to my surprise, it aged into a respectable red wine with some Pinot Noir qualities. At .75% RS it is too sweet, which was my error in judgment. For some reason it has a slight caramelized flavor.

Six-Month Aseptic Juice Johannisberg Riesling

LABEL: 21.2°B. sugar; 3.00 pH; 8.3 grams total acid; 93 ppm sulfite.

DAY 1. Poured contents into 7-gal. glass carboy containing Steinberg lees from prior fermentation of Gewurztraminer. Added ½ tsp. DAP. Held overnight at room temperature.

DAY 2. Fermentation underway. Took to garage to cold ferment.

4 WEEKS. Still fermenting, but very slowly. Hydrometer reads negative. Set in warm room to complete fermentation. If the sugar had been higher initially, I might have stopped fermentation at 1% RS. But at 21°B., the alcohol level will only be 11%, so I need not be concerned about high alcohol. It is easier just to add sugar back. Another option for adding a bit of residual sugar after fermentation would be the concentrated conditioners marketed by some of the concentrate kit companies, which is pure grape concentrate (fructose) with potassium sorbate to discourage renewed fermentation.

5 WEEKS. Fermentation is complete. Clinitest reads .1%. Removed the air lock and immediately replaced with a solid rubber stopper, wrapped in plastic wrap to give it a good seal. Set the carboy in the garage to settle for a week or two. There is almost a "gallon" of head space in the carboy, which is filled with almost pure carbon dioxide. It is imperative that the stopper not be removed until racking as air would get in. Even if it is not opened, the wine will not be safe for more than two weeks. It would be safer to sparge the headspace with argon.

6 WEEKS. The gross lees have settled out. Racked and sulfited with ⅛ tsp. per 5 gallons. Have 5 gal. plus ½ gal. Sealed with rubber stopper and set outside to cold stabilize for a few weeks.

8 WEEKS. No further clearing. TA = .86%. Made Sparkolloid™ slurry (7 tsp./5 gal. since it was quite cloudy) and racked, adding 17.5 g. of calcium carbonate (to lower TA by .14%). No sulfite. The wine cleared overnight. Much crystallization, which compacted

the Sparkolloid™ lees.

9 WEEKS. TA = .74% — the carbonate lowered TA by .12% rather than .14%. This is a normal deviation. pH = 3.2.

3 MONTHS. Racked, sulfited (⅛ tsp.) and added 6 oz. of sugar to raise RS to 1%.

4 MONTHS. Wine is crystal clear. Bottled. This turned out to be a pleasant wine that one would never guess was not made from fresh grapes!

Six-Week Wine Kit Johannisberg Riesling

DAY 1. Mixed the bentonite in the blender per directions and put into primary fermenter (10-gal. can). Emptied the 15-liter foil bag into a 6-gallon (U.S.) pail. Rinsed the bag with warm water to dissolve the rest of the concentrate and sugar; added more warm water to fill the pail. Dumped the pail into a primary fermenter and stirred. Sugar tested 21°B., which is just right for a Riesling. Rehydrated the Red Star Premier Cuvee yeast (Prise de Mousse) that came with the kit. After sprinkling the starter solution over the surface, I sprinkled another package of the same yeast in dry form directly onto the surface, for good measure. This wine was fermented at room temperature, but there is no reason it could not have been cold fermented over a longer period of time.

DAY 2. Fermentation underway.

DAY 4. Sugar down to 6° B.

DAY 8. Sugar at 2° B. Racked into a 5 gallon carboy and 1.5 liter jug and topped with air locks, discarding the bentonite and yeast lees. I could have fermented it to dryness at room temperature and added sugar back to sweeten it, but I chose instead to set it outside where the cool spring temperatures would slow down final fermentation.

DAY 14. Clinitest indicates that residual sugar is at 1%. Since this is the minimum level of residual sugar one would want in a wine of this type, I racked and sulfited (¼ tsp.) to stop fermentation. The yield was slightly over 5 gallons, the loss in volume being attributable to the use of bentonite. Left it outside so the gross lees could settle.

DAY 28. Very little clarification to date; the wine still looks viscous. Fined with Sparkolloid™ slurry at the rate of 1 tsp per gallon. The directions say to add meta, sorbate and isinglass at this stage, but I chose Sparkolloid™ instead, intending to use the isinglass later if necessary.

MONTH 2. It needs a higher level of residual sugar for good balance. Racked, adding ⅛ tsp. of sulfite and 6 ounces of table sugar to raise residual sugar from 1% to 2%. This seemed about right for my taste. The wine has cleared noticeably by now, though it will never be brilliant, due to the Sparkolloid™.

MONTH 3. Bottled. This is a pleasant semisweet Riesling. It would not win any awards, but most people would regard it as drinkable, if not enjoyable. I anticipate that it will improve somewhat with six months in the bottle.

MONTH 8. This has developed into a nice Riesling without a trace of the "caramelized" flavor normally associated with a concentrate. The only shortcoming is that it is far too sweet for my palate. I should have left the residual sugar at 1%.

Six-Week Wine Kit Zinfandel

DAY 1. Emptied the 15-liter foil bag into a 6-gal. (U.S.) pail. Rinsed the bag with warm water to recover any remaining sugar and filled the pail with warm water. Poured into a 10-gal. primary fermenter and stirred. The pH tested 3.55 and total acid measured .69%, both of which are good numbers. The sugar was low, however, at 18° B. Trusting the producer, I resisted the temptation to add more sugar. As a source of yeast and hopefully some added bouquet, I added approximately 1 gallon of skins of Cabernet Sauvignon (with the seeds shaken out using a nylon hops bag)—I had pressed a batch of Cabernet Sauvignon the same day.

DAY 2. Fermentation started. The cap will be punched down once or twice a day from now on.

DAY 6. Fermentation has come to a near standstill. Dipped the skins out with a stainless steel kitchen strainer and pressed by hand in a coarse nylon hops bag. Transferred the wine to glass containers. Attached air locks and stored at room temperature. Have 5 gal. carboy + 1 gal. jug, both almost full.

DAY 9. Almost dry. Residual sugar tests .2% using Clinitest.

DAY 22. Set outside to chill.

5 WEEKS. Racked and sulfited— ¼ tsp. / 5 gal. Some tartrate salts

have already precipitated. Net yield was 5 gal. + 3 liters. Stored at room temperature for further settling.

10 WEEKS. Bottled. I cheated a little by adding ½ tsp. of my raspberry liqueur (Appendix E) per bottle. TA = .66%. RS = .15%. pH = 3.49. Should be a very drinkable table wine in a few months.

NOTE: Malolactic fermentation is generally not advised for kits. In most cases the manufacturer will have increased or decreased the amount of malic acid to get the optimum level and balance of acids. In addition, it would be difficult to initiate malolactic fermentation with the relatively high level of sulfite in kits.

Chapter Sixteen

Blending

lending can be a very exciting adventure because two well-balanced wines having no defects can often be blended solely for the purpose of getting a better wine. You can start with wines that are good to great and with the right blend end up with something that is even better! In Europe, the advantage of blending has been recognized for many generations, and it will probably become even more common there as trade barriers fall within the European Common Market. Blending is just beginning to find acceptance in the United States, where straight varietals have been promoted since the inception of the premium wine industry several decades ago.

Blending is a complex topic on which there will not be much consensus beyond a few basic considerations. Here are a few of them to get you started down this interesting path. You can add to them as you go!

Blending different varieties

As a general rule, one wants to avoid blending two varieties where each has a distinctive varietal characteristic in its own right. They are likely to compete with each other—stick with varieties that harmonize with each other. Cabernet Sauvignon and Merlot may be the most classic of all blends. A blend of the two will almost always have more complexity and character than either one by itself. The Merlot will soften the Cabernet Sauvignon, which is inherently quite tannic and slow to mature. Or, depending on the proportions, the Cabernet Sauvignon will add some backbone and character to the Merlot, which the latter usually needs. Other Bordeaux varieties also blend well: Merlot and Cabernet Franc, Cabernet Sauvignon and Cabernet Franc. The less common Bordeaux varieties of Malbec, Petit Verdot and Carmenere are also good blenders.

The classic Rhone wine is a blend of up to thirteen varieties, including four white wines. Two of the principal red varieties — Syrah and Grenache — blend very well, and the blend can often be improved with a small percentage of Viognier, a white grape with unusual characteristics. Viognier emphasizes aroma and extends the after taste.

Blending is by no means limited to the classic Bordeaux or Rhone varieties. Witness the tremendous growth of Cabernet Sauvignon–Syrah and Syrah–Cabernet Sauvignon blends. Syrah has good mouth feel and aromas and shares these qualities nicely with other red varieties.

Straight Zinfandel seems to lack complexity and in my opinion is improved by the judicious blending of lesser amounts of other varieties, such as Grenache, Cabernet Sauvignon, Carignane or Syrah. As a rule, 5 to 10% of another variety can be blended without diluting the varietal characteristic of the main wine. At levels above 15%, however, the varietal characteristic starts to become less distinct. If you add 25% of Grenache or Syrah to Zinfandel, for instance, the blend will be more complex but will have less Zinfandel character. There is almost always a trade-off associated with blending.

Similar considerations apply to the blending of white varieties. As a rule, you will get a better result by blending a neutral or semi-distinctive variety with a distinctive one — they harmonize better. Sauvignon Blanc and Semillon are often blended, and either can be blended with Chardonnay, although it is not commonly done with premium Chardonnays. You can raise the aroma profile of Chardonnay by blending in a small portion of Riesling or Viognier. Except in the case of sparkling wines, it is difficult to improve Chardonnay by blending.

I sometimes press a small quantity of Pinot Noir without crushing and use the resulting *blanc de noirs* for blending with other white table wines, such as Sauvignon Blanc and Semillon. Adding 5 to 10% of white Pinot Noir seems to give a Sauvignon Blanc or Semillon more body. When using Pinot Noir in this fashion, you want the varietal characteristic to be low, so grapes with sugar in the range of 19-20°B. should be used. These are the same grapes that one would want for making a sparkling wine. The next time you make a *blanc de noirs* sparkling wine, make a little extra and try some sample blends to see how you like it!

Methodology

Wines to be blended should first be individually evaluated. Which wine do you want to improve and in what way? Is it too dark or too light in color? Is one of them overly fragrant? Do you want a higher fruit profile? Do you want more tannin for a longer "window of drinkability?" Do you want an austere wine? Are you looking for a big bouquet? A lingering aftertaste? It's easy to get confused in the midst of evaluations if you are only trying to decide which blend is "best." Most of the time you will get an outcome more to your liking if you decide beforehand what the goal is. Your attention in this respect is directed to the last section of this chapter. The input of others can be invaluable in defining the goal of the blend, as well as evaluating the final outcomes.

Since there is no universal approach to finding the right blend and ratio, you will have to adopt and revise your own technique as you go. I have settled upon four different combinations (80:20, 60:40, 40:60, and 20:80) plus a control of each variety. The controls are a reference in case none of the blends are better than the individual wines — nothing is to be gained by blending unless the result is better.

Some winemakers do more sample blends in finer increments, which is a good practice. I do essentially the same thing later in the second round of blending. I keep the increments rather limited in round 1. If 80-20 seems optimum, for instance, I do a second series of 90:10, 85:15, 80:20 again and 75:25, etc. This way I not only confirm my initial impression, but I might find a better blend in the process. If the optimum blend on the second round is not somewhere in the middle of the pack, then I have reason to question my initial impressions. Finding the right blend can be elusive, so it is good practice to confirm the results.

Blending several wines

All that has been said thus far concerns the blending of two wines. What if you want to blend three wines? Theoretically, one would devise a matrix of the various ratios of the three varieties. This quickly escalates into numbers that far exceed my goal in blending! When blending more than two wines, I usually do a master blend of what I regard as the two main wines. For instance, let's assume that I have done my sensory tests and found that 90% Cabernet Sauvignon and 10% Merlot is the optimum combination. Now I want to see if it can be improved with some Cabernet Franc. Instead of doing a sample blend of all possible combinations of the three wines, I adopt the more modest goal of seeing whether I can improve on my 90-10 master blend with small additions of Cabernet Franc, such as 5%, 10% and 15%. As long as the end result is a better wine, I am content. This is not to say that when the third wine is added, some other ratio of the first two might not be better. Let's assume that my master blend of 90% CS–10% M is improved by adding 5% CF. This produces a blend consisting of 5% CF, 86% CS and 9% M. It could very well be, for example, that 85% CS, 5% M and 10% CF would be even better. But I am satisfied any time I can improve on the master blend.

Remedial Blending

Blending can be an excellent way to deal with flaws, such as too much or too little acid, residual sugar, sulfite, alcohol, astringency, color, pH and the like. These qualities can be altered by blending wines of either the same or different grape varieties. The astute blender will always do sample blends and attempt to optimize the sensory outcome as well as the readings.

Maybe you have one wine where the total acid is too high and another where it is too low. Blending is an ideal way to correct both problems. Similarly, an excess of residual sugar in one wine can be remedied by blending with another that has too little. Both of these cases can be calculated mathematically.

Let's assume that you have two carboys of dry white table wine, one with total acid (TA) of .8% and one with .5%. Obviously, if you wanted to end up with .65% TA, you would blend equal amounts of each. More likely, the acid levels will not fall into such a neat range or you won't want the midpoint. If one wine is .9% TA and the other .45% TA and you have determined that you want to end up with .6% TA, how are the quantities to be calculated? The following formula is the easiest way I have found to calculate quantities. The result is the *ratio* of the *volume* of one wine to the other.

$$TA_1 + TA_2 X = TA_b (1 + X)$$

Where:

TA_1 = Total acid wine no. 1

TA_2 = Total acid wine no. 2

TA_b = Desired total acid of blend

X = Ratio by volume of wine no. 2 to wine no. 1

Example. Total acid of wine no. 1 is .9. Total acid of wine no. 2 is .45. You want a blend having total acid of .6.

$$TA_1 + TA_2 X = TA_b (1 + X)$$
$$.9 + .45 X = .6 (1 + X)$$
$$.9 - \mathbf{.6} + .45 X = .6 - \mathbf{.6} + .6 X$$
$$.3 + .45 X = .6 X$$
$$.3 + .45 X - \mathbf{.45 X} = .6 X - \mathbf{.45 X}$$
$$.3 = .15 X$$
$$2 = X$$

The result, X, is the *ratio* of wine no. 2 to wine no. 1. In this case, two volumes of wine no. 2 are needed for one volume of wine no. 1 to end up with acidity of .6%. The calculations would be done the same way with one batch having too much residual sugar and another having too little. Just substitute sugar percentages for acid percentages.

Most measurements lend themselves to the above formula, including alcohol, total acid, residual sugar, and parts per million of sulfite. The one notable exception is pH, which is a logarithmic function. If you blend a gallon of pH 3.8 with a gallon of pH 3.4, you will not get 3.6. The pH will be closer to 3.4 than 3.8 because the 3.4 wine will have a disproportionately greater concentration of H^+ ions.

There is a good interactive chart for blending at www.winemak-ermag.com.

Bench trials

Rather than arbitrarily deciding that you want a total acid of .6%, it is always better to do bench trials first to determine what acid level tastes best. You might think that a TA of .6% will be optimum, but why not try some blends slightly above .6% and some slightly below? Bench trials can be particularly helpful when correcting total acid in white wines because residual sugar is another variable that must be taken into consideration.

My suggestion is that the formula (or www.winemakermag.com) be used to identify some sample blends that are likely to be in the ballpark. Use it to determine how many milliliters of one wine versus the other is needed to result in .55% TA. Then do the calculation for .60%, .65%, etc. After calculating the ratios, mix a few milliliters of each at .55%, .60%, .65% and .70%. I use medical syringes from the drug store (or pipets) for blending small volumes because they conveniently measure in milliliters. Once you have decided on a blend, the same ratio will apply to blending in gallons as in milliliters. If I were working with large quantities, I would use 375 ml bottles, cork them and do the taste evaluations in a month, after they have partially recovered from the disturbance. Having been sparged with argon, the carboys will be safe in the meantime.

Note that blending does not always pay off. If one lot is well balanced and promises to be exceptional, think twice before sacrificing it to salvage a substandard lot. It might be better to keep the promising wine intact and find some other way to deal with the lesser one. For one thing, you have to blend a much greater volume of the wine having normal acid or residual sugar to correct one that is significantly outside the desired range. It's just the way the numbers work. In any event, I would certainly do bench tests to make sure that the reserve quality wine will not be unduly compromised by the blending and that the lesser one is sufficiently enhanced. It has to be worth the trade-off.

When to blend

There are three times when blending is most commonly done: (1) before fermentation; (2) shortly after it falls still; and (3) right before bottling. Blending before fermentation would have the advantage of allowing everything to integrate during fermentation but is impractical unless you have cold storage, because grapes will seldom ripen at the same time. And there is an inherent disadvantage in not knowing anything about either of the wines-to-be before the blend. As a result, most blending is done after fermentation.

You could start as early as the first racking. However, the wines will still be very yeasty and astringent. A better assessment can be made by waiting a few more months. Late spring is a good time to get serious about blending because the wine temperature will be higher, the flavors more pronounced and the wines less astringent.

Some who barrel-age their wines like to blend, based on tannins, just before the wine goes into the barrel. This allows the wine tannins to integrate with the wood tannins. However, there can be an advantage in waiting until just before bottling to blend because one of the wines might turn out to be an exquisite, single-vineyard wine that needs no help. You would not know that before barrel aging because the wine would not have developed its individuality yet.

I suspect that most of the time you will have wines of several different varieties or vineyards and will be trying to "craft" a blend, as discussed early in this chapter. This can best be done late in bulk aging.

Additional considerations

Never blend to correct flaws such as oxidation, acetaldehyde, ethyl acetate or acetification — or you will end up with twice as much troubled wine. Some authorities make an exception for volatile acidity (VA) that is only slightly high, since some VA is said to be desirable. This depends on how high the VA is and your tolerance for it. My tolerance is extremely low, so I would never attempt to dilute detectable VA by blending.

There should be no residual sugar or malic acid remaining in any blending wines that were inoculated with MLF bacteria. Of course, if you are dealing with wines that have never been exposed to ML bacteria and kept properly sulfited, this will not be a consideration.

Although oak tannins will mellow over time and are desirable in the background of the finished wine, if you oak before blending, the oak flavor and tannins will mask a lot of the fruit and bouquet. This in my opinion interferes with the evaluations. It works better to concentrate on evaluating the fruit and bouquet and blend to maximize those qualities. Then add the oak.

Sensory evaluation

Each individual wine should be evaluated before being sample blended so that you can decide what changes you want. The blends should also be carefully evaluated. This is where your friends come in! A tasting session is a nice occasion to have friends over and solicit their opinions. Hopefully, they will be experienced wine tasters and be familiar with the varieties at hand. If there is a particular commercial wine that you would emulate, by all means include a bottle in the array. Tell them what you hope to achieve by the blend and get their thoughts on what they would do.

Taste evaluations should be done in a clean, well-lighted room, away from socializing and odors, such as tobacco or perfume. Each person should have wine glasses of uniform size and shape, and the wines should all be the same temperature. Bread and water are fine to renew the palate, but if you are tasting a large number of samples, don't swallow. Encourage everyone to spit and dump to keep their taste buds alive longer. Have pens and paper available and ask them to give the reasons behind their preferences. I usually do a blind tasting, in that no one knows what the blend is. The order could be totally random, but your feedback might be more focused if the blends are arranged in ascending or descending order.

When you are reflecting on all the input, take the consensus of the group into account, but also factor in the differences in their palates. You know what you like and how you want your wine to turn out. Let the final decision be your own!

TESTING PROCEDURES

Testing sugar content

This is the easiest of all tests. All it requires is a hydrometer and a cylindrical jar to hold the sample. Take the reading from the bottom of the meniscus (page 20). Note that pulp and solids suspended in the liquid will cause an artificially high reading. If you test right after pressing, deduct 1½°B as a rule of thumb. A better reading will result if the test sample is settled overnight and only the clear juice tested the next day. Precipitation can be hastened by chilling the sample and decanting the clear juice, which will be used for the three principal tests: sugar level, total acid, and pH. The degrees of sugar in a must is a rough indicator of the potential alcohol level — the actual alcohol level will be roughly 55% of the Brix reading (e.g., 20°B will result in a wine with 11% alcohol, more or less). A hydrometer will not read the actual alcohol level; a vinometer is required to do that.

The two most common scales for measurement of sugar are Brix and the older Balling scale. The two are essentially the same, except that Brix is standardized at a temperature of 20°C (68°F), whereas Balling is standardized at 15.5°C (59°F). The difference is not significant, so I treat the two scales as equals.

The calibrated temperature is marked on most hydrometers. If the temperature of the must is higher than the calibrated temperature, add approximately .25°B to the reading for each 9°F (5°C); if

the must temperature is below the calibrated temperature, deduct
.25°B from the reading for each 9°F (5°C) of difference.

Testing total acid

It's important to know the level of total acid of the must, starting
at the time of the crush. Plan to do your own titration test when
the grapes arrive, even if the vineyard gave you its reading. Your
reading, even if less accurate, is the more important reference point
for later measurements of the change in acid level after cold stabilization, during malolactic fermentation or after acid adjustment.

Acid titration tests require minimal equipment and can be purchased in kit form or assembled:

TIP

Small beaker or jar
.1N or .2N sodium hydroxide
Previously-boiled distilled water
Phenolphthalein
Burette (or 1-ml pipets)

*To slow down deterioration of
your sodium hydroxide, store it
in your refrigerator.*

WITH BURETTE. A 50-ml burette and Erlenmeyer flask is the most
common equipment used for acid titration. For most accurate titration results, the test sample, hydroxide and equipment should all
be at the same temperature. A must sample should also be settled
to eliminate the pulp. It is easiest to read the color change against
a white background, such as sunlight reflected off white paper.

After getting the burette set up and clearing the air out of the
channel so the hydroxide will flow freely, add 5 ml of wine or
must sample to the flask or beaker using a 5-ml pipet. Add 3 or 4
ounces of hot distilled water and 6 or 8 drops of phenolphthalein.
Make note of the level of hydroxide in the burette, measuring from
the bottom of the meniscus. Drip hydroxide in and swirl the flask
until it turns faint pink and holds for 20 seconds. Measure the new
level in the burette, subtract to determine how many milliliters
were required and multiply the result by .15. If 7 ml of .1N NaOH
was needed to neutralize the 5-ml sample, total acidity is 1.05 (7
X .15). If you used .2N hydroxide, use a factor of .3. Half as much
hydroxide would have been required, so you have to double the
factor to get the same result of 1.05 (3.5 ml x .3 = 1.05).

WITH 1-ML PIPETS. Unless I have numerous samples to test, I usually use 1-ml pipets (class A) for titrations. It's faster than a burette because you avoid the setup and cleanup. You could even get by with an eye dropper — one drop quite consistently equates to .05 ml.

If you have .1N hydroxide, start with 1 ml of sample wine or must. (There are too many solids in musts to use fine-pointed class A pipets, so use a disposable pipet.) If you have .2N hydroxide, start with a 2 ml of sample. When adding either hydroxide or wine sample, the excess should be wiped off the outside of the pipet so an extra drop does not sneak in. Add the sample to a beaker and then add about an ounce of hot distilled water. Add 3 or 4 drops of phenolphthalein. Slowly drip hydroxide from the pipet into the beaker, swirling continuously, until you reach the endpoint, which will be indicated when the phenolphthalein turns faint pink and stays pink for 20 seconds. Multiply the ml of hydroxide used by .75, and the result is the total acid in grams per 100 ml, measured as tartaric. For example, if you started with 2 ml of sample wine or must and used .8 ml of .2N hydroxide, the total acidity would be .6 (.8 ml X .75). Note that you would get the same result if you started with a 1 ml sample and used .1N hydroxide; .8 ml of hydroxide would have been used and the acidity would be .6%.

In the case of red wines it is difficult to identify the titration endpoint because the phenolphthalein indicator is the same color as the sample. So you have to watch carefully. As the hydroxide is dripped in the test solution will gradually turn lighter pink, then slightly gray and then almost clear. The endpoint will be indicated when it turns faint pink again and holds for 20 seconds.

pH METERS. A pH meter is the most accurate way to detect the endpoint when titrating red wines. If you are titrating with a pH meter, the endpoint will occur at 8.2pH (but there will be very little difference between 8.1 and 8.3 when the TA number is calculated). Remember that the pH meter will not know how you got to the endpoint; if your hydroxide is weak, the reading will be overstated because more hydroxide will have been required. In addition, if you are using a pocket pH meter, be sure to calibrate it before testing.

DISTILLED WATER. Tap water contains chlorine as well as some trapped carbon dioxide, with some localities being worse than others. I recommend using distilled water, but even that will contain some trapped carbon dioxide, which will alter the pH. At a minimum, you should boil your water before using it to dilute the wine or must sample to be tested.

Standardizing sodium hydroxide

Sodium hydroxide loses its strength through exposure to carbon dioxide in the air. The weaker the solution, the faster it deteriorates. The best practice is to divide a new 16-ounce bottle into four ounce bottles and use one at a time. This works acceptably well for acid titrations, even though it will be weaker toward the end of the bottle. Be aware that you can also buy ampules of concentrated hydroxides or acids which store well and which will make a solution of exact strength when diluted to 1 liter with distilled water. Again, break it down into small lots and share with fellow winemakers.

My preference is to open a fresh bottle more often and not worry about standardizing. But in a bind, sodium hydroxide can be standardized against a stable acid of known strength, such as hydrochloric acid (HCl) or potassium acid phthalate (KaPh). This allows one to ascertain the exact strength of a hydroxide, and to adjust titration readings accordingly.

PROCEDURE FOR STANDARDIZING 0.1N NaOH
WITH POTASSIUM ACID PHTHALATE, 0.1N

Pipet 5 ml of 0.1 N KaPh into a beaker or small glass. Add 3 or 4 drops of phenolphthalein and titrate with your 0.1N NaOH until it turns faint pink and holds for 20 seconds after stirring. The normality of your hydroxide is determined by this formula:

$$\frac{\text{ml of KaPh x Normality KaPh}}{\text{ml NaOH}}$$

If 5.2 ml of NaOH were required to neutralize 5 ml of the phthalate, the normality of the hydroxide would be 0.096N:

$$\frac{5\ ml \times 0.1}{5.2} = 0.096$$

A total acid reading, for example, would have to be adjusted downward by multiplying by the factor of 0.96 ($\frac{0.096}{0.1}$).

PROCEDURE FOR STANDARDIZING
WITH HCl 0.01N

When working with very dilute solutions, it is good practice to neutralize some distilled water before the test. Bring about 100 ml of distilled water to a boil, add 5 or 6 drops of phenolphthalein and neutralize with a dilute base until it turns a faint pink and holds. Now add 5 ml of 0.01N hydrochloric acid and titrate with the subject sodium hydroxide to the same faint pink. Since hydrochloric acid is also a mono-acid, the formula for calculating normality will be the same as for potassium acid phthalate:

$$\frac{\textbf{ml of acid std. x Normality acid std.}}{\textbf{ml of test hydroxide}}$$

If it took 4.8 ml of hydroxide, the normality of the hydroxide would be 0.0104:

$$\frac{\textbf{5 ml x 0.01}}{\textbf{4.8}} = \textbf{.0104}$$

If you were doing the titration in a vacuum aspiration test, for instance, the reading would have to be increased by a factor of 1.04 ($\frac{0.0104}{0.01}$).

Testing residual sugar

Clinitest tablets are a simple and reliable way to measure the level of unfermented sugar left in a wine, commonly referred to as residual sugar, or RS. They come packaged with two color charts — 0 to 2% RS, and 0 to 5% RS. However, the older Dextrocheck chart, if you can find one, is better, as the color patches are on an ideal scale for the testing of dry wines of 0% RS (blue) to 1% RS (orange). This scale is more convenient and accurate for dry wines than the charts packaged with Clinitest kits. Some wine supply shops or distributors have Dextrocheck charts available upon request. The three charts are summarized on the next page.

In addition to Clinitest tablets, you will need a test tube and a ½-ml or 1-ml pipet (or at least an eye dropper). To test using the Dextrocheck chart, drop ½ ml (10 drops) of the sample wine into the bottom of the test tube, drop a Clinitest tablet in and watch the color change from blue to green and possibly to orange as the

CHART	RS Range	No. of Drops	Volume
2 drop Clinitest	0–5%	2*	.1 ml
5 drop Clinitest	0–2%	5*	.25 ml
Dextrocheck	0–1%	10	.5 ml
* Plus 10 drops of water			

reaction goes to completion. After the reaction stops, wait a few seconds and compare the color against the chart. Using ½ ml (10 drops) of test solution, dark blue will be zero RS on the Dextrocheck chart and orange will represent 1% RS.

If the reaction continues after the solution turned orange, the sample has more than 1% residual sugar. In that case you will need to dilute a sample and test again. Use .25 ml of sample wine (5 drops) and add .5 ml of water (10 drops) for additional liquid. Read the new result directly off the 5-drop color chart that comes packaged with Clinitest to get the percentage RS. Or, double the results read off a Dextrocheck chart.

Clinitest tablets have many uses. They will confirm that your wine in the carboys fermented to completion; check before adding sulfite! They can be used to test residual sugar after sugar addition, but you have to wait a few weeks until the sucrose has been converted into fructose and glucose.

Clinitest tablets are indispensable if you want to stop fermentation at a predetermined level, such as 1%, before all sugar ferments. This will keep the alcohol level slightly lower and can be used to advantage where the grapes had excessive sugar that might result in an overly alcoholic wine. For example, if the grapes arrive at 26°B, the progress of fermentation can be monitored with Clinitest tablets and fermentation stopped at 1% residual sugar by racking, sulfiting and chilling. The alcohol level will be approximately .55% lower than it would be if fermented to dryness and sugar added back to raise RS to 1%. A slow-fermenting yeast must be used in order to determine when to intervene and stop fermentation.

Paper chromatography

Chromatography is an easy way for the home winemaker to determine whether or not malolactic fermentation has gone to completion. Fortunately, chromatography test kits are fairly inexpensive

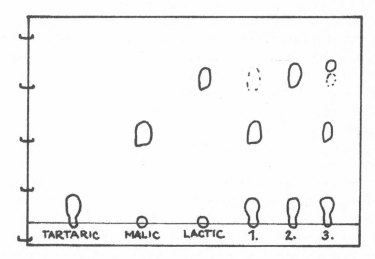

Chromatography Paper Test

and easy to use. A kit will include the following essentials:

- Whatman paper (#1 or #20) — 8" X 10"
- capillary tubes
- capillary tube holder
- chromatography solvent
- wide mouth jar — 1 gal.
- malic and lactic acid reference solutions (0.3%)
- tartaric and citric acid reference solutions (0.3%) (optional)

The acid reference solutions can be purchased or else prepared by dissolving 300 mg of the acid in 100 ml of water. In addition, you will need a pencil and ruler and a stapler to fasten the paper into a cylinder.

Start by drawing a pencil line along the length of the Whatman paper, 1" from the bottom. Place dots at 1" intervals on the line to mark where the liquids will be spotted. A piece of paper will accommodate 3 acid samples and 7 wine samples marked in this manner. Identify each dot on the line with a pencil — "M" for malic, "L" for lactic, "T" for tartaric, etc. Also identify each wine sample to be spotted on the line and tested.

Now dip a capillary tube in the malic acid reference until it is about half full and touch it lightly to the "M" dot. You only want to release enough liquid to make a ¼" circle, so lift it the instant any liquid soaks into the paper. Do the same with the lactic acid reference and all other acid or wine samples, using a separate tube for each. Keep each circle as small as possible because that will result in a more clearly defined result. Replace each capillary tube in its ordered slot in the tube holder so they don't get mixed up.

Let the spots dry, which might take 10 or 15 minutes. Repeat the spotting process about three more times in the same places so that an intense acid mark is left at each dot on the line. Hopefully, none will be more than ¼", but there's no need to start over if a little too much liquid happens to escape the tube. It's just that the smaller and more concentrated the circles are, the easier it will be to interpret the outcome when the paper dries.

Spot the paper four or five times. When the acid spots have dried, shape the paper into a cylinder and fasten it with staples. The edges should not overlap because then the acid spots will not move vertically. The pencil line along the base should line up where the paper edges meet to form a cylinder.

Now pour about 2 ounces of the chromatography solution into the wide mouth jar. Be careful not to breathe the fumes. Stand the paper cylinder upright in the jar, pencil line at the bottom, and put the lid on. The solvent will gradually travel up the paper. Although nothing will be visible until the paper dries, the solvent takes the acid spots with it as it moves upward. Lactic acid travels the most, followed by malic, citric and tartaric, in that order.

Leave the paper in the solution for 6 to 10 hours — until the solution has traveled almost to the top. It will take longer for Whatman #20 than #1. Then remove it and hang it to dry away from all chemical fumes. Spots will start to become visible after 2 or 3 hours of drying and will be quite conspicuous when the paper is completely dried. The Whatman paper becomes blue-green and the acid spots are yellow. The lactic reference acid will be closest to the top and the malic spot right below it. The tartaric reference spot will be nearest the pencil line.

Here's how you interpret the results (see illustration page 179). If the wine has not started malolactic fermentation, it will show only a malic spot at the same height as the malic acid reference spot, and no lactic spot, or a very faint lactic spot (see sample no. 1). In the case of sample no. 2, the lactic spot higher up with no malic spot indicates that it has gone completely through MLF — i.e., no malic remains, all of it having been converted to lactic. If it has both a lactic spot and a malic spot, then MLF is partially complete (see sample no. 3). In the last case, if the malic spot is bold and the lactic spot much lighter, then MLF is just underway, or maybe hasn't even started. If the lactic spot is bold and the malic spot faint, then MLF is nearly complete. In this limited sense, the test is quantitative.

The chromatography solution can be poured back into the bottle after the test and reused. The solvent will last a year or more. When the paper turns orange rather than blue-green, the solvent is getting weak. Wash and dry your hands before handling the paper. Store the paper away from chemical fumes.

Note that if any artificial malic acid was added to the wine, as by using an acid blend, a malic spot will always appear. That's because artificial malic acid has a different chemical makeup from natural malic, and only half of the artificial version will be converted to lactic. Some malic will always remain, so chromatography is not a valid test.

Titrets for free SO_2

At the levels discussed in this book, excess SO_2 will not be a problem. But curiosity or a need to know the level of free SO_2 could arise. Checking the level of free SO_2 is a good procedure because the manufacturer may have added more or less than they represented. Maybe you are having trouble getting malolactic fermentation started and want to know the level of free SO_2 (or total SO_2, which, if too high, can impede MLF.) Or maybe you want to adjust free SO_2 at bottling time—red wines

Titret ampule and slide-on stem

should have 20-30 ppm of free SO_2 and white wines 40-50 ppm. The sealed glass ampules marketed by Chemetrics as Titrets® are a convenient way to test free sulfite in dry white table wines that have not been put through malolactic fermentation or been exposed to ascorbic acid. They have good shelf life if kept in the box and not exposed to sunlight. Be aware that they tend to significantly over-state the amount of free sulfite — I always deduct 15 ppm from the reading, even for white table wines.

The instructions that come with each package of ten vials are quite good. Push the flexible tube up the slender tippet of the ampule until it reaches the white line. Then gently snap the tippet below that white line. Stick the end in the sample and draw some of the sample up by pinching the glass bead in the flexible tube.

WHITE WINES. The ampule will turn dark blue the instant any sample is drawn in and will gradually lighten as more sample is admitted. Titrate until it turns clear, which is the endpoint. Invert the ampule and read the free SO_2 in parts per million.

RED WINES. The endpoint is very difficult to detect using Titrets® in red wines. As with white wine, the ampule will turn dark blue as soon as wine is admitted. Again, you titrate to the absence of blue. The problem is that the wine will not be clear at the absence of blue; it will be the same shade of red as your original sample. It might help to dilute the sample with an equal part of distilled water (and double the reading), but it is almost as red as before and any error is magnified when you double the reading. It also might help to use side lighting against a yellow background.

The best reference is probably a spent Titret vial filled with some of the original sample. Carefully crunch off the tippet with scissors or pliers so the vial can be drained and refilled with the sample to be tested. A pipet can be used to refill it. When titrating, look for the point where it ceases to become a lighter gray and is the same depth of red as the original sample in the vial. Even then, the read-ings will vary widely from one person to the next.

Vacuum Aspiration

In addition to the problem of detecting the endpoint in red wines, the Ripper method, including Titrets®, has another major shortcom-ing in that pigments, tannins, acetaldehyde, ascorbic acid and MLF by-products react with the iodine and cause an artificially high reading. Ripper might read 30 ppm, when in reality you could have as little as 10 ppm. Those who want to closely control the level of free SO_2 will do well to invest in the equipment and chemicals to test by vacuum aspiration, although sending a sample to a lab for analysis always remains an option.

The following equipment and chemicals are needed to test free SO_2 by the vacuum aspiration method, also known as aeration-oxidation. Some of the laboratory supply distributors sell kits containing everything that is needed.

Equipment	Chemicals
Support stand & rod	SO_2 indicator solution
Sidearm flask & clamp	H_3PO_4 phosphoric acid, 25%
Impinger tube & clamp	NaOH, sodium hydroxide, 0.01N
#1 stopper with pipet	*H_2O_2, hydrogen peroxide, 30%
#4 stopper with glass rod	HCl, hydrochloric acid, 0.01N
2.5 watt aquarium pump	Distilled water
Vacuum tubing	Very dilute acid
20 ml volumetric pipet	Very dilute base
Variable-volume dispenser	
(or pipet safety cup)	
1 ml graduated pipet	*Store it in the freezer to keep it fresh.
100 ml measuring device	

The cost can be reduced by substituting plastic stands to hold the sidearm flask and impinger tube. This eliminates the considerable cost of a metal stand, rod and clamps.

Phosphoric acid is added to the wine sample (sidearm flask) to release the SO_2 to a free state. Air is then pushed (or pulled) through the sidearm flask and into the impinger tube, taking the gaseous free SO_2 with it. The SO_2 reacts with hydrogen peroxide in the impinger tube, forming sulfuric acid. The solution in the impinger tube is then titrated with a weak sodium hydroxide to determine the quantity of sulfuric acid. Based on the milliliters of hydroxide required to neutralize the sulfuric acid, the amount of free SO_2 can be calculated. It sounds complex, but after a couple of tests, you will find it to be very easy. Here are the steps:

1. You can use an aspirator pump connected to a faucet to pull air through the sidearm flask and into the impinger. I prefer an aquarium pump to push the air, but the two are functional equivalents.

2. Prepare 100 ml of 1% H_2O_2 by dispensing 3 ml of 30% H_2O_2 into

a graduated cylinder and adding distilled water to bring the total volume to 100 ml. This solution will keep overnight if refrigerated but otherwise should be prepared fresh for each testing session. Fill the impinger tube to the 10 ml line with the 1% H_2O_2 and add 2 or 3 drops of indicator solution. This should give it a blue-gray color. If it is aqua, add a drop or two of very dilute acid. If it is purple, add a drop or two of dilute base until it becomes blue-gray. Insert the stopper. Be sure that the tip of the glass rod is below the level of the liquid.

3. Now dispense 20 ml of wine sample into the sidearm flask. Then add 20 ml of phosphoric acid (25%) into the sidearm flask — this lowers the pH and releases the SO_2. If you do not have a variable-volume dispenser to measure the phosphoric acid and are using a pipet instead, be sure to use a pipet safety cup as THIS ACID IS CORROSIVE. Don't ever get it in your mouth. Immediately stopper the flask to retain the gas. Again, the tip of the pipet must be submerged so that air will bubble through the wine-phosphoric

Left: Vacuum aspiration apparatus with aquarium pump. *Right:* Variable-volume dispenser for measuring corrosive liquids.

acid solution. All the fittings should be tight as the reading will be low if gas is escaping.

4. Turn on the aquarium pump or aspirator and let air bubble through the setup for ten minutes. The solution in the impinger tube should turn purple after a minute or two; if it does not, there is no free SO_2 in the wine, and you can stop the test. If it does turn purple, stop the pump after ten minutes and remove the impinger insert, being certain to allow all the condensed liquid to drip back into the impinger.

5. Titrate the solution in the impinger tube with NaOH .01N until it turns approximately the same shade of blue-gray as it was before aspiration was started. (This point is neither as critical nor as difficult to detect as it is in the case of Ripper with red wines.) A 2ml graduated pipet works very well for this titration.

6. Calculate free SO_2 in parts per million as follows:

free SO_2 (ppm) = 1600 X ml of NaOH used x normality of NaOH

If your NaOH was exactly .01N, the formula becomes:

free SO_2 (ppm) = 16 x ml of NaOH used

You can prepare .01N NaOH by mixing 10 ml of 0.1N sodium hydroxide and 90 ml of distilled water. I always have 0.1N sodium hydroxide on hand because that is the strength I use for acid titration. (Alternatively, glass ampules of most chemicals can be purchased from chemical supply companies referenced in Appendix F and diluted to 1 liter for a solution with very accurate strength.) Note that hydroxide of such diluted strength as 0.01N is particularly vulnerable to carbon dioxide when exposed to air. It should be kept tightly stoppered and standardized if stored more than a day or two (see Standardizing sodium hydroxide, p. 176). I find it easier to mix a fresh solution than to standardize.

The indicator solution, which is light-sensitive and should be stored in darkness, has a shelf life of approximately six months.

Testing free SO2 by Ripper

Vacuum aspiration is the most accurate way to measure free SO_2, but it is also slow relative to the Ripper method. To get the best of both worlds, wineries having many dozens of barrels to monitor often test by both methods initially and make note of the difference between the two — Ripper will always read higher due to the interferences of pigments, aldehydes, *botrytis*, ascorbic acid, etc. Since the difference remains relatively constant, the more efficient Ripper method can be used during bulk aging by subtracting the known overstatement from the Ripper reading. Vacuum aspiration can be used again shortly before bottling to get an accurate reading.

The home winemaker will not have very many specimens to test, so the additional time required to run vacuum aspiration tests will not be a major consideration. The cost could be, however, as it costs two or three times as much for equipment and chemicals as for Ripper.

The following equipment and chemicals are needed to test by the Ripper method:

Equipment
250 ml Erlenmeyer flask
5 ml disposable medicine syringes (for sulfuric acid)
20 ml pipet
10 ml burette
10 ml pipet

Chemicals
25% sulfuric acid—CORROSIVE!! Use syringe or pipet safety
   cup.
1% or 2% starch indicator
0.02 N iodine solution (store in total darkness)
0.02 N sodium thiosulfate solution (store refrigerated)
dilute acid and dilute base

PROCEDURE FOR TESTING FREE SULFITE

1. Pipet 20 ml of wine into the flask.
2. Add 2-3 ml of starch indicator solution and approximately 5 ml of sulfuric acid using a disposable medicinal syringe.
3. Quickly titrate to a bluish endpoint with 0.02 N iodine solution—the color should hold for 30 seconds. Don't add the sulfuric acid until you are all set to titrate. Test samples one at a time.

Titrating Formula:
$$\frac{(\text{ml iodine used}) \times (\text{N of iodine}) \times 32000}{\text{ml of wine sample}}$$

Example: 3.9 ml of our iodine solution was required to titrate 20 ml of wine sample. Free SO_2 =125. 3.9 x 0.02 x 32000/20=125. However, iodine loses strength and should be standardized frequently.

PROCEDURE FOR STANDARDIZING IODINE

Iodine starts to deteriorate instantly if exposed to direct sunlight, less quickly under less intense light. Since a very dilute solution is being used, it should be calibrated frequently, preferably before each testing session and the final SO_2 reading adjusted accordingly.

Pipet 10 ml of iodine to a 50 ml Erlenmeyer flask or beaker. Titrate with .02N sodium thiosulfate until the brownish color is almost gone. Then add 2 -3 ml of starch solution, which will turn it blue. Continue titrating with thiosulfate until it turns clear and holds. Calculate the total volume of thiosulfate used.

Standardizing Formula: The following formula will give you a factor (F), which can be applied to all SO_2 readings for that particular day. N = normality; ml = volume used in milliliters.

$$\frac{(\text{N of thiosulfate}) \times (\text{ml of thiosulfate})}{(\text{assumed N of iodine}) \times (\text{ml of iodine used})}$$

Example: 6.5 ml of 0.02N thiosulfate was required to titrate 10 ml of iodine having an assumed normality of 0.02. F = 0.65. This iodine has lost strength; rather than being 0.02 N, it is only 65% of that strength. The factor of 0.65 must be applied to all free sulfite tests run today. In the above example, free sulfite would only be 81 ppm (0.65 x 125).

Testing total sulfite by Ripper

Total sulfite is a lesser consideration in winemaking in that nothing can be done to lower it after the fact. It should be kept as low as possible, however, by never adding more than necessary because at higher levels it will inhibit malolactic fermentation and bind up some of the esters, which will reduce the wine's bouquet. This is true even if all of it is bound and none free. Since it takes considerable additional equipment to test total sulfite by vacuum aspiration, the Ripper method is most commonly used. A strong base must be added before the test to unbind the bound portion.

1. Pipet 20 ml of wine into the flask. **Add 10 ml of 1N sodium hydroxide (CORROSIVE—use medicinal syringe or pipet safety cup), mix, and wait 10 minutes.**

2. Add a few drops of starch indicator solution and 5 ml of sulfuric acid using a medicinal syringe.

3. Quickly titrate to a bluish endpoint with 0.02 N iodine solution — the color should hold for 30 seconds.

Except for the sodium hydroxide and 10-minute wait, everything else is the same for total sulfite as free sulfite, including the formula above.

If your starch solution becomes moldy, you can make a new solution by mixing 20-25 grams of ordinary starch into 500 ml of distilled water and boiling for several minutes. The commercial products contain a mold inhibitor.

Digital pH meters

A pH meter is an extremely helpful tool that you will want to get if winemaking becomes a serious hobby. Thanks to the digital revolution, you can get an accurate pocket pH meter for well under $100. When shopping, be aware that although they all read to .01, that does not mean they are accurate to that degree. The better ones are accurate to +/- .02, whereas most of the cheaper ones are only accurate to +/- .10, even though they all read to .01. It's worth the extra cost to get the more accurate model. The Hannah PHEP 5 may be the most common model among home winemakers and it has a replaceable electrode.

You will also need to get small bottles of pH 7 buffer, pH 4 buffer, and electrode storage solution. A pH 10 buffer is not needed for testing wines, even if you use the meter for identifying the end- point in acid titrations (pH 8.1-8.2). Get your distilled water at the supermarket. I use 1-ounce plastic medicine cups from the drug store to hold the buffers and samples.

CONDITIONING A NEW METER. A new meter needs to be conditioned before its first use. Follow the manufacturer's instructions, which are likely to include rinsing the white crystals off the electrode in running water and then soaking the electrode for an hour or two in distilled water or a buffer solution.

CALIBRATING. Pocket pH meter should be calibrated and the slope set before each testing session. Just follow the instructions on the readout window, which will call for first calibrating in the 7.01 buffer. The digital reading should stabilize in a minute or two. If the meter does not automatically lock in the 7.01 reading when it stabilizes, it will tell you to push the "Confirm" or "Hold/Confirm" button. This is the point where the concentration of free hydrogen H^+ ions exactly equals that of the hydroxyl OH^- ions and there is zero conductivity.

If your buffer becomes contaminated, as could happen if you poured used buffer back into the bottle to economize, the actual pH will be something other than 7.00. The meter will not know the difference and will set itself to read 7.01 even though the actual pH of your buffer is more or less than 7.01. The inaccuracy could be magnified in the pH 3-4 range of wines and musts. So always discard used buffer solution.

Most meters have automatic temperature control (ATC) and automatically compensate for the difference in conductivity for samples with different temperatures. This is a great convenience, but I let my samples warm up to room temperature to narrow the temperature spread.

SETTING THE SLOPE. After being calibrated to pH 7, the slope must be set. That is, the meter must be instructed that "this is pH 4.00." After rinsing the electrode with distilled water, hold it in pH

4.00 buffer until the digital readout stabilizes. If the meter doesn't lock in the stabilized reading, follow the instructions and push the indicated button. Now the meter's minicomputer will take over and set the slope between pH 7 and pH 4 and points above and below.

Most contemporary digital pH meters automatically calibrate to pH 7.00, pH 10.00 and pH 4.00. All you have to do is to submerge the electrode in the buffer and wait until the meter locks in the reading or push the button. Some of the older meters have a manual set screw. If so, turn the set screw with a jeweler's screwdriver until it reads 7.00, 4.01, 3.00 or whatever known pH you are calibrating to.

To test for accuracy, I keep a buffer of pH 3.00 on hand. You could also use a fully saturated solution of potassium bitartrate (cream of tartar from the grocery store), which always has pH of 3.56. Just mix a teaspoon or so of potassium bitartrate in 4 ounces of distilled water and shake it well to dissolve as much as possible. As long as some undissolved white powder remains on the bottom, you know the solution is saturated. If the meter reads close to pH 3.56 and/ or 3.00, you are ready to measure the pH of your samples.

TESTING. The actual testing is easy — just submerge the electrode, wait for the reading to stabilize and note the reading. The electrode should be completely submerged in the sample wine. Always rinse the probe with distilled water between samples.

RINSING. As mentioned, any and all contaminants should be rinsed off the electrode before it is used for the next test or stored.

STORAGE. The electrode should be kept wet during storage to prolong its life. Some meters have a watertight cap over the electrode, which makes this easy. Always use a buffer solution for storage. Never use distilled water or pH 7 buffer.

CLEANING THE ELECTRODE. The electrode may become coated with tartrates and pigments, particularly if you test a lot of red wines. If you can see a film or coating on the electrode, hold it under running tap water for a couple of minutes and then very gently stroke it with a wet Q-Tip. The electrode is the most delicate and expensive component in the meter and is very fragile. So use only the slightest pressure. Rinse it again in running water and finally soak it in a dilute hydrochloric acid solution (0.01 N). If you don't have hydrochloric acid on hand, use storage solution or pH 4 buffer solution.

PROBLEMS. If the readings are not consistent and drift around, you may only need new batteries. Or the electrode may need cleaning. Eventually the electrode will wear out and have to be replaced. The manufacturers advise not to expect more than about two years out of an electrode. However, wines are not very corrosive and with proper care a digital pH meter might last for three years. If the electrode is clean and batteries are fresh and the readings jump around or it will not calibrate, chances are that the electrode is worn out, particularly if you can see tiny air bubbles in the electrode. If so, it's time to replace the electrode or buy a new meter.

Bench trials

Bench trials are advisable before adding most chemicals or fining agents to your wine or must, and in some situations bench trials are critical. I normally don't bother with bench trials when fining with bentonite or isinglass since they function independently of each other and are benign. In the case of tartaric acid and calcium carbonate, I try to avoid formal bench trials by making the additions in small increments when I rack, taking note of the result and using that as a basis for the addition at the next racking. If I need to raise the acid by .1%, for example, I add enough to raise it by .05% and run a titration test before the next racking to see what actually happened. Then I make another small correction when I rack again if my palate confirms the numbers.

This approach, of course, does not work well when lowering acidity with potassium carbonate because you won't know the full effect of the addition until the wine has been cold stabilized. So I add about 80% of the calculated amount and fine tune the acid after cold stabilization with a bit more potassium carbonate, or some tartaric acid if I over corrected. With these exceptions, I run bench trials before treating the main batch of wine.

The goal of a bench trial is to find the minimum addition that will produce the maximum benefit, whether the objective is increasing clarity, reducing astringency or bitterness, or correcting an organic flaw of some type. This is done by methodically adding the chemical or fining agent at different rates to small samples of the subject wine or must and evaluating the result. Once the optimum rate has been determined, you can apply the result to the entire batch. The more wine you are fermenting and the better the quality of the grapes, the easier it will be to justify the investment of time and patience.

Here is an example of a very simple bench trial. After crushing and pressing some white grapes, it was obvious that the acid was low. I blended tartaric acid and, since I had no plans for malolactic fermentation, an equal part of malic acid. I drew out one gallon of must and added 1 tsp. of tartaric-malic blend. After running a titration test, I added another ½ tsp. of the blended acid to the same gallon of must and took another measurement, etc. As it turned out, another ¼ tsp. raised total acid to approximately .7%, which was what I wanted. Since I had 15 gallons of must, I knew that I needed approximately 24 more teaspoons for the remaining 14 gallons (14 X 1.75). It was a simple matter of dissolving 12 tsp. of tartaric acid and 12 tsp. of malic acid in the gallon sample and mixing it back into the main batch of wine. This should be done after the solids have settled and the supernatant must has been racked off.

Most of the time the bench trial will have to be more exacting. Here are my suggestions on equipment:

1. Two Class A graduated pipets, 1-ml. This is the most practical way to run one or two titration tests and to dispense many liquid additives. Dissolve the needed grams of a chemical in water and dispense it in liquid form with a pipet.

2. Disposable serological pipets, 1-ml. These can be re-used if you remove the cotton wad after the first use, although it is difficult to control the flow. They have a wider tip than the class A's and are needed for dispensing musts or anything else with solid particulates.

3. A scale capable of weighing to tenths of a gram will be appreciated, but you can muddle by with measuring spoons that have been checked for accuracy. They vary in volume, even though 1 tsp. should be 5 ml.

4. Several one-liter jars, or 100-ml cylinders. I have 5 or 6 plastic hydrometer tubes with the 100-ml, 200 ml, and 250 ml levels marked in permanent ink. This is less expensive than 100-ml graduated glass cylinders, and they don't break.

Conducting bench trials with gelatin-Kieselsol or chitin-Kieselsol to clarify a white wine is a much more involved procedure because each is more effective in the presence of the other, and you do not know the optimum rate of either one before starting. But in the case of Kieselsol and gelatin, it is known that one liter of 30% Kieselsol per 1,000 gallons of wine will be in the ball park and that 2 to 4 ounces of gelatin will be required to counterfine 1,000 gallons of wine (0.15-0.30 g. per liter). To work with measurable quantities, 99 ml of distilled water should be added to 1 ml of Kieselsol to bring it to a total of 100 ml. Shake it well and immediately mix 26 ml of the dilute solution into 1 liter of wine (2.6 ml if you are working with a 100-ml sample). Do this with three different samples, each at the rate of 1 ml per thousand gallons. Shake the samples well to thoroughly mix the Kieselsol with the wine.

Wait a few hours and then add the gelatin. Prepare a dilute solution of gelatin by dissolving 5.6 grams of gelatin to 100 ml of warm distilled water. This would be sufficient for 50 to 100 gallons of wine, so you have to reduce the volume. Add .26 ml to the first 1-liter wine sample, .39 ml to the second 1-liter sample and .52 ml to the third and shake them all for good dispersion. Inspect them the next morning for clarity or taste to evaluate the change in astringency, as the case may be. Pick the best of the three samples and run the numbers for the main batch of wine. If the container is bigger than the sample, I usually give it a puff of argon and cap the container to minimize air contact, but it's a necessity only if you plan to wait longer than overnight before evaluating.

Most home winemakers, the author included, will let it go at that. But a commercial winemaker not wanting to filter might go through the same procedure using .75 liters of Kieselsol per thousand gallons and 1.25 liters per thousand gallons. The ratio of gelatin (2-4 ounces per thousand gallons at 1 liter of Kieselsol) will stay in the same range. So just decrease gelatin by .75 or increase it by 1.25.

It's often more convenient to use 375-ml bottles for bench trials because they can be corked and held for a few weeks before evaluating.

TROUBLE SHOOTING

Stuck fermentation

If there is no sign of fermentation 36 hours after inoculating, something may be amiss. If sulfite was kept within limits, temperature is the most likely culprit. If the must temperature was below 60°F (16°C), the temperature should be raised to 65-70°F (18-21°C). If you cannot raise the room temperature or move the must to a warmer room, drop in plastic milk jugs filled with warm water. Or you could dip out a couple of pails of the must, set them in a hot water bath, and dump them back in when warmed and fermenting actively.

If temperature is not the problem, aeration will accelerate yeast multiplication. Add a teaspoon of yeast food per 5 gallons. Rack or pour the must into another container, aerating it as much as possible in the process. Keep the temperature up and it should start.

On rare occasions, usually in the late stages, fermentation will slow prematurely and then stop with a few points of residual sugar. This is less likely to happen if you gave it 1 tsp. of a yeast food when fermentation peaked and another ½ tsp. when the unfermented sugar dropped to about 10°B. Or, it could occur if it was subjected to cold temperatures for too long. Or, it could be that the grapes were deficient in nitrogen. If you suspect temperature, warm it up to 70°F (21°C) again. Fermentation will always speed up when the temperature is raised; the question is whether the yeast have enough vigor remaining to ferment to dryness. If fermentation does not rebound to a healthy rate, then temperature is presumably not the culprit. If the Brix is less than 5°, the next step is to re-inoculate with a new yeast starter. It's too late to add more yeast food.

But first, treat the must with lysozyme at the rate of 1½ grams per gallon to slow down the increase of volatile acids and with yeast hulls (3 grams per gallon) to absorb fatty acids. This is a precaution while you get the new yeast starter going. Prise de Mousse would be a good choice, but Fermichamp or Uvaferm 43 would be better. The most convenient choice would be ProRestart®43, which is Uvaferm 43 in encapsulated form. Uvaferm 43 is a little more tolerant of high alcohol, and encapsulated yeast are so convenient.

If not using an encapsulated yeast, you will need a new starter solution about twice the size of the original starter; i.e., about 4% of the must volume. If you have 20 gallons of must to be re-inoculated, you will need almost a gallon of new starter, comprised of 1½ quarts of water, 1½ quarts of fresh grape juice (Thompson seedless grapes from the grocery store if need be) and 1 quart of the stuck wine. City water should be carbon filtered to remove any chlorine. Add about 2 grams of Fermaid K® to the concoction and get the temperature up to 75°-80°F (24-27°C) to minimize the temperature difference after you rehydrate the yeast and mix them together.

Rehydrate the yeast per instructions — probably 1 packet in a cup of water at 100°F. Add a pinch of Fermaid K® and give it about 20 minutes to come to life. Make sure the starter solution is close to 80°F and then add the rehydrated yeast. You want the temperature difference to be less than 10°F to avoid stunting the yeast. Let the starter ferment down to about 3°B per your hydrometer. Now it's ready to take on the stuck wine. Add an equal volume of stuck wine, again at approximately the same temperature of 70°F or so. Wait until you see signs of fermentation and then double it again. Keep on doubling, keep your fingers crossed and it should go to completion.

If you are concerned about the dilution caused by a starter, and the stuck must is in excess of 5°B, you could try a much smaller starter solution by doubling in the same manner. A stuck must with higher sugar should be easier to re-start than one with less than 1% remaining. Regardless of which technique, be sure to wait until it is actively fermenting before doubling again; don't get impatient.

But not all stuck fermentations can be reactivated. The sooner the problem is detected and corrective measures taken, the more likely is success in restarting fermentation. If these steps are not successful in restoring a vigorous fermentation, start planning what to do with a sweet wine, such as bottling sweet or blending with next year's dry wine.

Hydrogen sulfide

Hydrogen sulfide, or H_2S, smells like rotten eggs and can be the beginning of *major* problems. Hydrogen sulfide is most likely to be encountered with grapes that had excess sulfur on the skins at the time of crushing, although there are other causes too. The sooner the problem is discovered and addressed, the easier it will be to correct and the less the quality of the wine will suffer. If left to run its course, what starts out as hydrogen sulfide will convert into mercaptans, which are harder to deal with, and then into disulfides, which are even more challenging. The chemical remedy for dealing with mercaptans/disulfides in an advanced stage is beyond the scope of this book as it involves qualitative sensory tests using cadmium sulfate, which is highly poisonous, and using ascorbic acid to convert the disulfides back to mercaptans so that copper sulfate will work. The advice that follows assumes the problem has been detected and addressed early on and has not progressed to the disulfide stage.

If H_2S is detected early in fermentation, the fermenting wine should be racked off the lees and pulp immediately and a balanced yeast food or diammonium phosphate added at the rate of 1 tsp per 5 gallons. This may solve the problem. If the smell returns, rack it a second time and a third time, but omit the chemicals. The object of racking is to separate and discard the pulp on the bottom of the carboy as it contains most of the H_2S-generating constituents. If H_2S is not generated until late in fermentation, the D.A.P. probably will not help. But two or three rackings still might take care of the stink.

As soon as Clinitest confirms that fermentation is complete, the wine should be racked off the lees. Extended aging on the lees is an invitation to post-fermentation conversion of hydrogen sulfide compounds into mercaptans. So rack and sulfite soon after the wine has fallen still, even if the odor has disappeared.

Copper should not be added during fermentation, but it is safe and advisable to add a minute amount of copper after fermentation is complete. Add .3 ml (6 drops) of copper sulfate (1% $CuSO_4 \cdot 5H_2O$) per U.S. gallon (.08ml per liter), which will add .2 ppm of copper. **(Caution - be sure you are using 1% solution and not 10%).** Stopper the carboy and set it in a cool place.

As long as the stopper stays seated, the problem is probably under control. If the stopper starts popping out, the hydrogen sulfide compounds are most likely being converted into mercaptans. Promptly rack again, but this time the wine should be racked into an air-free atmosphere if possible — i.e., displace the air with CO_2 or argon before racking. Add ¼ tsp. of ascorbic acid per 5 gallons when racking. The next day stir in another .15 ml of copper sulfate per gallon. If the smell persists, add another .15 ml per gallon a few days later. Even with two or three small additions of copper, after the reaction you will end up well under the FDA limit of .2 parts per million residual. If you added more than .4 ppm of copper sulfate, the wine should be fined with bentonite at some later time to strip out any excess.

The odds are high that these measures, taken promptly as needed, will solve the problem. Some of the compounds may have progressed to the mercaptan stage, but none to the disulfide stage. So the rackings and copper addition should deal with it. However, it is a good precaution to bring a small sample to room temperature and smell carefully from time to time during bulk aging.

Off Odors and Flavors

Browning in a finished wine is a sign of oxidation. Excessive exposure to air could have resulted from fermenting too long in an open fermenter before transferring to carboys or from storage in carboys that were not filled to the top. Fining with Polyclar VT (and sulfiting, of course) after the fact might help reduce the browning.

If your wine has a vinegary taste, the flaw is acetic acid. Since

some of this volatile acid is always formed during primary fermentation, it will be present in low levels in virtually every wine, and
is not objectionable at low levels. However, at higher levels, which
vary from one palate to the next, it becomes a flaw. The acetic acid
resulting from fermentation will usually not rise to that level. But
if the ever-present acetobacter are given enough time in the presence of oxygen, they will convert ethanol into acetic acid and very
likely ruin the wine.

If your wine tastes vinegary and exposure to air was not the
cause, perhaps the grapes were overripe or had too much bunch
rot, or the pH was high and it was fermented too warm. If a must
is fermented warm without sulfiting first, spontaneous malolactic
fermentation might have started with one of the undesirable strains
that generates acetic acid.

As alcohol is oxidized, the first stage is acetaldehyde. Acetaldehyde is present in all wines and at low levels contributes to
complexity. At higher levels it will make a wine seem "flabby" or
"flaccid" (i.e., lacking in fruit and varietal characteristic and seem-
ingly sweet). If ethanol is oxidized further, acetic acid will result
and finally ethyl acetate. Ethyl acetate is an ester having a most
unpleasant odor, like nail polish remover or airplane glue. It is,
to me, the vilest of all organic flaws, although I know people who
seem not to detect it or be bothered by it. Although acetaldehyde
will bind with sulfite, there is no cure for ethyl acetate in even the
smallest amount.

Note that for the most part, there is no satisfactory "cure" for any
of the organic defects discussed above. Prevention in the form of a
proper pre-fermentation acid level (at least .6% TA), sulfite and air
avoidance is by far the best remedy. It is natural to think that by
blending, the flaw will be diminished. Depending on the problem,
it usually does not work that way—normally the blend is just as
flawed as the problem wine. If you have one of these organic defects
and sufficient volume of wine to make it worth the effort, consult
with someone locally who can give you some perspective, as these
problems are difficult to diagnose and treat. Or, send a sample to
one of the labs listed in Appendix F. A heavy dose of sulfite (100
ppm) may be the best palliative. After that, you could consider
trying to mask some of the defect with oak flavoring or a higher

level of residual sugar.

Finished wines that have a "pruney" flavor were usually made from overripe grapes with high sugar and were fermented too hot. A pruney flavor right after fermentation will diminish with time but will not always disappear. If your grapes have abnormally high sugar, keep the temperature in the 70s if you can; don't let it rise to the high 80s. Be sure to sort out all raisined and spoiled grapes before crushing. And give the must a dose of lysozyme at the rate of 1½ grams per gallon.

Excess Astringency

If a wine is left in contact with the seeds too long, it will become excessively astringent due to the tannin and could take years to mellow. The tannin level can be reduced by fining with egg white, isinglass, potassium caseinate or gelatin, all of which are protein-based and attract tannins. Some of these fining agents deal with astringency more effectively and others deal with bitterness.

Appendix C

Sulfite Management

You need to use potassium metabisulfite if you aspire to making world class wines. Although the dosages recommended earlier in this book are fine for wines with a normal pH, the optimum amount of sulfite varies with the pH of the wine. Those who use barrels will be particularly interested in sulfite management because the level of free sulfite drops about twice as fast in barrels as carboys, and a certain minimum level is needed to protect both the wine and the barrel itself from contamination.

Molecular sulfite

Sulfite binds with acetaldehyde, yeast, bacteria, sugars and oxygen, but has a higher affinity for some of these constituents than others. It binds most irreversibly with acetaldehyde and proteins, and less so with sugars. Some of the esoteric forms of sugar will eventually release SO_2 that was initially bound. The sulfite that is not bound is known as "free" sulfite. "Total sulfite" is the sum of the bound and free portions, all being expressed either as parts per million or as milligrams per liter. As you will note at the top of the chart on the next page, a miniscule portion of free sulfite consists of "molecular" sulfite. The portion may be tiny, but molecular sulfite is actually the most significant component because it is molecular

200

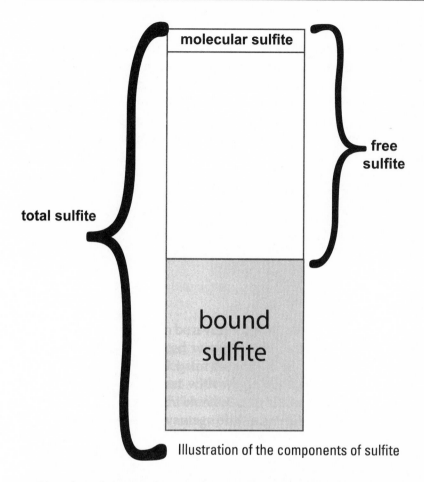

Illustration of the components of sulfite

sulfite that delivers the preservative effect attributed to sulfite in general. Molecular sulfite has a very high affinity for oxygen and reacts immediately with it.

The goal in sulfite management is to maintain just enough free sulfite to get the preservative benefits of some molecular sulfite, but not so much that its negative attributes come forward (namely, the odor). The maximum preservative effect is attained at 2 ppm molecular, but at that level the sulfite odor is objectionable. Balancing odor against preservative benefits, the optimum level is generally regarded as 0.8 ppm molecular. At that level you get adequate antioxidative benefits without suffering an unacceptable odor. Since they contain significant amounts of tannin, dry red table wines need a little less sulfite, with 0.5 ppm molecular generally being regarded as sufficient.

Molecular sulfite cannot be measured by conventional means, but there is a direct relationship between pH, free sulfite and molecular sulfite which allows us to derive the molecular amount. If the pH and free sulfite levels are known, the parts per million of molecular sulfite can be determined. This graph shows the level of free SO_2 required to maintain 0.8 ppm and 0.5 ppm of molecular sulfite at differing pH levels:

It is at once obvious that the higher the pH, the more free sulfite is needed to get the requisite level of molecular sulfite. At pH 3.6, for example, 45 ppm of free sulfite is needed to maintain 0.8 ppm molecular, whereas only half as much free sulfite is needed at pH 3.3. That is the main reason that wines with pH 3.6 and higher are such a problem — you cannot use enough sulfite in a high pH wine to get the necessary preservative effect without suffering an offensive sulfite odor.

Determining the amount needed

It is assumed that you have the ability to measure both the level of free SO_2 and the pH. The pH is measured with a pH meter, of course. Pocket-sized digital pH meters are available at very reasonable prices these days (see Appendix A). Free SO_2 is measured by the Ripper method (including Titrets®) or preferably by vacuum aspiration, both of which are explained in Appendix A. As an example of how you work the numbers backward, assume that you have a barrel or carboy of white wine which measures pH 3.4. Vacuum aspiration test indicates that free SO_2 has dropped to 10 ppm. From the above graph for 0.8 ppm, you know that the desired level of free SO_2 at pH 3.4 is 32 ppm — this is the approximate level that will deliver the optimum 0.8 ppm of molecular sulfite. An additional 22 ppm is needed to get it back up to 32 ppm.

The basic formula to calculate the amount of potassium metabisulfite needed is:

$$\frac{\textbf{ppm needed x liters of wine}}{\textbf{0.57}}$$

The divisor of 0.57 is needed because only 57% by weight of this compound is the active ingredient, free SO_2. In the above example, if you had a 228-liter barrel of wine, the grams needed would be calculated as follows:

$$\frac{.022 \times 228}{0.57} = 8.8 \text{ g}$$

Adding 8.8 grams of potassium metabisulfite to the barrel will raise the free sulfite by approximately 22 parts per million. This addition, plus the existing 10 ppm already in the wine, will bring free sulfite up to the 32 ppm that the chart indicates is necessary to result in 0.8 ppm of molecular sulfite.

If you are using Efferbacktol or Oensteryl tablets, be aware that "5 grams" on the package means 5 grams of total sulfite; divide by 0.57 to determine the total amount.

Note that when you do the calculations, you cannot just use the raw number "22" in the equation. You have to move the decimal point three places to the left. That's because one part per million is actually 0.001 grams per liter, and twenty-two parts per million is 0.022 grams per liter. This is important because if you are off by only one decimal point, you will get ten times too much SO_2, or one-tenth, either of which could be a disaster.

If you are working with 5 U.S. gallons, you have to first convert the gallons into liters. One gallon is 3.785 liters. Five gallons is 19 liters: (5 X 3.785 = 19)

$$\frac{0.022 \times 19}{0.57} = .73 \text{ g}$$

What if free sulfite does not measure 32 ppm after the addition? This will happen almost every time for two reasons. Sulfite decomposes fairly quickly and will invariably be less than it's theoretical strength of 57% the day you buy it. In addition, you never know until after the fact exactly how much of a sulfite addition will become bound with aldehydes, sugar, yeast, etc., and how much will remain free. A significant but unknown amount of sulfite is needed to bind with the aldehydes, proteins and sugar, and only after those needs have been satisfied will the extent of unbound or free sulfite be known. Fortunately, this variable diminishes as the wine ages. At crushing, almost all of a sulfite addition will bind with the sugar and none will remain free at the end of fermentation. At the first racking about 40 to 60 per cent of an addition will become bound; the rest, by definition, is free sulfite. The percentage becoming bound will go down further with later additions because the wine will have fewer proteins and solids. And much of the remaining solids will already be bound with sulfite from the previous addition, so the wine will have considerably less capacity to absorb another addition. Almost all of it will be free. As a result of this residual nature of free sulfite, it is good practice to run another vacuum aspiration test three or four days after the addition. If it is close to 32 ppm, leave well enough alone. Otherwise, add a little more.

10% stock sulfite solution

Rather than using the above formula to calculate the grams needed and then weighing it and dissolving it in water, it is easier to prepare a 10% stock solution ahead of time. A pre-mixed solution is easier to work with and less prone to error. A 250-ml brown glass bottle with screw cap works well. Fill the bottle half full of warm water and add 25 grams of potassium metabisulfite (4 tsp.). Shake it until the crystals are dissolved and then top up to 500 ml with cold water. A 750-ml brown wine bottle also works well if the sulfite quantity is also increased by 50%. **This stock solution will only stay fresh for 2 or 3 weeks** and then should be remixed. Due to its short life, I only use a 10% stock solution during the crush season and use the leftover stock to fill airlocks.

Here is a guide as to the volumes of stock solution required for various sulfite levels and volume measurements:

PARTS PER MILLION OF FREE SO$_2$ DESIRED

Milliliters of 10% sulfite solution required per:	10 ppm	30 ppm	50 ppm
Per liter	.18 ml	.53 ml	.88 ml
Per U.S. gal.	.67 ml	2.00 ml	3.33 ml
Per Imp. gal.	.80 ml	2.40 ml	4.00 ml

EXAMPLE 1. If you had just crushed grapes, had 20 gallons U.S. and wanted to add 45 ppm, multiply 20 X 3.32 = 66.4 ml of the 10% stock solution.

EXAMPLE 2. In the pH example above, where you had only 10 ppm, but wanted 32 ppm of free sulfite, you have to add 22 ppm. For a 225-liter barrel, you would add 87.5 ml, calculated as follows: .53 X [22/30] X 225 = 87.5 ml.

Whether you are dissolving it each time or are using a 10% stock solution, you have to stir the must or wine thoroughly to disperse it. This is particularly the case with a must containing skins and pulps. The sulfite will not mix without considerable stirring.

Efferbacktol packets and Oenosteryl tablets are handy waya to boost the level of sulfite in barrels without have to stir. They generate a fizz to help disperse the sulfite. They are marketed in 2-gram and 5-gram sizes:

Tablet Size	Per U.S. gal. Total	Free	Per 5 U.S. gals. Total	Free	Per 228 liters Total	Free
2-gram	500	300	100	60	9	5
5-gram	1300	750	250	140	22	12

The manufacturer of Oenosteryl advises against using only a portion of a tablet because there is no assurance that the sulfite will be evenly dispersed throughout the tablet.

If you added way too much sulfite to a must or wine, you can neutralize the excess with hydrogen peroxide. Add 1.9 ml of 1% H_2O_2 per gallon (0.5g/liter) for each 10 ppm of free sulfite that you want to neutralize. This requires that you get an accurate measurement of free sulfite via vacuum aspiration. If you added only a little too much, you can usually deal with it by racking/aerating.

Grape Varieties

There are hundreds of different grape varieties; the list that follows contains only the more common types, along with some yeast suggestions. Be sure to go on-line to read more about your yeast strain as some will need nutrient additions.

Vitis vinifera

Vitis vinifera is rightfully regarded as the elite species for winemaking. The better ones have no equal. In addition to California and the Pacific Northwest, *vinifera* acreage is increasing in the Northeast and Mid-Atlantic regions of the U.S. and in parts of Canada.

Red vinifera

CABERNET SAUVIGNON. The blue berries of this premier wine grape variety are very small. The resulting high skin-to-juice ratio produces a wine that is very dark, intensely flavored and tannic. Since the skins are tough and the clusters are loose and easily aerated, this variety will survive bad weather before harvest with minimum susceptibility to mildew or bunch rot. Although it takes a fair amount of heat to ripen Cabernet Sauvignon to the point where the wine will have the classic black currant overtones, the grape will grow in cooler climates and produce a respectable red wine. However, if not sufficiently ripened, or if the canopy is so heavy as to restrict aeration and sunlight, the wine will have a vegetative bouquet and flavor. Cabernet Sauvignon buds later than Merlot and is less vulnerable to late spring frosts. The juice is clear when first pressed and makes a wonderful rosé — if you can bear to part with a full-bodied wine! It blends well with Merlot, Cabernet Franc, Syrah, and other Bordeaux varieties.

Suggested yeasts: D80, D254, D21, RC212, Pasteur Red, BDX, FRE, BM45

MERLOT. The plump black grapes of Merlot make a soft, fruit-forward wine that is very deserving of its current popularity. Merlot is lower in acid and tannins, ripens about a week earlier and ages faster than Cabernet Sauvignon. It usually improves Cabernet Sauvignon to blend in 10 or 15 percent Merlot to soften the tannins. It also tolerates cool, damp soils better than Cabernet Sauvignon, but its thin-skinned berries are more subject to mildew and rot in the event of early fall rains. When Merlot and Cabernet Sauvignon are blended, the result is often better than either one alone. The crop set can be erratic and is adversely affected by spring rains right after budding.

Suggested yeasts: D21, D80, Pasteur Red, D254, RC212, BDX, FRE, BM45

CABERNET FRANC. This very cold-hardy red grape does very well in parts of the Northeast United States, Long Island and Ontario's Niagara peninsula, as well as the West Coast. Cabernet Franc is lighter in color and tannin, quite aromatic and ripens earlier than Cabernet Sauvignon. Cabernet Franc tends to overproduce and become herbaceous if over-cropped. It has traditionally been used in Bordeaux for blending with Cabernet Sauvignon and is gaining in popularity in the United States, both as a straight varietal and for blending with Cabernet Sauvignon, Merlot and other Bordeaux grapes.

Suggested yeasts: D254, Assmannshausen, Prisse de Mouse (Premier Cru, EC1118), Pasteur Red, ICV-GRE, RC212, BM45, GRE, W15

PINOT NOIR. Pinot Noir is the most difficult variety to grow and to ferment. It should be racked infrequently and do not stir the lees during malolactic fermentation. Almost never do the results equal the fine red Burgundies by which Pinot Noir wines are inevitably judged. However, with ripe grapes, a very good red wine can be expected. The grape is inherently low in tannin and light in color, and the color diminishes further as the wine ages and bottle sediment develops.

For a lighter wine that emphasizes the grape's delightful fruitiness, try "cold-soaking" for several days after crushing, but before fermentation. This is widely believed to produce a wine with softer flavors, more fruit and a deeper, more stable color. You could also ferment 10-20% whole clusters in the must to emphasize the fruit. By pressing early, say at 5°B, you would avoid the harsher tannins that would be extracted at higher alcohol levels.

For a bigger-bodied wine that will take longer to age and have less fruit, but more complexity, crush and de-stem rigorously to macerate the grapes as much as possible. With fully ripe grapes, 10 percent of the stems could be returned to the must before primary fermentation to increase tannin. I once put some Pinot Noir through extended maceration and pressed at exactly the wrong time. The wine was initially so harsh as to be undrinkable. The tannins eventually softened but it took seven years, by which time I had almost none left. I mention this because that wine was one of the best I have ever made! Pinot Noir is generally not given extended maceration.

It is usually necessary to put Pinot Noir through malolactic fermentation as a means of getting total acidity down into the desired range. I like a limited exposure to toasted oak; it improves this wine in my opinion.

The many clones of Pinot Noir all tend to have tight clusters and tender skin, which makes them susceptible to mildew and bunch rot if damp weather sets in just before harvest. To hedge against this possibility, you might want to pick some at 18-20°B, as Pinot Noir makes an excellent sparkling wine. Press without crushing first, and the juice will be white. This juice is excellent for blending with white wines, such as Semillon, Sauvignon Blanc, and Chardonnay.

Suggested yeasts: RC212, Assmanhausen, W15

SANGIOVESE This is the staple grape in Tuscany and it is catching on here in the U.S., even though it is very site-specific and difficult to grow. Good grapes will give you a delicate, fruit-forward wine with medium body. It makes a wonderful rosé!

When lining up a source, remember that Sangiovese is a late ripener, and you want to avoid fruit that is under-ripe as a result of cool weather or over-cropping. You want woody stems/brown seeds, as under-ripe grapes are more likely to result in a wine that is herbaceous, overly acidic and/or overly tannic. After cold soaking for a few hours, draw off about a fourth of the juice to make a rosé. See page 111. Ferment the rest as a big-bodied wine. If you have excess Syrah or Cabernet Sauvignon on hand, blend about 5% into the main Sangiovese wine to give it a little more backbone and mid-palate.

Suggested yeasts: D254, RC212, BM45, SYR, D21, D80, Assmannshausen, GRE

SYRAH, a.k.a, Shiraz. Serious California wineries are starting to bottle Syrahs that rival the fine wines of Hermitage and Côte-Rôtie, albeit with more fruit and lower tannin. At its best, Syrah makes a big, spicy and complex red wine that takes many years to mellow. In small proportions it will enhance Sangiovese, Cabernet Sauvignon, Merlot and Zinfandel.

Suggested yeasts: D80, D21, D254, SYR, W15, ICV-GRE, L2226, BM45, BDX, Assmannshausen

ZINFANDEL. When the yield per acre is limited, Zinfandel makes a spectacular, spicy full-bodied wine. "White Zinfandel," so popular with the American public, is fermented from heavily cropped Central Valley grapes. Serious winemakers will want grapes originating farther north in California, where cooler weather will allow for slower, more even ripening. When fermenting overripe Zinfandel, be sure to cull out those that are raisined and carefully monitor the fermentation temperature to avoid a "pruney" flavor. Try to keep the wine temperature below 80°F. during fermentation. It's okay to leave around .5% of residual sugar in this red wine, as the commercial wineries often do.

Suggested yeasts: D21, D80, D254, Assmanhausen, Uvaferm 43, RC212, BDX, SYR, BM45

White vinifera

CHARDONNAY. It should come as no surprise that the grape that gives us the great Meursaults and Montrachets of Burgundy is so widely planted throughout the world. It is quite hardy and adapts to a wide range of climates. The problem with Chardonnay is that unless it is well ripened, it has little inherent varietal characteristic. And the quality of the wine falls off rapidly as the tonnage surpasses the optimum yield per acre, which will vary from one region to the next. Its tight clusters are not easily aerated, making it quite susceptible to mildew and bunch rot in damp weather.

It is best, in my opinion, to soak Chardonnay grapes on the skins for 24 hours before pressing and fermenting. I am partial to cold fermentation with Steinberg yeast, but wineries typically ferment with more vigorous yeast strains at 65°F (or start lower and let the temperature rise after the sugar drops below 10°B). Although I confess to liking the buttery flavor that results from malolactic fermentation, I have mixed emotions about MLF because it eliminates so much of the fruit flavor. It also seems to make the wine more difficult to clarify. When I do opt for MLF after primary fermentation, which is usually when total acidity is high, I keep the temperature fairly warm and stir the lees once or twice a week. This imparts the maximum yeasty flavor in addition to promoting MLF. Note that if you want to keep the temperature abnormally warm during MLF, avoid the vigorous yeasts; otherwise, autolysis is likely, where the yeast cannibalize each other after the sugar is gone and leave a bad flavor. Sometimes I flavor a Chardonnay with French oak and sometimes not, since the oak flavoring masks some of the fruitiness.

Suggested yeasts: D47, D21, D254, VL1, VL2, BA11, GRE

SAUVIGNON BLANC. The vines of Sauvignon Blanc are very vigorous and if not pruned to give the grapes some air and sunlight, the grapes will develop an overwhelming grassy quality. Going to the opposite extreme, many U.S. wineries maximize exposure to air and sunlight by canopy management and put the wine through malolactic fermentation as well. The resulting wine will more easily pass for a Chardonnay than a classic Sauvignon Blanc that goes so well with seafood. Sauvignon Blanc is sometimes blended with Semillon and marketed as "Fumé Blanc."

Suggested yeasts: VL3, BA11, K1, Uvaferm 43, Prise de Mousse, ICV-GRE

SEMILLON. Semillon is one of the most widely planted white

grapes in the world. It is the basic grape of white Bordeaux and of Sauternes (it is very prone to *Botrytis cinerea*, the "noble rot"). Semillon is commonly blended with Sauvignon Blanc to round out the flavor of the latter and with inexpensive Chardonnays as an extender. With the right grapes, Semillon will make a serious white wine capable of long-term aging.

Suggested yeasts: K1, Pasteur white, Pasteur Champagne, ontrechet, VL1, VL3

PINOT GRIS. This relative of Pinot Noir is known as Tokay in Alsace and as Pinot Grigio in Italy, where it produces an excellent, dry white wine with a pleasing lemony quality. In the United States it can make a high quality white wine rivaling Chardonnay or Sauvignon Blanc in quality. If well ripened, Pinot Gris wines have a pleasant spicy quality; but if allowed to get overripe, the grapes tend to lose character and will turn red if left to hang too long. Pinot Gris tends to have high acid and low pH, even at high sugar levels. Malolactic fermentation can often be used to good advantage to add some body to the wine. Pinot Gris is less susceptible to mildew and bunch rot and ripens earlier than Chardonnay.

Suggested yeasts: D21, D80, D254, Uvaferm 43, RC212, BA11, 71B, W15, Steinberg, BA11, D47, GRE

JOHANNISBERG RIESLING, a.k.a, White Riesling. This is a great one for home winemakers to ferment! It is more widely available than other varieties because the vines are very hardy and will thrive in cooler climates, such as the northeast United States and southeast Canada. It does extremely well in New York. Even if it is harvested early and sugar is added, Riesling will make a nice wine with a distinctive aroma. It can be made dry or sweet or in between and is a good grape for sparkling wine. Riesling can be left hanging longer than other varieties because the berries are highly resistant to frost. If healthy grapes are left to hang, with luck they might become infected with *Botrytis cinerea*, and you will have the makings for a delicious sweet wine! (Note that in hot climates Riesling ripens too quickly and loses much of its quality.)

Suggested yeasts: BA11, 71B, Steinberg, W15, D47, GRE

GEWURZTRAMINER. I have never figured out why Gewurztraminer lacks commercial appeal because it can make such fine wines — perhaps the majority of the buying public has never had a good one. Gewurztraminer is similar to Riesling in that it excels in cool climates and makes a good dry wine as well as sweet. The berries are small and pink and the wine is full-bodied, aromatic and easy to recognize. The acid level tends to fall rapidly as Gewurztraminer ripens, so a 50-50 mix of tartaric and malic acids is often needed at crushing to raise acidity. I am partial to an overnight soak on the skins, but I know others who go in the opposite direction by pressing without first crushing. Ferment cool. If the grapes were picked a little early, the wine tends to have a slightly bitter after-taste. Fining with gelatin, Kieselsol or isinglass might help deal with that tendency. Use a bottle to good avail to top up dry white table wines when racking.

Suggested yeasts: W15, Steinberg, VL1, VL3, 71B, Epernay 2, BA11 W15, D47, GRE

French hybrids

There are dozens of different French hybrids, interspecific hybrids and French-native American hybrids under cultivation in the Midwest, Southeast, and Northeast regions of the United States and in parts of Canada. They generally were selected over *Vitis vinifera* varieties for their greater cold hardiness, tolerance of humidity, and/or resistance to fungal diseases, rot, pests and mildew. They are superior to *Vitis labrusca* because they are less foxy and make far better wines. However, if allowed to over-ripen, some hybrids will develop a "cotton candy" and foxy flavor. It is critical that they be harvested at the right level of ripeness. Commercial wineries often deal with these unwanted flavors by heat treatment and/or carbonic maceration. Avoid extensive skin contact during fermentation of red hybrids and plan to press as soon as the wine has developed sufficient color.

Hybrids for the most part are diminishing in importance as more is learned about cultivating *vinifera* varieties in different locales. The white hybrids are generally of higher quality than the reds.

Following is a list of the better hybrids for winemaking:

White French hybrids

CAYUGA WHITE. Cayuga White is a relatively new cross which is productive, disease-resistant and very versatile. It can be fermented into a fruity, off-dry white wine or, with oak aging, into a more complex, dry table wine. It's also good for sparkling wine. Don't let it get too ripe or it will develop some foxiness.

VIDAL BLANC, a.k.a Vidal. With fully ripened grapes Vidal Blanc will make a good fruity, floral wine reminiscent of Riesling — dry, semisweet or sweet. It is popular in Canada as a late-harvest dessert wine. It is a heavy producer and needs a long growing season, so cluster thinning is required.

SEYVAL BLANC. This is a good white hybrid of long standing. It ripens early and can be fermented in various styles — crisp, dry, fruity or put through MLF for a more complex wine. Seyval Blanc is productive and does well in cool climates, but it is very susceptible to bunch rot.

VIGNOLES, a.k.a Ravat. Vignoles ripens to a high sugar level while retaining high acidity, making it an excellent choice for late-harvest and ice wines. It can also be made into a dry white table wine. In addition to its versatility, Vignoles is a very hardy and is seldom affected by frosts since it has a late budbreak. Its principal drawback is that very compact clusters make it highly susceptible to bunch rot.

TRAMINETTE. This is a new variety developed at the NYS Agricultural Experimental Station by Cornell University. According to all reports, it should not be stigmatized as a "hybrid." It is just starting to become commercially available and is expected to establish itself quickly because the wine, similar to Gewurztraminer, is high quality, has a good balance of sugar, acid and pH, and ages well. The vines are cold hardy and the berries quite resistant to rot and mildew.

Red French hybrids

CHAMBOURCIN. This is a relatively new hybrid that makes a full-bodied wine of good quality when the grapes ripen fully. The wine is fruity and aromatic, slightly herbaceous. Due to high yields per acre, it should be cluster thinned. Chambourcin will tolerate humidity and is cold hardy. It ripens mid-season.

CHANCELLOR, a.k.a Seibel 7053. Though not quite as well regarded as Chambourcin, this transplant from the Rhone Valley makes good reds and rosés. It is moderately hardy. Clusters should be thinned to promote ripening. It is susceptible to mildew.

BACO NOIR, a.k.a Baco No. 1. Makes an intense red wine with some aging potential, despite low tannin. It is very vigorous but disease-prone and frost-prone due to early budbreak.

MARECHAL FOCH, a.k.a Foch. This winter-hardy hybrid has been around a long time. It ripens very early and its black berries produce a fruity red wine with some Burgundian qualities. It lends itself to carbonic maceration.

Vitis labrusca

The wines made from Vitis labrusca tend to have a "foxy" quality which experienced wine drinkers find objectionable. The riper the grape, the more pronounced the foxiness; so with these varieties, it is better to harvest a little too green than too ripe. However, if picked green they will be quite acidic. As a result, 3 or 4 parts of the must is commonly diluted with one part of water sweetened to about 20°B with table sugar. Foxiness is also reduced by pressing immediately after crushing to minimize skin contact. It's a good idea to line the press basket with fiberglass mesh as the tough slipskins make pressing difficult. Pressing is made easier and the yield increased if pectic enzyme is used.

DELAWARE. The small pink berries of Delaware ripen early and are used to make sparkling wines in particular, but also dry, sweet and ice wines. Delaware has a spicy, musky aroma and is probably the least foxy labrusca.

CATAWBA. Since they are quite foxy, these pink grapes are usually converted into white or pink dessert wines, of which the quality can be quite good. They are also used for super-sweet ice wines. The grapes are acidic and the wine will improve somewhat with age. They require a long growing season.

NIAGARA. This white grape is quite foxy and aromatic. It is usually used to make a sweet version, but sometimes dry. The vines are vigorous and productive.

CONCORD. This is probably the least desirable labrusca, due to foxiness and harshness. It has high acid and is best made into a sweet wine.

Fermentation Notes

CABERNET SAUVIGNON
MALOLACTIC FERMENTATION
Extended Maceration

DAY 1. Crushed and destemmed 130# Cabernet Sauvignon. Tested 25° B. right after pressing, with pulp (probably about 24° B. without pulp); .83 TA; 3.43 pH. Sulfited @ ¼ tsp./5 gal. of volume; used pectic enzyme to hasten maceration. Added 1 tsp. of diammonium phosphate. Soaked overnight on skins. Grapes had little flavor.

DAY 2. Brought into warm room — used space heater to raise ambient temperature to 75-80°F (24-27°C). Inoculated with Pasteur Red starter solution sprinkled over surface. Fermentation was visible in a few hours.

DAY 3. Cap starts forming.

DAY 4. Deep cap. Since malolactic fermentation is desired with the acid being .83, this is the time to add ML starter and yeast extract. Note that it is normal for the temperature of a fermenting wine to run 5-15°F (3-8°C) above ambient temperature. This is due to the heat generated by fermentation. You want the fermenting wine temperature to run up to 80-90°F (27-32°C) for two or three days during active fermentation in order to maximize extraction of flavors and color. Monitor with a floating thermometer or an indoor-outdoor digital thermometer and don't let it exceed 90° (32°C). Wine should be punched down three or four times a day during this stage of vigorous fermentation.

DAY 10. Cap is greatly diminished. Unfermented sugar is slightly over 1%, per Clinitest. Room temperature and wine temperature are almost the same now at 75°F (24°C). It could be pressed now, but I am putting this batch through extended maceration. Covered the cap with a layer of plastic wrap after punching down, to keep air away.

DAY 11. Punching down once a day now and covering with plastic wrap.

DAY 14. Wine is dry. Clinitest turns slightly yellow, but the red pigment is so overwhelming that a reliable reading on residual sugar is not possible. Hopefully, the slight bubble formation is a sign of malolactic fermentation, but it might just be trapped CO_2 escaping. Tastes bitter and tannic.

DAY 16. Still some bubbles escaping. Cap floating on surface, so no need to punch down. Wine mellowed; has spectacular flavor and fruit — should be excellent wine!

DAY 17. Wine bitter again.

DAY 20. Ran chromatography test: malolactic fermentation is complete. Pressed lightly and sulfited — ¼ tsp./ 5 gal. Ended up with 5 gal. + 3 gal. + 3 liters, some of which will be lost as pulp and lees at the next racking. Placed outside to cold stabilize (optional with red wines) and clear. The wine is bitter and tannic again, but has an immense amount of fruit. In hindsight, I should have racked on Day 16, as it was sweeter then, but an extra 4 days on the skins will not make much difference.

5 WEEKS. Wine has good color and clarity. Tastes tannic. pH = 3.65.

9 WEEKS. First racking. There was a mild hydrogen sulfide odor, so I aerated during racking by trickling the wine down the side of the carboy and added .1 part per million copper sulfate (.15 ml/ gal. of 1% $CuSO_4 \cdot 5H_2O$). Some of the H_2S might have converted to mercaptans, but not to disulfides, given the short time on the lees and faintness of the odor. Although there should not be a problem with this wine, this is a good example of the importance of monitoring a wine during the days and weeks immediately after

fermentation ceases. The more pulp and sediment, the greater the risk of problems. Had I left it unattended for a few more weeks, the H₂S would have been converted to mercaptans and possibly disulfides. Have 5 gal. + 2.8 gal. + 1.5 liters. TA tests .73.

16 WEEKS. TA tests .735% and will have to be lowered chemically. Have 5 gal. + 3 gal. The small carboy is earmarked for blending with next fall's Merlot, and will not be adjusted now. Racked 5 gal., adding 12.5 g. calcium carbonate (to lower TA by .1%). No sulfite. May have to add a bit more at the next racking.

17 WEEKS. TA = .62%. Has good flavor, but not much bouquet.

18 WEEKS. TA = .69%. pH = 3.88—the carbonate raised the pH far more than I wanted or expected. Since the pH is already higher than I would like, I will live with high total acidity. It does not taste acidic.

5 MONTHS. Racked, added 2 cups American oak chips to 5 gal. carboy and 45 ppm sulfite and 1½ grams of lysozyme/gal.

8 MONTHS. Racked both carboys.

10 MONTHS. Bottled 5-gal. carboy. Due to the high pH, I added 75 ppm of sulfite at bottling. Holding 3-gal. for blending.

CHARDONNAY
COLD FERMENTATION
Malolactic Fermentation

210 pounds of Chardonnay, 21.5°B at pressing, acid and pH not tested. Grapes had some bunch rot from recent rains, which I sorted/cut out with as much patience as I could muster. Grapes taste sweet but not much flavor. With sugar at this relatively low level, the acid level will be high, and malolactic fermentation looks like a good way to lower it.

DAY 1. Crushed, dissolved and added ¼ tsp sulfite per 5 gal. of volume. Covered with plastic wrap and soaked on skins for 24 hours to pick up additional flavor.

DAY 2. Pressed, giving the must another half dose of meta (⅛ tsp./5 gal.). Sugar dropped to 21°B after pressing (because pressed juice is slightly lower in sugar than the free-run juice tested yesterday). Inoculated with Montrachet yeast starter. Must has peculiar odor.

DAY 4. Still no sign of fermentation (wine has been in cold garage). Added some yeast lees which were siphoned from a different batch of wine containing Steinberg yeast. Steinberg is active at lower temperatures.

DAY 5. Fermentation under way. Could be either Montrachet or Steinberg — it's probably Steinberg, but it doesn't matter.

DAY 6. Fermentation very active. Transferred to carboys, ¾ full; topped with air lock.

DAY 13. Fermenting slowly.

4 WEEKS. Fermenting slowly.

5 WEEKS. Fermenting slowly; still tastes fairly sweet. Combined carboys. Note that with Steinberg yeast it would take several weeks for the last 1% of the sugar to ferment. So I brought it to room temperature to ferment it to total dryness faster. Fermentation picked up as soon as the temperature started to rise.

6 WEEKS. Being held at approx. 70°F (21°C). Fermenting very slowly.

7 WEEKS. One carboy is still, the other ferments slowly.

8 WEEKS. Both carboys are still. Raised ambient temperature to 75-80°F (24-27°C). The next day I stirred in 1 tsp. yeast extract per carboy and malolactic starter (Chr. Hansen *Viniflora® Oenos*). Stirred up lees and replaced air lock. The wine will be maintained at 75-80°F (24-27°C) and the nutrients stirred up with a slender dowel until malolactic fermentation is complete. MLF will lower total acid, and the diacetyl produced as a by-product of MLF will give the wine a distinctive "buttery" quality. Stirred twice the next day. It was apparent in two days that MLF had started — carbonization was evident when the lees were stirred up.

9 WEEKS. Effervescence has been slowing of late — very little when I stir the lees.

10 WEEKS. No more effervescence. MLF complete? TA = .73%, which is higher than I would expect after complete MLF. Moved to the garage to cold stabilize and start clarification. Wine tastes very dry, lacks fruit. Needs some character!

11 WEEKS. Chromatography test shows that MLF was just underway when it stopped. The temperature must have dropped lower than I realized (the carboys were sitting directly on the floor). Put the carboys back into the heated area, set on wood blocks to keep it off the floor. Raised ambient temperature to 80° and MLF restarted right away.

12 WEEKS. I stir the lees two or three times a week. The efferves-

cence is a good sign of MLF.

14 WEEKS. Effervescence has slowed noticeably.

15 WEEKS. MLF complete per another chromatography test. Set in a cool place to allow the gross lees to settle. Tastes thin, no fruit, does not seem to have much promise.

16 WEEKS. TA = .69%. Has some Chardonnay character.

17 WEEKS. TA = .675% and .69%. pH = 3.39. RS is well under .05%. Tastes even better, like it has some potential! First racking—sulfited (¼ tsp/7 gal), added 8.75 g of calcium carbonate to lower TA by about .05%, and fined with Sparkolloid™ (1 tsp/gal). Brought inside so it will warm and clear faster.

19 WEEKS. Wine appears clear, but still contains residual haze from Sparkolloid™. Stuffed 2 cups of French oak splinters into one carboy, none in the other carboy.

6 MONTHS. Racked, adding 1.8 oz. of table sugar to the carboy with oak (to raise TA to about .2%), ⅛ tsp sulfite and fined with 2 oz of liquid beermaker's isinglass per carboy. The carboy without oak received 1.2 oz of sugar for a different style.

8 MONTHS. Bottled with no further racking, even though there was visible haze. The necessary sulfite was added by rinsing the bottles with an intense sulfite solution, draining thoroughly and then adding 1 ml of pre-mixed sulfite solution (¼ tsp. sulfite per 25 ml water). The wine does not seem to have much fruit at this stage, but probably will be very good in a couple of years.

FROZEN MUST

CABERNET SAUVIGNON
MALOLACTIC FERMENTATION

Extended Maceration

DAY 1. Picked up 5 gal. frozen must, Sonoma Mountain Cabernet Sauvignon, with skins. Label: 26.5°B sugar; .64 total acid; pH 3.45.

DAY 2. Opened pail — mostly thawed. Dissolved and added ¼ tsp sulfite.

DAY 3. Completely thawed; almost to room temperature. Stirred thoroughly. My readings: 22°B sugar; approx. .9% total acid. (The variance from the label results because one bucket of grapes could have come from any corner of the vineyard and not reflect the average.) The must has a great deal of flavor. Added 1 tsp diammonium phosphate and pectic enzyme. Hydrated 1 pkg. Pasteur Red yeast in ½ cup warm water and sprinkled over surface.

DAY 4. Definitely starting to ferment — cap forming. Dumped from pail into 10-gal. primary fermenter and covered. Wine temperature is 67°F (19°C). Took to small heated room which will be heated to approx. 75°F (24°C) for a few days, so the wine will ferment at 80-90°F (27-32°C). Cap will be punched down twice daily from now on.

DAY 5. Fermenting vigorously. Wine temperature is 93°F (34°C), so lowered the room temperature. Added 1 tsp. yeast extract and malolactic starter.

DAY 8. Almost still. Wine temperature just under 80°F (27°C). Wine should be tasted daily from now on to see when it mellows.

DAY 12. Very slight cap. RS over 1%, per Clinitest. Chromatography test shows ML is complete. Lowered room temperature to 70°F (21°C).

DAY 14. RS less than .5%. Seems to be still. Tastes more mellow —perhaps.

DAY 15. Tastes harsher — ? If this was the awaited mellowing, it was not very pronounced. Pressed out of concern about the mild hydrogen sulfide odor that has been present for the past several days. This was resulting from autolysis; i.e., active yeast cells consuming other yeast cells. (If the odor had been caused by excess sulfur on the grapes, there would have been an unmistakable rotten egg stink.) To be on the safe side, I added .1 ppm of copper (.15 ml per gal. of 1% $CuSO_4 \bullet 5H_2O$). Ended up with 3 gal. + 750 ml + 375 ml. Set outside to cold stabilize and let gross lees settle.

4 WEEKS. First racking. There was so much pulp and lees that I got less than 2.8 gals. of wine from an original 5 gallons, which included skins. Very dark color.

7 WEEKS. Tests .72 TA; .2% RS; pH 3.55. It tastes acidic; the acid will probably need to be lowered.

11 WEEKS. TA tests .73%. TA must be lowered since it still tastes acidic. TA can be lowered chemically using potassium carbonate or with greater accuracy using calcium carbonate. Since the wine will not be bottled for several months, the calcium carbonate will have plenty of time to settle out. I would like to end up with TA

just under .6%, but will err on the cautious side initially by adding only enough to lower it by .1% (2.5 X 2.8 gal. = 7 g). Dissolved the calcium carbonate in ½ cup of water and added while racking. Set in the corner of a closet until the next racking — calcium carbonate will not precipitate at cold temperatures.

12 WEEKS. TA = .645%. Has nice bouquet, but not much flavor.

13 WEEKS. TA = .67% pH = 3.80. Would like to lower the TA a bit more but will not tinker with it, since the pH is already higher than I would like. It does not taste acidic.

6 MONTHS. Racked.

9 MONTHS. Bottled. Due to the high pH, I used 75 ppm of sulfite at bottling.

2 YEARS. Excellent wine. Took third in a tasting, beating some very pricey California wines!

Lowering pH before fermentation

This is how I handled a different vintage of frozen must, where the pH was high:

Two pails of Sonoma Mountain Cabernet Sauvignon grapes arrive partially thawed. Brix and pH are high, and total acid is low. I plan to lower the pH to approximately 3.50 by adding tartaric acid, regardless of how much it takes or how much it raises total acid. I will lower total acid chemically after fermentation if necessary to get it into the .55–.65% range. Right now, before fermentation, my concern is the high pH — I have to correct it now because I might not be able fully correct it after fermentation.

After the grapes are fully thawed, I blend the 2 pails and mix thoroughly. Dipped out 1 gallon and added 1 tsp. of tartaric acid. This lowered the pH to 3.70. Added another ½ tsp. of tartaric, which lowered pH to 3.60. Added another ¼ tsp., which lowered it to 3.50. Based on this result, I know that each additional gallon also needs 1.75 tsp of tartaric to lower the pH to 3.50. Pre-fermentation adjustments are always a little inexact due to the skins, stems, seeds, etc. but at least it's in the right ballpark. The acid tested .85%, which is fine because I plan to put it through malolactic fermentation, which will lower total acid. Acid will drop a little during fermentation and cold stabilization. I will lower it with carbonate later if necessary. The carbonate will raise the pH, but not by much.

Raspberry Liqueur

Raspberry liqueur is the only fruit wine I continue to make. It is so good that I want to pass along my recipe for the "essence of raspberry," as I call it. If you like port wines or dessert wines, such as Sauternes, ice wines, late harvests, or sweet muscats, this should appeal to you.

If you reveal the recipe first, your friends are guaranteed to snicker—but not after they taste it! The secret is bananas. A pure raspberry liqueur without bananas would be one dimensional and unexceptional. The bananas broaden the raspberry flavor and round out the overall impression of the wine. The more bananas, the mellower the wine will be. Although the ratio of bananas to berries will have an effect on the flavor, the ratio is not critical to success. The following is only a suggestion to be followed on your first attempt. If you want a slightly different result the next time, change the recipe accordingly.

The goal is not to dilute the raspberry flavor and bouquet any more than necessary during the course of fermenting the alcohol level (up to approximately 16%). Always try to minimize the amount of water added; try to get by with the liquid from the sugar syrup, the yeast starter and later from spiking it with Everclear or brandy. You don't get very much wine, but the flavor is intense.

Here are the ingredients which will be needed initially:

1 flat fresh raspberries — approx. 12 lb.
5-7 lb. *ripe* bananas
3 lb. raisins
Pectic enzyme and potassium metabisulfite
Sugar syrup
Tokay yeast, which will ferment to a higher alcohol level than
      most other wine yeasts (Prise de Mousse would also be a
      good choice)
1 cup "Everclear" (190 proof ethanol) per gallon of finished
      wine or 2 cups of brandy

Mash the raspberries in a small primary fermenter and add the raisins. Slice up the bananas and add them. Raspberries have wonderful flavor and bouquet, but contain little sugar and little liquid.

The raisins will be a source of sugar as they break down, but more sugar and a little more liquid will be needed. Make a very heavy sugar syrup by dissolving 4 pounds of cane or beet sugar in 2 quarts of boiling water. Add enough of it to the mashed fruit mixture to raise the Brix of the must to approximately 35-40° B. The heat will help rehydrate the raisins and also help break down the berries. If the Brix is much above 40° after the mixture cools, add a little water to lower it. Store the extra syrup in the refrigerator for use later in fermenting or sweetening. After the mixture has cooled, add ⅛ tsp. of meta plus pectic enzyme.

Activate the yeast as described in Chapter 2 and inoculate the must when active. The cap should be punched down two or three times a day, as though red grapes were being fermented. This will extract more flavor out of the berries as well as frustrate the aerobic bacteria which might otherwise get established on top of the cap.

Check the remaining unfermented sugar with your hydrometer, and when it drops to 5°B, add more sugar syrup sufficient to raise it to 10-15°B. Try not to exceed 15°B because that seems to be the maximum desired sweetness in a fortified wine and very little of the additional sugar will ferment anyway due to the high alcohol-sugar level.

When fermentation slows to the point where little CO_2 is being produced, pour the entire contents of the pail into a nylon mesh bag and press it by hand (using rubber gloves, of course). Then pour it into a small carboy or gallon jugs to finish fermenting. The jugs should be as full as possible. If you need to fill some air space, add more sliced bananas! Top with an air lock.

When fermentation has slowed to a trickle, it is time to fortify. You want to end up with a liqueur having an alcohol level of approximately 20%. At that level of alcohol, it will be stable and immune to air. This will require about 1 cup of Everclear or 2 cups of brandy per U.S. gallon. You also need to take the volume of pulp into account when spiking. If one-fourth of the wine is pulp and solids, reduce the amount of alcohol to be added by one-eighth. The solids will not absorb the alcohol, and you don't want the final product to be overly alcoholic.

You can leave it in the jugs to settle. The extensive volume of pulp will compact in a few weeks, and the liqueur will be clear and ready to bottle. This liqueur has a very intense bouquet, so I usually bottle in tenths rather than fifths, or even smaller bottles. The quantity is limited, but the flavor is so intense that small bottles work well.

As mentioned, the final product can be altered by changing the ratio of the ingredients. My first effort consisted of equal amounts of berries, bananas and grapes. I added a small amount of water and sugar syrup as needed and spiked it. The resulting flavor was less concentrated than the above recipe, but I had more wine. It was indistinguishable from a high quality California port. Lower the ratio of bananas to berries and minimize the volume of water going in, and you get a more intense raspberry bouquet and flavor.

Blackberries could be used, but red raspberries are better. Black raspberries should also be good.

Supply Sources

Frozen musts

Peter Brehm has been crushing, pressing and freezing grape musts from Washington and California for many years. Local home wine-makers arrange to pick up their fresh grapes or frozen musts at the site; distant winemakers can have frozen musts shipped to them. He also sells through a few distributors around the country that have freezer facilities and keep some in stock. It is an expensive proposition, but Brehm goes out of his way to deliver quality. It is a good way to get blending varieties, such as Cabernet Franc, Grenache, Syrah, Carignane, etc.

BREHM VINEYARDS
932 Evelyn Avenue
Albany, CA 94706
Phone: 510-527-3675
FAX: 510-526-1372
e-mail: grapes@BrehmVineyards.com
www.brehmvineyards.com

Equipment and Supplies

PRESQUE ISLE WINE CELLARS
9440 W. Main Road
North East, PA 16428
814-728-1314 (information)
800-488-7492 (orders)
FAX 814-725-2092
e-mail: info@piwine.com
www.piwine.com

Supplier of grapes, must, fermenting equipment and supplies, plus basic lab glassware and chemicals. Services small wineries as well as home winemakers. Breaks down some less common additives into practical quantities for home winemakers.

MOREWINEMAKING.COM
995 Detroit Avenue, Unit H
Concord, CA 94518
800-823-0010
www.morewinemaking.com

Equipment and supplies for the home winemaker, including boutique yeasts in 8-gram packets, and encapsulated yeasts. Excellent manuals on the website.

THE BEVERAGE PEOPLE
840 Piner Road #14
Santa Rosa, CA 95403
phone orders 800-544-1867
FAX orders 707-544-5729
advice 707-544-2520
www.thebeverage people.com

Supplier of grapes, must, fermenting equipment and supplies, plus basic lab glassware and chemicals. Services small wineries as well as home winemakers. Breaks down some less common yeasts and additives into practical quantities for home winemakers.

GUSMER ENTERPRISES, INC.
Analytical Services
640-D Airpark Road
Napa, CA 94558
707-224-7903
866-213-1131
FAX 707-255-2019
sales@gusmerenterprises.com
www.gusmerenterprises.com

Services small wineries as well as home winemakers. In-depth analyses of musts and wines. Website has troubleshooting articles.

SPAGNOL'S WINE & BEER MAKING SUPPLIES
1325 Derwent Way
Delta, BC
Canada V3M 5V9
800-663-6954
FAX 800-557-7557
www.rjspagnols.com

Supplier in Western Canada of wine grapes, must, concentrates, fermenting supplies and equipment. Website has a blog plus articles on numerous aspects of interest to home winemakers.

CYNMAR CORPORATION
21709 Route 4 North
P.O. Box 530
Carlinvelle, IL 62626
800-223-3517
217-854-3517
FAX 800-754-5154
www.cynmar.com

Check out their prices for lab equipment and glassware.

NAPA FERMENTATION SUPPLIES
P.O. Box 5839
575 Third Street - Bldg. A
Napa, CA 94581
707-255-6372
FAX 707 255 6462
www.napafermentation.com

Supplier of fermenting equipment and supplies for small wineries and home winemakers. Carries imported presses and crusher-stemmers. Also carries basic lab glassware and chemicals.

VINQUIRY
7795 Bell Road
Windsor, CA 95492
Ph. 707-838-6312
FAX 707-838-1765
e-mail: vinquiry@aol.com
www.vinquiry.com

Labware, chemicals, reagents, fermentation supplies and equipment for wineries and advanced home winemakers. Analytical testing of wines and musts.

ALL WORLD SCIENTIFIC
17120 Tye Street, Ste. D
Monroe, WA 98272
Ph. 800-289-6753
FAX 425-776-1530
www.awscientific.com

Labware, chemicals, reagents and test equipment for commercial and advanced home winemakers.

Oak supplies

STAVIN INCORPORATED
P.O. Box 1693
Sausalito, CA 94966
415-331-7849
FAX 415-331-0516
www.stavin.com

Excellent quality oak beans, staves, stave segments, sleeves and infusion tubes for barrels. Available in American, French and European (Hungarian) oaks — medium, medium + and heavy toasts. Sells 228 liter barrels, but nothing smaller.

DEMPTOS NAPA COOPERAGE
1050 Soscal Ferry Road
Napa, CA 94558
707-257-2628
FAX 707-257-1622
www.demptos.fr/en_v2/

Makes 7½, 15 and 30 gal. barrels, French medium toast only (except heads are not toasted). Also sells American oak chips, but no staves. Website has pages on barrel selection and repair.

OREGON BARREL WORKS
2750 S.E. St. Joseph Rd.
Box 748
McMinnville, OR 97128
503-472-8883
FAX 503-435-2445
www.oregonbarrelworks.com

Makes 15 and 30 gal. barrels — French or American oak. Makes Oregon oak barrels but only in 228 liter size. Sells Oregon oak chips in small quantities, all 3 toasts.

BARREL BUILDERS
1194 Maple Lane
Calistoga, CA 94515
707-942-4291
800-365-8231
FAX 707-942-5426
www.barrelbuilders.com

Sells barrels in French, Hungarian and American oaks, including 30-gallon sizes. Inventories used barrels.

INNERSTAVE
21660 8th Street E.
Sonoma, CA 95476
707-996-8781 / 888-996-8781
FAX 707-996-1157
www.innerstave.com

Barrel alternatives in numerous forms.

TABLE OF EQUIVALENTS

1 oz.=28.4 g	1 g. = .0353 oz
1 lb.=454 g	1 kg. = 2.20 1b
1 fl. oz. =29.6 ml	1 gal. = 128 oz. = 3.785 L
1 qt.=.95 L	1 Hecto liter (100 L) =
	26.4 U.S. gallons

One part per million is either 1 gram per million milliliters or 1 milliliter per million milliliters. Similarly,

5 g/hL = 50 ppm
10 g/hL = 100 ppm
15 g/hL = 150 ppm
20 g/hL = 200 ppm
30 g/hL = 300 ppm

TO RAISE TOTAL ACID BY .1%
tartaric acid — add 3.8 g/gal.
malic acid — add 3.4 g/gal.

TO LOWER TOTAL ACID BY .1%
calcium carbonate — add 2.5 g/gal.
potassium carbonate — add 3.8 g/gal.
potassium bicarbonate — add 3.4 g/gal.

BRIX TO SPECIFIC GRAVITY

Brix	Specific Gravity	Brix	Specific Gravity	Brix	Specific Gravity
0	1.000	9	1.035	18	1.070
1	1.004	10	1.039	19	1.074
2	1.008	11	1.043	20	1.078
3	1.012	12	1.047	21	1.181
4	1.016	13	1.050	22	1.085
5	1.019	14	1.054	23	1.089
6	1.023	15	1.058	24	1.093
7	1.027	16	1.062	25	1.097
8	1.031	17	1.066	26	1.101

Volume-to-weight table

Here is a summary of the weight-per-teaspoon of the most common chemicals used by winemakers. Please bear in mind that these are necessarily approximate because some absorb moisture out of the air and some samples will be more compacted than others. As a result, a teaspoon from one source will not weigh the same as a teaspoon from another source. In addition, there can be a sizeable difference from one "teaspoon" to the next. Some spoons vary considerably from 5.0 ml. A scale would obviously be better, but you can get by using these equivalents.

ADDITIVE	GRAMS/TEASPOON
Potassium metabisulfite	6.3
Tartaric acid	4.8
Malic acid	4.5
Gelatin	3.0
Potassium carbonate	5.9
Potassium bicarbonate	3.5
Diammonium phosphate	4.3
AR 2000	2.9
Potassium sorbare	3.3
Fermaid K	4.8
Bentonite	5.4
Bentonite – prilled	3.7
Lysozyme	1.8

Appendix H

Websites of Interest

http://www.americanwinesociety.com	American Wine Society
http://wineserver.ucdavis.edu/	University of California at Davis
http://www.makewine.com	Amateur Winemakers of Ontario
http://www.vawa.net	Vancouver Amateur Winemakers Assn.
http://www.cellarmastersla.org	Cellarmasters
http://www.sachomewine.org	Sacramento Home Winemakers
http://www.hr/wine/link/	World Wine List
http://winemaking.jackkeller.net	Jack Keller's website
http://www.geocities.com/lumeiseman	Lum Eisenman's website
http://www.scottlaboratories.com/	Scott Laboratories
http://www.lallemand.com/	Lalvin Yeasts, Laffort enzymes
http://www.wyeastlab.com/	Wyeast Labs
http://www.winemakermag.com	Winemaker Magazine

Index

acetaldehyde, 24, 86, 171, 182, 198, 200

acetic acid, acetification, acetobacter, 109, 110, 127, 155, 171, 198

acid blend, 71, **90**, 126, 181

acid test kit, 20, 34, 174

acidity. *See* total acid.

aeration-oxidation. *See* vacuum aspiration.

amelioration, 37-38, **91-92**

argon, **22**, 52, 55, 57, 110, 111, 113, 121, 153, 160, 170, 193, 197

ascorbic acid, 181, 182, 186, 196, 197

Balling. *See* Brix.

barrel fermentation, 101, 147-148, 154, 155, 156

bench trials, 22

before blending, 170

fining agents, 60, 61, 66, 193,

calcium carbonate, 93, 191

tannins, 115, 117, 118

bentonite. See fining agents

Bisulfite. See potassium metabisulfite.

blanc de blancs, 133

blanc de noirs, 133, 137, 167

blending,

varieties, **165-172**, 208, 209, 218, 226

sensory evaluation, 173

ratio equation, 169

to adjust acidity, 35, 40, 53, **85-86, 91,** 101, 115,

to correct flaws, 155, **168-170**, 196, 198

botrytis cinerea, 24, 43, 97, 98, 104, 116, 186, 211, 212

bottle fermentation (sparkling wines), 132-137

bottling, **79-84**

timing of, 48, 57, 65, 66, 77, 154

sulfite level, 2, 181

equipment, 19, 21, 22, 83-84

free/molecular sulfite levels, 218, 222

Brix :

vs. Balling, 173

measuring with hydrometer, 20, **173-174**

red grapes, 70-71

white grapes, 33, 34-35

sparkling wines, 132

late harvest/ice wines, 103-104

to specific gravity, table, 231

bulk aging, 47-50, 77

burette, 21, **174-175**, 186

Cabernet Franc (grape variety), **208**

blending, 166, 168, 226

Cabernet Sauvignon (grape variety), 7, 44, 80, 86, 111, 114, 146, 162, **207-208,** 216, 220

blending, 165-166, 208, 210

calcium carbonate (chalk), 22, 36, 71, **92-93**, 123, 161, 191, 218, 220, 221, 222, 230

Campden tablets, 24, 31

cap, punching down, 67, 72, **73-75**, 108, 217, 224

carbonic acid, 53

carbonic maceration, 94, **112-114**, 215

casein. *See* fining agents, potassium caseinate.

cellaring bottled wine, 83

chalk, precipitated. *See* calcium carbonate.

Champagne. *See* sparkling wines.

chaptalization. *See* sweetening musts.

Chardonnay (grape variety), 7, 10, 35, 36, 44, 45, 50, 80, 96, 100, 121, 129, 131, 132, 133, 145, 146, 147, 148, 154, **210-211,** 218, 220

blending, 166, 209, 211, 212

chitin (chitosan). *See* fining agents.

chromatography test. *See* paper chromatography.